STALKING
IRISH MADNESS

STALKING
IRISH MADNESS

SEARCHING FOR THE ROOTS OF
MY FAMILY'S SCHIZOPHRENIA

PATRICK TRACEY

A BANTAM BOOK

STALKING IRISH MADNESS
A Bantam Book/September 2008

Published by Bantam Dell
A Division of Random House, Inc.
New York, New York

Book design by Catherine Leonardo

Bantam Books is a registered trademark of Random House, Inc., and the
colophon is a trademark of Random House, Inc.

Library of Congress Cataloging-in-Publication Data

Tracey, Patrick.
Stalking Irish madness : searching for the roots of my
family's schizophrenia / Patrick Tracey.
p.   cm.
Includes index.
ISBN 978-0-553-80525-3 (hardcover)
1. Schizophrenia. 2. Schizophrenia—Ireland. 3. Irish American families.
4. Irish—Mental health. 5. Irish Americans—Mental health. I. Title.

RC514.T67 2008
616.89'80092—dc22
2008013064

Printed in the United States of America
Published simultaneously in Canada

www.bantamdell.com

10 9 8 7 6 5 4 3 2 1
BVG

ACKNOWLEDGMENTS

A big thanks to all who helped, and especially Marie France for watering the seeds; James Warren for feeding the soil; John Thornton of the Spieler Agency for his steady care; Mark Newell for the wisdom of the *seanchai;* Sue Warga and Amy Brosey for superb copyediting; Philip Rappaport, my editor at Bantam, for believing in this story all the way; and finally to Alan Green, the first to encourage me, for showing me that the marathon is run one step at a time.

CONTENTS

I THE TWISTED STRAND

II THE IRISH ROOTS

III THE HAZE OF THE HOMEFRONT

STALKING
IRISH MADNESS

PART I

THE
TWISTED
STRAND

༄

AWAY
WITH
THE FAIRIES

It's dark and murky inside Ireland's Cave of the Cat. A muddy abyss in the heart of bog Ireland, the Cave of the Cat, or the Oweynagat, as it's known, is no ordinary grotto. A royal shrine in the second century, this natural limestone fissure was said to be a local doorway to the "otherworld" of the fairies, a race of paranormal beings reputed, among other things, to possess the minds of the insane.

I crept in here just before midnight, searching—vainly, I suspect—for clues to the madness that has mauled my family for generations: the victims include two of my four sisters, along with one uncle, one grandmother, and her great-grandmother before her, a perfect storm of schizophrenia that follows a maternal line stretching from Boston back here to County Roscommon, our ancestral homeland.

Inside the cave, the silence is split only by the drip-drop of water, the emptiness of the place and the steady pounding drip unleashing in me small pangs of paranoia. But the limestone is my lodestone, drawing me into its black depths because this is as far back as the fairy myths of madness go in Ireland. According to 1,100-year-old manuscripts, the *sidhe* (pronounced "shee")—the mischievous fairy people who capture minds from those who lose them—set the nearby palaces of mortals afire and ran into this cave. It's all too fantastic to believe, but I'm trying to be receptive.

Unlike those Irish Americans who dig after genealogical clues, I have no sentimental attachment to my forebears. Instead, I feel I'm chasing much bigger game here, stalking the madness that stalks my family in a direct line down to—but not including—me. Of all the caves in Ireland (and there are thousands), the Oweynagat is the one that gets the most attention in the early Irish literature. Psychotic cats, a symbol of the devil in ancient Ireland, were said to prowl the countryside from here; curses were probably cast here as well by robed Druids, the old wizard priests of Ireland who gathered at this spot for royal pagan feasts. Back when all madness was seen as a punishment, as payback for crossing some deity—first pagan and then Christian—so phantasmagoric were the myths surrounding this cave that to step into its darkness was to enter "Ireland's hellmouth."

I'm here with my own hellish story of sorts, because I know of at least three ancestors who suffered—as two of my fifth-generation Irish American siblings do now—from schizophrenia, a savage psychosis for which there is no cure or effective treatment. Statistics reveal that one of every four people worldwide suffers from some type of mental illness— one in one hundred from schizophrenia, the most severe form, its victims typically tortured by voices and other hallucinations that give rise to bizarre and demented behavior. I pick my steps carefully, groping in the darkness for the widening cave walls, yet my quest feels as slippery as the muddy clay floor that dips then rises toward the neck of this bottle-shaped chamber.

The fairy cave and a massive network of Druid ring forts that surround it are a short distance north of where my mother's side—our schizophrenic side—hails from, an area thick with archaeological sites that hold secrets of the past. Tonight is Halloween, known here for thousands of years as the Samhain (pronounced "sow-when"). The pagan new-year feast day, the Samhain in Ireland marks a fresh start for the year ahead. But it's also that most bewitched evening of the Celtic calendar, the Feast of the Dead, when the veil dividing our world from the next is thought to be at its thinnest. Of the four major pagan festivals, the Irish are most uneasy about this one, with mortals going to the otherworld and the dead returning here. It is said that tonight, from here at the stroke of midnight, our ancestral ghosts are let loose to roam the earth.

As the hour nears, I can't help wondering about the haunts of my own schizophrenic lineage. The thought of them lurking here in the cave's darkness gives me the shivers. One might be Mary Egan, who limped out of bog Ireland, a twenty-four-year-old already driven insane in the midst of the Great Famine that pushed her with her husband, John, to Boston. Or so goes the family lore.

Another schizophrenic ghost might be her great-granddaughter, my grandmother May Sweeney White. She never set foot in Ireland, but her gene string stretches back here to Mary Egan and forward in time, with little mutation, to my mother's brother and two of my four sisters. We are a busy nest of schizophrenia, all wrapped up in a twisted strand of DNA. I count myself as a genetic near miss. But for the sake of the next generation, I'm out here probing the hereditary horizons, monitoring the schizophrenic frontier. And this cave is as close as I'll ever get to the psychic origins of the mysterious "voices" that afflict my family like nearly no other.

To my mind, May Sweeney's story was the scariest and therefore probably the most "schizophrenic" of all. Her "incident," as my mother called it, happened on a crisp autumn day in 1924. There was already some doubt about May's rickety state of mind that morning, but by evening it was obvious that she was the latest victim. The twenty-nine-year-old mother of six must have thought it was a special day, because she picked out her best outfit—a dark shawl thrown over a chiffon dress, a velvet cloche hat, and a pearl necklace. Slipping on a pair of white kid gloves, and without leaving a note, the poised-looking beauty set off through the leafy streets of Providence, just an hour's drive down the old Post Road from Boston.

No one saw her slip out for the day, and by twilight her husband had grown worried. Jack White waited at their modest Hannah Street bungalow in the heart of the Olneyville section of town, watching from the window in the gathering dusk. Normally, Big Jack was a sea of calm, but today he was concerned for a host of reasons. For one, May had not been eating properly; for another, it was past sunset and unsafe in the city at night, and it was not like a young woman to stay out so late, her whereabouts unknown. Out in the unlit parts of the neighborhood or on the hidden banks of the river, bad things were known to happen. Mostly, though, it was that May had not been herself lately. Once cheerful and lighthearted, she'd grown aloof and lifeless in the months since her sixth child was born. The melancholy—a listless sort of head fog that had come over her—now hung like a dark bank of clouds.

At last Jack sees May's figure approaching in the darkness. In her white-gloved finery, she moves up the walkway. But something is amiss: she is clutching her shoes; her hat is cocked, her makeup smudged. May stands in the middle of the road, her shoeless feet swollen and reddened, hard-worn, it would seem, from hours of walking. She says nothing, but as Jack goes out the gate to meet her, her slow grin says it all: every tooth has been wrenched from May's head—her gums a swollen and bloody mess.

Jack drops his teacup, shocked by the sight of her. "Jesus Christ!" he shouts. "What has become of your goddamn teeth?"

May, it turns out, was nobody's victim. She had gladly paid for the dental surgery, she said, to stop the voices in her head. The voices had grown in power and strength until she could no longer bear them. The voices told her they would go, happily, if she would free them from her dental cavities. Whether extensions of her mind or enemies in her head, these strange voices lied, though; they were still chattering, her empty gums still bleeding, as May collapsed into my grandfather's arms and was carried inside to an old Victorian fainting couch.

May had been wobbly leading up to the incident. For months she'd endured a settled depression. Now it was plain to see that something far more serious if initially less obvious was at work. May had swerved off, though *swerved* may be the wrong word because it suggests a sudden deviation, that the route can be regained, that May might be able to merge back into the lanes of life. *Flipped* is wrong too, as she was never able to flip back over to lead a normal existence. *Swirled,* then, may best capture what happens with this enigmatic psychosis, for whoever May Sweeney White was—or thought she was—that day she went swirling off forever, the pieces of her personality dancing like autumn leaves in the breeze.

I never got to meet my insane grandmother, who was

hospitalized until her death thirty-one years later. She and her fellow patients at the Rhode Island Institute of Mental Health, outside Providence, were some of the earliest patients studied since the clinical term *schizophrenia* was coined in 1911 by the renowned Swiss psychiatrist Eugen Bleuler. He believed that schizophrenia, which had earlier been known as dementia praecox, was not an organic deterioration of the brain, as most had thought, but a "disharmonious" state of mind. The general feeling of the day was that schizophrenics were best left out on a pastoral site, away from city chaos. So on a hill above the Pawtuxet River, May had her own room in a large asylum on the Howard campus, where my mother and sisters went to visit every other weekend.

The full consequences of my grandmother's dental catastrophe were never divulged. My grandfather, Jack White, a Teamsters leader in the style of Jimmy Hoffa, had good reason to keep mum. It was whispered he'd had the dentist whacked, payback for his wife's surgery. "Good man," his sister (my great-auntie Rose) said, nodding. "And who could hardly blame him?"

As Rhode Island's top Teamster, the business manager for Local 57 of the International Union of Operating Engineers, he was a guy who could get the job done. Gruff and no-nonsense, my maternal grandfather actually had a heart of gold that only the closest could see. Grampa White used to visit our house like clockwork on weekdays, arriving between 10:00 and 10:30 A.M. for tea and raisin toast with my mother. When school was out, I'd always wait to catch him coming out of his black, chauffeur-driven Chrysler Imperial. Jack White cut a tough-guy figure in his big black car, while a large hat gave him a gangster-like air of authority.

Big Jack White, as he was known in Teamsters circles, was a union boss right out of central casting. With his name hitting the front pages for the embezzlement charges the FBI could never make stick, he and my lawyer mother had a lot to talk about in the 1970s. But I could never get Grampa White to tell me much about his bride, May Sweeney, the mad mother of his six children. All he said was that her hideous face was the most frightening thing he'd ever seen. He said her madness had been handed down from Ireland, and passed it off by joking that if I ever wanted to go back there to shake the family tree, lots of lunatics would fall out.

Right up until a couple of years ago, the idea held zero appeal. I wish I could say I had a passionate devotion to my ancestral homeland, a sentimental view of the Emerald Isle like so many Irish Americans, but I never could traffic in the tourist myths. To me Ireland was never the land of happy-go-lucky leprechauns, never a place to follow dogs across rolling green fields. To me, it was a dark and doomed place—the bog of no return. The less I thought about it, the better, because Ireland to me was the source of the same inexplicable storm of madness that kept rolling, taking two of my four sisters.

As a boy, before my sisters went mad, I did wonder innocently about the dentist getting whacked. Grampa White's reticence only tickled my curiosity, the noir scene unreeling in my mind like an old black-and-white movie: a poised, well-dressed woman appears at the dentist's door. She is a dark stranger, in a hurry to have her mouth looked at. The dentist examines her but sees nothing wrong. She insists she wants her teeth out—all of them, top and bottom. He refuses. She insists. Finally, the lady tells the dentist that she'll pay him well—so well, with the wad she produces from her ample breast, that he reluctantly agrees to do it. He loads her up with a syringeful of morphine and, working well past sunset, he does the deed.

In the next scene that unfolds in my mind, Grampa White is a young man now, just thirty, and he is pacing the floors of his Hannah Street home, plotting revenge, and then serving it cold months later when some of his goons in big hats and overcoats push into the dentist's office. The pencil-thin dentist squirms, begging for his life in his own dental chair. "How was I to know she was mad?" he pleads. "How was I to know that she was the wife of Big Jack White? She certainly looked fine in her expensive clothes. How was I to know that she was some schizo?"

Indeed, May was a real head turner when she set off that day, bewitchingly beautiful with her jet-black hair, her sparkling blue eyes, her radiant smile. When she got home, she was in bits. As shocking as it was, losing her teeth was the least of it. May had lost her mind too, and what could be worse? May had schizophrenia, an apocalyptic form of madness because it robs its victim of our most precious human gift: the ability to separate the real world from the unreal and to trust one's thoughts as true.

Schizophrenia is not a case of snapping back and forth between different personalities—a common misconception. Schizophrenia is the hearing of voices, but the hallucinations can be seen, felt, and smelled as well as heard. It's fright night for life for many, an all-consuming terror that never ends.

Though the women have been hit hardest, not all the men have been spared. After serving in World War II, my mother's brother, Robbie White, came home altered; whether he was shell-shocked (as combat stress was then referred to) or schizophrenically damaged wasn't entirely clear. Within weeks, Robbie was taken out on a stretcher from that same Providence home that May had disappeared from, eventually to live on his own in a home for mentally ill veterans, on a farm out on the state line. I was four or five when I learned that. I was with my mother and my sister Austine (pronounced "aw-steen"), who was a year older. There were cows and horses at the farm, making visits there as much fun as two small kids could have. Though Uncle Robbie had little to say and seemed lost in space, he introduced us to farm animals we'd only ever seen in picture books. Then one day he turned on me.

It was on my third visit, and Uncle Robbie had offered to teach me how to milk a cow. I still hadn't lost my sense of skittishness, but his presence was reassuring as he guided my hand up to the animal and encouraged me to stroke her. And then, without warning, he slapped me hard across my cheek. I was too stunned to feel much pain, and hesitated to say anything to my mother. But Austine had been a witness and told her when we marched in from the field. It was the last time we were ever brought out to see our uncle Robbie again.

On the ride back to Boston, I ask Mom, "There's something wrong with Uncle Robbie, isn't there?"

Behind the wheel of her big Cadillac, Mom lights a Tareyton charcoal filter. "Yes," she says, taking a drag on her cigarette, "there is." She uses a big word that hangs in the air, that sounds like a sheet of glass being cut slowly. She tells us that the real Uncle Robbie did not strike me—his schizophrenia did. Young as I am, I get it. The slap was something beyond Uncle Robbie's control. Coming from his schizophrenia, it was more like a will foreign to himself, outside his own volition.

"Robbie is unwell," Mom goes on, more simply now.

Unwell is a euphemism I will come to hear with alarming frequency in the years ahead. In fact, in time the notion of wellness will come to seem an odd barometer, with its degrees of health, its good days and bad, whereas every day is pretty much the same for the chronically schizophrenic. Unlike with depression, say, one does not fall somewhere along the spectrum of schizophrenia; you are either schizophrenic or you are not. In my family, at least, it allows no middle ground. *Cracked* is more like it. Uncle Robbie is cracked.

"Like your grandmother," my mother finishes explaining to us. "Your grandmother was not well either."

On the rest of the ride, and without going into the details of her own mother's crack-up, Mom elaborates on the family misfortune, filling Austine and me in on a place called Ireland where there was a valley, and in it a healing well where the cracked are made whole. Mom does a little play on words. She tells us that by drinking its waters and feeding on the shamrocks that grow around it, the unwell are made well.

When Robbie died shortly thereafter, Mom said he was better now. I missed him in a way. I missed the big farm animals, and I missed planning to find this faraway valley where schizophrenics can all go together, to heal in the kinship of common schizophrenic suffering. "Jesus probably has a miracle waiting there for Uncle Robbie," Mom told us, putting the best possible spin on his demise. She said we should imagine his face glistening in the waters of the well out on the edge of Ireland. From then on, I liked the idea of Robbie in a valley, cupping water from its magical well.

With Robbie gone, we were schizophrenia-free for the first time in forty years. Over the next decade, Mom rarely spoke of it, shunting the subject aside whenever it did arise. "What is without remedy should be without regard," she said, quoting from *Measure for Measure*. Mom was wrong on that score, because like those things about which little is ever said, I knew schizophrenia was a horrible thing—possibly a family curse. I knew of curses. Boston kids are reared on the Red Sox curse of the Bambino, for having traded Babe Ruth, but this curse is worse, a big bat that knocks a hanging change-up over a tall wall, never to be seen again.

From time to time, memories of Robbie appeared and vanished—small reminders Mom would have us ignore, at least until the schizophrenics began springing out of the family traps again. Mom had kept a lid on things, but now her own children were losing it, one after another, and only she had a real inkling that some of us might be destined. I believe Mom was always scared of it, but she tried not to show it. Schizophrenia had already cast a shadow down from the previous generations. The only question was whether it would press on.

As the two youngest, Austine and I formed a separate clique within the family. The last-born, and the only boy, I had a special status at the foot of the pecking order. Austine and I were "the babies" and were shielded from as much as possible, including the truth about our grandmother. Grampa White said little more about the episode, except that the insanity that tore through our grandmother's side had sliced like a knife through old Ireland too.

The notion that madness had favored the Irish had been kicking around since the 1850s, when a seeming prevalence was first noticed among immigrants in New York and Boston. The toll was so high that, between 1817 and 1961, no other nation had produced, in proportion to its population, so many who were sent to asylums, workhouses, and jails for the conditions we now call manic depression and schizophrenia. In the sixty-five years that followed the famine, Ireland's per capita asylum population saw a sevenfold increase, an unparalleled expansion.

Genetically speaking, the Irish are no more at risk than any other people. But in their darkest hour their rates of insanity were pushed to extremes. The story was the same on both sides of the Atlantic. Not long after my ancestors hit Boston in 1847, the mental wards were swamped with Irish lunatics, most of them hard-drinking laborers. Until then the Irish population in America had been largely Protestant and comparatively well screwed on. These newer arrivals, these Irish Catholics, were another thing altogether. "We are not so successful in the treatment of them as with the native population of New England," conceded doctors at New York City Lunatic Asylum on Blackwell Island, which was constructed in 1839.

This trend had alarmed medical observers, because it was feared that the frontiers of insanity had shifted west. If America was going mad, then maybe it had the Irish to blame. Some whispered that the Irish were a doomed race, preternaturally mad, even cursed. Others said that if the Irish were mad, they had only the British to blame. The British had brought together Ireland and Britain as a single political entity, the United Kingdom of Great Britain and Ireland, during that time, and then booted the peasants out, basically. Not only were the Irish starved out, the colony's own Gaelic language was outlawed. As late as 1886, as Britain continued to run its regime from Dublin Castle, a new island-wide network of county asylums had been erected. Still, there was, in the words of one government inquiry noted in the *Journal of Mental Science,* a "large number of individuals of unsound mind, or whose sanity is doubtful, wandering about Ireland...not under public supervision."

By the turn of the twentieth century, on both sides of the Atlantic, insanity was being called the second curse of the Irish. Anyone could point the finger of blame—at the long history of famines and the malnutrition they spread, at drink, at religion, at emigration, at British inhumanity. Whatever the cause, my family had a place in this history. As they made the voyage out of Roscommon, with them came the madness. As I return there, with me comes a need for answers.

I know that for most people, the idea of going insane is unthinkable. For most families sanity is a given, as easy as breathing, as sure as seeing the sun rise in the eastern sky. For too many of us, however, there is a creaky gate that swings open at the cusp of adulthood, and on the other side is madness. On us sanity rests no more securely than a hat blown off in the wind. In our family, schizophrenia hangs the moon and tells the sun when to set.

I visited the cave earlier that evening, first with students from an Irish folklore class at Galway's National University of Ireland, all of us crawling on our bellies through the small opening under a hawthorn hedge. I learned from the group's professor that the Oweynagat may be the Grave of the Cat, rather than the Cave of the Cat, because ancient Irish had the same word *(owey)* for "grave" and "cave."

Cave or grave, once inside, the professor leads the students in summoning the fairy spirits with music played on traditional Irish bodhran drums and replicas of Bronze Age trumpets discovered several years earlier in an old bog marsh in Armagh, far north of here. He tells his students that the music combines energies to forge "a stronger connection between this world and the next." I push my skeptical thoughts aside and open my

15

mind to the possibility that fairies do play a part. The fairies were called the "good people" more out of fear than favor, I suspect, because they might blight your crops or inflame your mind. I see no fairies, but old farmer Paddy might be my guide. He has joined the festivities just for kicks, turning up earlier on an old bicycle with a flask he removes from his sports jacket. Old Paddy has no doubt about the fairies. Unscrewing the cap, he spills a few drops of whiskey on the cave floor for them, an ancient tradition, and offers me a swig, another ancient one.

"No, thanks. I'm off it," I reveal, wondering whether the whiskey helps to conjure this fairy otherworld at all.

"Yerra," he mutters, swigging from the flask and looking around. "And ain't they a bother."

Paddy has seen no fairies himself, as it transpires, but he has a sort of sixth sense about them, he says, beaming. I wouldn't know a fairy from a fruit fly, but when pushed further, Paddy says they must be real. "It must be," he insists. "'Cause it come down from the ancestors, so it has to be." Ireland may be changing rapidly, but here in old Ireland, regard for ancestry still has the zeal of hero worship, and the infallible and the definitive rarely converge. "Would have to be," Paddy says, nodding genuinely. "Been handed down like that, so it would have to be."

In Ireland since the early Tuatha De Danaan people, the *sidhe* were thought to live in the wind, *sidhe gaoithe* meaning "gust of wind" or "whirlwind." Also called the wee folk, the good folk, or the fair folk, they came to be known as fairies. Other names were banshee, leprechaun, and puck. The fairies were feared as thieves who stole people, leaving a changeling in their place, a look-alike who was an imposter. There was even a curse of madness that preceded the Gaels, arriving with Druidry, the oldest psychospiritual tradition in Ireland: a balled-up wisp of hair in your face, a quick incantation, and a curse of madness was conjured for generations. Or so the ancient curse of the Druid Fullon goes.

Davey Patton, a thirtyish wood sculptor and pagan scholar whose property abuts the cave, takes a more nuanced view. "I'll agree with yer man here," he says. "There may be more to it than meets the eye." Davey guesses that fairies, like so many other paranormal phenomena, may be expressions of "transcendental visions" known only to mystics and madmen, and here only to the saints and schizophrenics of a now-vanishing Ireland. Like me, Davey had a schizophrenic uncle. "He saw angels and demons and he broke doctors' ribs," he recalls. "I was a wee lad. They said he was on his way, so we hid upstairs."

Or fairies may just offer an explanation where there is none, especially if kids are within earshot. If those who have seen fairies or heard the wail of the banshee then go mad, as some suppose, then the explanation has a convenient plot twist that eliminates any reliable witness. It also allows the story to repeat itself, to be told and retold over the generations. So when Big Jack White—sipping his tea at our kitchen table, buttering his raisin toast with those big meaty hands—told us that our grandmother, May Sweeney White, had been "away with fairies," it was just his way of saying, with a wink and a nod to my mother, that the talking was over. Away I was shooed, as clueless as a kid then as I am this Halloween in a damp, cold Irish cave, just past midnight.

CHAPTER TWO

ى

MADNESS GALLOPS

I pitied my grandmother. Apart from the onset of schizo-phrenia, the circumstances that dictated her life could not have been easy. The daughter of Margaret O'Grady and Charles Sweeney, an Irish wool weaver, she grew up in Woonsocket, Rhode Island, just across the Massachusetts line. She was just a teenager in 1912, when both parents died of tuberculosis within seven weeks of each other. May then went to live with her older sister Elsie, who ran a boardinghouse for immigrant Irish mill workers. May married young and, in rapid succes-sion, bore five boys and a girl, my mother, Millie. May's lot may not have been comfortable, but neither was it unbearable. Who knows what heights of happiness she might have reached had she not gone mad.

Even as a young girl, my mother was aware of May's be-coming mentally ill. Mom spoke of the anxious ache she felt as she watched her mother grow slowly aloof. May developed a faraway look, as if the air itself might hold answers. While her six children ran wild, she grew ever more listless. Though barely five at the time, my mother remembered how her mother had stopped ironing, darning socks, or doing the dishes, and how she began exhibiting certain other strange behaviors. For instance, although my mother was the only girl, May confused her with her brothers. Even when Mom stood right in front of her, May was apt to call her John or Raymond, Robbie, Danny, or Charlie.

And while there were other clues, nobody really thought May was going mad. She'd always been of sound mind—or so it seemed to my great-auntie Rose, ever the optimist, who wrote off her sister-in-law's slump to postpartum depression. "It will pass in time," Rose said, even as poor May became more remote, not less, until that fateful autumn day.

I felt sorry for my mother too. Forced to endure the loss of her mother, her brother, and then two of her four daughters to clinical insanity, she saw schizophrenia swing from vine to vine in her lifetime. Mom was five when May was sent away, and she visited her every other Saturday at the mental hospital. It was a ritual she continued as an adult, hiring a driver to take her and her three oldest girls—Elaine, the oldest, and Seanna (pronounced "shaw-na") and Michelle, the twins—on the hour-long trip south to the Institute of Mental Health. The girls dreaded the highway journey to the complex of brick buildings; forbidden from speaking about their grandmother to friends, they obediently kept details of these weekend outings to themselves.

After arriving at the hospital, the girls waited in the parking lot until our grandmother appeared in a window with Mom beside her. Delighted, May would point down at them, calling each by name (and, as often as not, by the wrong name). May knew her granddaughters, at least collectively; it was as individuals that she got them confused. As May's head tilted forward from the window, the girls waved back up, as instructed. It was as if the grandchildren on the ground and the grandmother above were stretching to fill the empty space between them. Tragically, it seemed like Chelle was waving up at her own grim future too. Schizophrenia hadn't arrived in our immediate family yet, but on those Saturday drives to the asylum, it was standing on the back bumper, hitching a ride.

As the years slid by, May's condition never improved. She grew into a gray-haired Hitchcockian curtain twitcher up there in the window. For a couple of hours each day, she was escorted to the grounds for some fresh air. On visiting days she may have noticed her granddaughters growing up, but she never let on. Time never passed for her, and as far as my mother was concerned, it was all just as well. She humored May, but with no truly effective treatments available then as now, she made little effort to rehabilitate her mother. Mom and her five brothers had visited their mother frequently until the boys went off to fight in World War II. After the war ended, only Mom and Grampa White kept up the visits.

Mom's big worry was that she might pass her mother's madness down to her own children. She suspected it was genetic, built in, that the mental illness that apparently runs in families ran rampant in ours, and she knew full well the risks. Schizophrenia swoops offstage the one you thought you knew. In his or her place comes a sad alternative, like a changeling. It throws a long shadow too, the spared suffering from an almost hypochondriac obsession that they too could be carriers.

So Mom had not planned to have children, had not even dreamed of us. Instead, she hung her hopes on a career in the legal profession, inspired by Shakespeare's cross-dressing Portia and the legal trap she set for Shylock in *The Merchant of Venice*. At the end of World War II, however, her head was turned by a tall, dark, and handsome charmer dead set on having his own big Irish Catholic brood. She balked at my father's plans. It was an instinctive feeling that something was not right, a fear fed on familiarity. She knew she'd be tossing the dice, that some of her children might be marked out for schizophrenia before they were born. Even the family doctor advised against having children. Schizophrenia runs in families, he said, and one day science would prove it.

Nonsense, my father said. Half Irish and charmingly persistent, he pushed for and got a second opinion from a New York City specialist, who insisted that the faulty brain wiring that seemed to pass through our maternal generations might not be triggered if they were good, caring parents, raising us in a stable household. That was our best bet, one our dad quickly forgot. A strong Roman Catholic, my mother had put her faith in God to keep her children from developing schizophrenia. But with Mom's second pregnancy and the birth of twins, Michelle and Seanna, schizophrenia already had a paw in the door.

We had two family physicians who made house calls. Neither saw it coming, but left to the mercies of our errant gene bank, Michelle, the oldest twin by several minutes, and Austine, seven years younger, were somehow destined for the disorder. As for Elaine, Seanna, and me, there are not many days when one of us isn't counting our own sanity as beating the odds. It's as if God flipped coins, three of five falling favorably in our family.

Our chances must have been on Mom's mind when she and Dad bought their first house, a three-story brick colonial in Milton, Massachusetts, soon after marrying. Like millions of other postwar Americans, they'd gone to the suburbs in search of the higher social status that such neighborhoods conferred. On the south edge of Boston, Milton was a nice upper-middle-class 'burb, with plenty of foliage that went up in brilliant flames of color before the icy winters, with their snowy blankets, froze us in. We mowed our lawn, had backyard barbecues, were sent to good private Catholic schools. Our parents were accepted into the Woodlawn Country Club with the other well-to-do Boston Irish. We had a milkman, a fruit and vegetable man, a bakery man, an ironing lady, and a cleaning lady to do the floors.

Michelle and Seanna were born two years after Elaine on the eve of the fifties, in the early hours of New Year's Eve day. The delivery room doctor pronounced the pair identical, because the afterbirth was that of only one baby. How could that be? How could they have come from one split egg instead of two separate eggs when there was so little physical resemblance between them? If there was another egg, then where was the other afterbirth? At their first checkup, Michelle was still nearly bald, with just a tiny light-brown tuft atop her head, whereas Seanna already had thick, jet-black hair. Things were mixed up from the start. When our mother was heralded in 1960 as the first mother of five in Massachusetts to be sworn in as a lawyer, the front-page story in the *Boston Globe* wrongly reported that the twins were "identical."

My parents settled in Milton partly because Auntie Rose was there. My mother had formed a strong bond with her aunt, although more out of need than love, and Rose had limited sympathy for her mad sister-in-law; like many of her day, and many still today, she saw mental illness as a personal failing. Watch those girls, she warned my mother presciently. One day they could turn out like May Sweeney, just as May Sweeney had wound up like Mary Egan. Rose was dead right—it was the destiny of two of the four of those girls to go schizophrenic.

When her husband lost his position as an executive at the Gillette Company, Rose took a job behind the makeup counter at Filene's Basement, Boston's famous department store, in the heart of the downtown shopping district. There she met Rose Kennedy, another proud Irish American, whose son would soon occupy a seat in the Senate and, of course, the White House. The two Roses became somewhat friendly. One helped the other stage fashion shows for charitable causes. Most of those shows were held at the Ritz-Carlton Hotel, overlooking Boston's Public Garden, and the little twins, Seanna and Chelle, were always the grand finale.

From the wings of the stage, Elaine would hiss, "Okay, go!" and the pair would skip to the end of the runway. They looked adorable with their hair in ringlets and their red long johns with rear flaps. When they wiggled their little bottoms and threw the bouquet, the place went wild with laughter. Upon finishing their bit, the twins always looked flummoxed, as if to say, *What do we do now?* "Come back," Elaine would shout, waving them in from the wings. "Hurry up," she'd say, and the little sisters would scamper her way.

After each show, my mother and her three young girls would stroll across the nearby Boston Common. Amidst the cry of city sirens and the rumble of streetcars, they made their way to Tracey's Religious Articles, Dad's place of business on Chauncy Street, just opposite Filene's. His shop sold everything from holy cards and rosary beads to crucifixes, chalices, and life-sized statues of the saints and Jesus and Mary. He did a brisk trade in gifts for all occasions Roman Catholic—baptisms, first communions, confirmations, Last Rites, and holy days of obligation.

Our own home was stuffed with religious goods, including a shellacked altar made of matchsticks. Our Bible was a big, red-leather-bound version with gilded edges, monograms, and a trio of little companion Bibles that surrounded it on a reading stand. Dad thought we'd wreck them, and prohibited us from taking them off the stand. As a result, we were more drawn to the books of Kahlil Gibran that Mom had spread around. The Lebanese mystic poet, a fad at the time, had taught that beauty lies in the mind and heart, not in the face or body. Mom had us sit in a big blue chair in the living room and read Gibran when we needed time out.

Dad's own father, who had started the religious-articles business, had made a bundle selling rosary beads during the Great Depression. Patrick Tracey the first, for whom I was named, had a contrarian impulse and a sixth sense in bad times. In those desperate days, many Roman Catholics could hardly afford an apple, much less a silver medal of a patron saint or a rosary made of rose petals, but folks dug deep for their redemption. Eventually he sold directly to the churches, his line of merchandise including custom-made, hand-embroidered vestments for the priests and more modest garments for the nuns and altar boys.

America may have been the great frontier of prayer—"one nation under God"—but France was the place to buy the finest rosary beads. Anticipating the Nazi invasion, my grandfather cornered the French market before the Führer could shut it down. Like so much of our history, my grandfather's success story was topsy-turvy. The way my father told it, here was his dad—mean as a bean and with masses of money—with his wife living high on the dime of the Roman Catholic Church when, at bottom, he was a nasty atheist. Crossing the Atlantic on ocean liners, my paternal grandparents were the original Ugly Americans, draped in fur and dripping in diamonds in the depths of the Great Depression.

Everything my grandfather touched turned to gold—or was gold in the first place. He was so smooth, it was said, he could literally talk the precious metal out of your teeth. During the war years, wealthy members of New England's large Catholic parishes offered up their jewelry so that their diocese could aid Uncle Sam. The most generous—or the most rash—even tossed their rings, watches, and brooches onto the collection plates that passed through the pews on Sunday mornings. Through his close connections at the high end of the clergy, my grandfather got hold of a certain amount of the finer jewelry, ostensibly to use to plate chalices. In fact, he hoarded his cache until he could arrange to have it melted down and transformed into gold bars that he stashed in safe-deposit boxes. He had come up as a poor Irish kid with only a third-grade education. He was smart, and he vowed never to chance poverty again. Gold was his guarantee.

At his own religious-goods store, Dad's genius was in courting the nuns. In town to visit the shrine or the cathedral, the sisters had no quiet, out-of-the-way place to rest after their pilgrimages, so Dad built them a plush hospitality suite in his store's basement, complete with a crystal chandelier that shone soft light over comfy sofas. (There was also a TV set and fully stocked bar for those visitors not quite so pious.)

Dad was a gregarious guy who greeted everyone warmly, remembering names like a good salesman. He looked at people squarely, and knew how to say exactly the right things. He stood just over six feet, and had to crouch to change his window display, which he did each week without fail. To him, image was everything, and he presented a warm and friendly one to the steady procession of bishops, priests, and nuns who crossed his threshold.

On Sundays, Dad always made sure we were a little late for Mass so that we could make a grand, head-turning entrance. Being seen with his five young children—the girls all elaborately coiffed and dressed to the nines—and with his wife, the attorney, was good for business. With me in one arm and Austine in the other, his three other girls and Mom— always in something tasteful from Bonwit Teller or Bergdorf Goodman—following in his wake, Dad marched us up the center aisle just as Mass was starting. The seven of us filled a whole pew for our weekly hour of worship. Dad liked to sing the hymns too loudly and deliberately off-key. He thought his clowning around was a hoot, but we all cringed.

After church, the girls were put to work responding to obituary notices in the *Boston Globe*. "Girls, time for the obits," Dad commanded, and they would get their assembly line going on the dining room table. One stuffed, one stamped, one licked Dad's direct-mail offerings of bereavement gifts for the dearly departed. In nice summer weather, it was a relief to head for the shore instead. "All right, girls, take off the finery," Mom would shout after Mass. Dad would pack a cooler stocked with lemonade and Italian cold cuts, and we'd all pile into the Ford Country Squire.

Dad called it the beach wagon, and he'd pilot it, merrily at first, toward Cape Cod or Rhode Island. These outings always started out fun, but sooner or later something would irritate him. Long, angry passive-aggressive silences seemed to be the main mode of communication between our parents. They rarely hugged, kissed, held hands, or showed even the most trivial display of affection. Dad's drinking and gambling were a big part of it. He was either wasted and happy or hung over and testy, depending on his winnings. Dad was a bit of a madman when it came to gambling. I once saw him toss a TV set out the window when the Celtics lost. Lord knows how much he'd had on the game. He'd get in so deep with the bookies that every few months they'd send a tow truck to hitch up his Cadillac. Contrite, Dad would skulk downtown to St. Anthony's shrine to take the pledge not to gamble. He'd put his hand on the Bible and swear to God to clean up his act. All would be well for a while, until Mom found the next betting slip from Suffolk Downs in a suit coat pocket.

My sisters learned to navigate the tense, angry atmosphere by having their own fun. I was only three when they taught me the new dance craze, the twist. It was the early 1960s, and the corny boredom of Perry Como's easy-listening style had given way to rock and soul. Dad wanted nothing to do with this sexy new music aimed at his teenage daughters, and would change the station immediately. "Now sing, girls," he'd bark, flicking off the car radio. That was their cue to break into the old Eddie Fisher hit whose most memorable lines went: "Oh, my papa, to me he was so wonderful. Oh, my papa, to me he was so good." Naturally, this was Dad's favorite song.

I remember those rides like yesterday. The girls sing so-called standards Dad wants to hear as he steers the car toward Mashpee, a Cape Cod beach community, or south toward Narragansett, Rhode Island. Worse than the songs is the air inside the car, as my mother chain-smokes her Tareytons. She puffs so relentlessly that we call her the "eternal flame." The windows cannot be rolled down, because Dad needs to hear his daughters' singing over the highway hum. Besides, the breeze might mess up their perfect beehive hairdos cooking in a toxic confection of Aqua Net and Tareyton smoke.

I badly need to crank the window in hopes of blowing perfume and hair spray out the rear of the wagon. It never happens, and I am invariably hit by a wave of nausea. I need air, but as the runt I have no sway. Finally Dad pulls to the shoulder. Mom taps her cigarette ash as I tear into the high grass to vomit. Back in the car, there is only silence; my parents are figures of iciness who rarely address each other. They are like giant parrots perched up there in the front seats, each echoing the other, saying the same old things.

"Sing, girls," my dad commands.

"Louder, girls," Mom seconds, indulging Dad. "Your father wants you to sing louder, louder, louder. From down here," she says, pointing to her diaphragm. "Not from the throat."

Elaine and the twins were all-American kids, the earliest prototypes of today's children who get shuttled between sports and dance and music lessons, the objective being to chisel all three into theatrical perfection. Austine and Chelle were child models for Polaroid, and Elaine and the twins were Boston debutantes. Dad had convinced himself his three oldest— Elaine and the twins, that is—would be the next Lennon Sisters, a quartet of wholesome sister-singers on Saturday-night performances on *The Lawrence Welk Show*.

The girls were all perfectly behaved whenever Dad was around. They didn't dare provoke him. On the rare occasion when they did get out of line—and even at times when they had done nothing at all—Dad would fly into a rage, swatting them around while Mom pleaded: "Not the head, Pat, not the head. You'll scramble their brains!" Mom was worried about more schizophrenia from the first, but she tried not to show it. Dad wasn't even thinking about it. He had his own issues, apparently.

Austine, the baby girl, was always his "little darling," while Elaine, the oldest, who resembled Elizabeth Taylor in her youth, was placed on her own special pedestal. "Elaine the fair, Elaine the loveable," my mother would say, quoting the Alfred Lord Tennyson poem "Lancelot and Elaine."

The twins' twelfth birthday was typical of our home life. Dad wasn't around, but I remember my mother and Elaine hatching a plan to get the two girls out of the house, so that their birthday cake—a Boston cream pie—could be decorated in secret. The twins, in matching red coats and scarves, are told to go rummage in the yard for some Christmas toy that the snowfall has hidden. Austine and I stand quietly at the ready in the kitchen, eager to be mother's little helpers and, if we're good, to get to lick the frosting. Our boxer, Mike, cocks his ears and lifts his head, and a growl grows in his throat.

Mom gives me the bowl to lick and hands Austine a tube of decorative icing. She squeezes, but nothing comes out. She hands me the tube. I examine it closely, squeeze it, and get a face full of frosting, which Austine thinks is the funniest thing ever. She collapses in a fit of laughter, and I fall down laughing beside her. Mike licks the frosting off me as Mom hides the cake. The twins come back in, stomping snow off their boots to the smell of wet wool drying in the kitchen's warm air. "Oh, you like to giggle, do you?" Chelle says. Elaine and Seanna follow. They hold us down and stare at us from above with silly grins. Austine and I are tickled until we ache. After dinner Mom comes in with the cream pie. "Happy Birthday" is frosted above candles that flicker. Austine and I get piggy-back rides; she takes Seanna and I climb up on Elaine, as Chelle skips and serenades us all. This was the part of my life I call the happy part, before the crazy part came. I loved all four of my sisters equally, though I was closest to Austine.

On the surface, it all looked fine, but it wasn't. The twins had the toughest time of it. As recounted in later years, Dad discouraged them even from having opinions. If anyone asked, they loved Eisenhower and the Kennedys and hated Nikita Khrushchev. But in general it was better for them to keep their mouths shut. "Jesus, Mary, and Joseph, don't ever open your mouth and have an opinion," Dad ranted, banging his palm on the steering wheel. "You'll only embarrass me."

When the twins got fed up, they'd go off to catch a film at the Oriental Theatre in Mattapan Square. Or Mom might find them at the Glamorama having their hair done. Or they might get out of the house by taking Austine and me for strolls. We always felt sheltered by our three oldest sisters. They were al-ways bouncing us on their knees, singing the Beatles or the Beach Boys, the Supremes or the Temptations. In an odd way, we defined ourselves as what our parents were not. We were sane and rational; it was Mom and Dad who could have used some counseling.

In 1967 we moved from Milton to Providence, where Dad opened a restaurant, called Patrick's. When that business went under, another casualty of Dad's gambling, he filed for bankruptcy and Mom filed for divorce.

The three oldest girls had gone back to Boston for college, but we all kept close. Elaine was friendly with some Boston Bruins hockey players and invited me to meet them at her apartment on Commonwealth Avenue. Chelle then went to

Paris, studying at the Sorbonne for her senior year, and then to Manhattan to pursue her acting career. When Austine and I visited her in New York as high school juniors and seniors, Chelle took us to off-Broadway shows and comedy clubs, to fabulous museums and hole-in-the-wall galleries in the East Village. Before long we were traveling to see Seanna down in Fort Lauderdale too, where she had moved after college, a perfect destination for our spring school breaks. Austine and I thought our place was with the others, that we'd join them in Boston or New York one day or maybe even down in Florida. We never once thought it would turn out otherwise.

Only later would I come to understand the taunts of our uncle Charlie, a short, muscular man with a clumsy sense of humor. On the rare occasion that he visited, he always made cracks about the madness. "The family tree is out of its tree," he used to say. I wanted to hear more about this, but Mom always hushed her kid brother. Looking back, I can see what she saw: schizophrenia, so familiar to her, was the trickster that still had its hand on more trap doors. With macabre humor, Uncle Charlie quoted Cary Grant from *Arsenic and Old Lace:* "Madness," he said, "doesn't just run in our family—it gallops!"

To Mom it was no laughing matter, nor something worthy of loose discussion. As an attorney, she liked to think all problems had a solution—even in spite of those schizophrenics who broke and crashed behind her. We were each to take steady steps, get on track, go to college, find a career, settle down, and be happy and satisfied. Deep down, though, Mom must've feared that some of us were like car wrecks waiting to happen. She had always said that Chelle was "a little different." By the time Chelle was just twenty-six, we'd all see just how "different" she was.

For most people, a schizophrenic is just another roadside

attraction, a spectacle that's worth a quick look before driving off. Occasionally the whole nation fixes attention, when something senselessly violent happens. Psychiatrists and other mental health professionals weigh in with speculation, and we all look on momentarily in numb bewilderment. When it's your own siblings, though, it's impossible to turn away. The tragedy stops you in your tracks, as it stopped me in 1976. I was an average eighteen-year-old, home for the weekend during my freshman year in college. When the phone rang, it was Keith, Chelle's boyfriend, calling from Manhattan to say Chelle was on a bus back home.

He keeps it short. "Michelle," he says, "is not well."

CHAPTER THREE

THE
FIRST
POUNCE

Mom puts down the receiver and thinks nothing of it. Everyone else goes out for the evening, as planned, and I take Mom's Ford Pinto to collect Michelle at the bus station. When I arrive, ten minutes later, I have no trouble spotting her: she's the one twirling around in a long, loose peasant dress, all eyes upon her. Her face is caked in thick layers of makeup, heavy on the rouge, and as she twirls she sings "The Sound of Music." Chelle is a stage actress, but her little cabaret is way over the top. I have not a clue what to do. She always had a sense of humor, but I never thought we'd see a performance from Chelle quite like this. It would have been a joke, too absurd for anything but to be laughed at. How unfunny she seems to be now.

As I cross the station, Chelle leaps and disappears behind a newsstand. Reappearing, her darting eyes challenging any man to dance with her, she again disappears from sight; moments later, the scene is repeated. Chelle does not stop singing and dancing until I approach. Then she turns and throws her arms around me as though she'd never been happier to see anyone in her whole life. Without too much ado, she takes my arm and we leave the station quickly, Chelle skipping off to the senseless melody line of her newfound madness. As we drive back home to our house on the east side of Providence, I go with her out of this world and into another one altogether.

In the passenger's seat, she brings me up to date on her love life: she has just finished a fling with Warren Beatty, the film star and well-known womanizer, dumping him for Jesus of Nazareth, a true gentleman, whom she believes to be the Romanian tennis star Ilie Nastase. Chelle says all of this with a voice so full of you-gotta-believe that I strain to follow her logic. She says the whole world is getting ready for her marriage to Jesus. From what I can gather, the wedding is to coincide with the end of the world as we know it. The event should all go off just swell, she says, if only Dad, who has the role of Satan, doesn't get drunk and spoil the day.

"I just had to end it with Warren," Chelle explains breathlessly. And what can I say? Dumping Warren Beatty, dating Jesus Christ—these would be high-class problems for any young actress. It could be worse, I tell myself; whatever's wrong will surely pass. Chelle will be back to her old self in a few days. In the meantime, at least I've landed a sympathetic role in her romantic comedy: I'm the best man, apparently, because Chelle says I'm John the Baptist. All right, then.

Chelle rants nonsense about Jesus and Ilie. Oh yes, she knows all about them and more things beyond my range of reason. I try to talk sense into her, but the whole effort seems self-defeating. How can a mind so far off the grid grasp my simple reasoning? Chelle has been transported into a way of thinking that is way out there. She is gonzo yet theatrical as ever as she gazes out beyond the ceiling to receive messages from her mysterious voices.

The voices are back in our family, apparently, but whose are they? Chelle is like any ordinary person who has all the senses of sight, smell, touch, taste, and hearing, except she seems to have another attunement, an extrasensory relationship with these odd voices that she alone can hear. Back home as I sit and watch her move from room to room, spinning and swirling, I am feeling nearly as dazed and confused myself. I wonder if she's tripping, but Chelle is the straightest of the five kids, the only one of us who never toyed with recreational drugs. Chelle didn't need them; she always said she was "high on life."

I keep an eye on her and say nothing, despite my instinct to try to fix her, to look for a way into her head, to guide her back out. I want to step into her head and sweep free the seeds of insanity, but her voices command the heights. Chelle does not speak one word of sanity. She shambles about, circling in and out of closets, smacking into walls. She is like a bird that has flown into your house. You want to come to her aid, but you worry about doing more harm than good—assuming you're clever enough to catch her.

As the evening wears on, Chelle grows even more agitated, not less, babbling about the wedding ring Jesus has for her. She is convinced that Dad has installed hidden cameras, even though he hasn't lived at home since the divorce. As a college kid in sympathy with things weird and absurd, I sit with my sister, eight years my senior, and try hard to make some sense of what she's telling me. Chelle has always been a free spirit, but now, like some mad conspiracy theorist, her reasoning is all a merry-go-round whose ending starts back at its beginning. That she is the bride of Christ, for instance. Who can prove she's not?

When my mother comes home later that evening, the expectant light in her eyes dies the moment her daughter's condition dawns on her. The sorrow that takes over scares Elaine and Austine and me, for what it says about Chelle. To me, Chelle is suffering from a temporary insanity of some sort, and that is the extent of it. As overwhelmed as I am, I assume that there are things that I don't understand about her condition, but that we'll learn about them by talking to doctors. She'll sleep it off; right herself in a day or two; take some pills; adjust her thinking. She'll be well, I tell myself, and everything will be cool soon, and there will be grounds again for laughter and relief. But then Mom uses that horrible word again—the word I haven't heard since Uncle Robbie passed away. "It's the schizophrenia," she says, shaking her head.

"Huh?"

"The schizophrenia."

The word is next to meaningless to me. Until now, schizophrenia has been just a bunch of blarney from the old sod, the legendary lunacy that was the stuff of Uncle Charlie's bent humor. Even if it were true, the curse struck at a safe distance—a vaguely remembered uncle from my boyhood, a grandmother I never met, and her great-grandmother, a nineteenth-century ancestor from County Roscommon. Schizophrenia is something my mother has rarely mentioned, I suppose because she hasn't wanted to feed into it. Into her own girlhood it first burst more than five decades ago; now the anguish in Mom's face begins to tell the full story. In a flash I remember the long-ago car ride away from Robbie's farm and my mother speaking of schizophrenia. All this time since Robbie's death, as it turns out, our madness has only been on furlough. Now the menace that went away is on the loose again, reborn before our eyes as Chelle flounces through our Taber Avenue home.

Seanna is away, but Austine and Elaine look on in disbelief. Dad, who is living nearby, is called to come see Chelle. He is a pretty big guy, but when he sees his daughter in her state, he dissolves in tears. Believing Dad is the devil himself, Chelle lets fly with her hellfire, swearing like a sailor at him. Dad takes off. Mom reassures us. "We'll work things out," she says. "She'll be well again. I'm sure she will."

This was the best possible spin. Between the divorce, the restaurant going bankrupt, and Chelle's breakdown, our world was crumbling like a house of dust. In the coming months, some of the facts of schizophrenia would be revealed. I would learn that Chelle's onset, in her mid-twenties, falls within the usual age range—fifteen to thirty-four—and that for the vast majority of schizophrenics, there's no such thing as full recovery. Many manage their illness through medication and live with less frequent and disturbing voices. For them the side effects of the medication can be as debilitating as the voices themselves. A rare few will live medication-free, without hearing the voices, but most are never the same again. The ones in our household have all been "recovery resistant." Complicating Chelle's chances of recovery, she would later also be diagnosed with bipolar disorder (aka manic-depressive illness), which causes unusual shifts in her moods and energy levels.

Prior to her onset, Chelle had been working as a waitress-actress in Manhattan. She hung out at Elaine's, the famed bistro near Eighty-eighth Street and Second Avenue that for years has been a magnet for show-business and literary celebrities. Chelle was like a starlet at a soda fountain. She chummed around with Christopher Reeve and knew Margot Kidder before they became famous. Leave it to Chelle to hook up with Superman and Lois Lane.

Chelle had both a special gift for seeing the world's beauty and a powerful intellect. She had already found kindred spirits in the existentialists, taking first place in a national high-school essay contest for her paper on Albert Camus, the Nobel Prize–winning author and philosopher who wrote *The Outsider*. Chelle was herself a bit of a philosopher, drawn to those on the margins and given to pondering the great questions of life: Why are we here? Where are we going? What's our place in it all? She always said we should imagine the world the way we'd want it to be. She was a sweet, doe-eyed charmer who was passionate about art and quietly intelligent about world affairs. Full of ideas, she was never full of herself.

Chelle was never discriminating, as likely to engage a street tramp in conversation as a literary know-it-all, and her generous nature made her an easy touch for New York's desperate beggars. She vowed to help them all one day when she made it. She calculated that she had until her thirtieth birthday to make it as an actress. Beyond fame and fortune, she wanted to be swept off her feet by her "handsome white knight." She sought out anyone who might be able to tell her when her breaks would come: priests, spiritualists, mediums—anyone who might know if her white knight or acting career were written in the stars.

Gradually Chelle's easygoing demeanor was subsumed by nerve endings too close to the big-city surface. She met a playwright—an older man with a drinking problem—and her world began to fragment. He was not her knight, but he felt safe. All that she encountered in New York was beginning to touch her deeply—the city's human suffering, its sometime brutality, its twenty-four-hour intensity. Out of that cauldron, the voices began to murmur. Chelle started to hear things, and to see things even, the visual and auditory hallucinations slowly consuming her.

Whether Chelle had tuned in to the voices or the voices had tuned in to her is hard to say. All she could later recall was that when she came out of her Lexington Avenue apartment one day, the ground began to shift beneath her feet. Like a rolling ribbon of concrete, the pavement sloped upward and contained Chelle within it. She was petrified by it. I can picture my long-legged sister trying to march downtown while the sidewalk is rising and rolling her back uptown, devouring her and never letting her get off her block.

The days that follow Chelle's homecoming are sheer bedlam for our household. Chelle takes up smoking, leaving lit cigarettes everywhere. She thinks nothing of running around nude, wafting around the house in colorful silk scarves alone. Her moods swing from joy to anger, her mind alighting on anything and everything, her manic preaching very much the insanity of the moment. We're all exhausted by it, but Chelle's nonstop rants always draw us from our beds at night. This goes on all summer, with Chelle going off like a lit box of firecrackers. It will surprise none of us if she drops dead from sheer exhaustion. She is off the wall.

In the middle of all this, we can't get her the professional help she needs, and only because the law presents a classic catch-22: As an adult, Chelle is the one who must commit herself, should she decide she is insane. Since she's too mad to grasp that fact, we're left to prove that she is violent, that she is "dangerous to herself or others," but we have no proof of that either. The law, designed to prevent the sane from being wrongly committed, prevents schizophrenics from getting the help they need so desperately at earliest onset.

More than anything, Chelle is suffering from religious delusions, a common symptom of schizophrenia. For a religious fanatic, though, she has a mouth like bile. No one takes it personally. Chelle's cursing is so out of character, it's like watching a five-year-old smoke. I feel her frustration, since she's virtually living under house arrest, or at least as much arrest as our freewheeling household can muster. But if we don't keep an eye on her, there's no telling what she might get into.

We cannot prove that Chelle is dangerous—though her volatility scares the hell out of us. We hide the kitchen knives, the matches, and the cigarettes. Because Chelle believes she is Christ's bride, my mother suspects spiritual possession. This is a case of wishful thinking, with Mom hoping for a less damning diagnosis. She calls in the local priest from St. Sebastian's, who arrives with an acolyte. Chelle looks like a cornered animal as they enter. I'm sent away, while my mother stays on as a witness. Prayers are read, apparently, but Chelle's spasms are as maniacal as ever, moving her from room to room with a fury and turbulence that eludes even the priests. It's not the devil that dwells in her; schizophrenia is her master, its voices her mad chants.

For Austine, what happens next is probably worse. So she can sleep without disturbance, I put an inside lock on her bedroom door. One night, when Austine forgets to latch it, she wakes to find Chelle on top of her. "I've got the family disease," she tells Austine, taunting her, "and now I'm passing it on to you."

That was it for Austine—she has graduated from high school and is free to go as she pleases. That autumn she drops out of fashion-design school and heads to Florida for a job with her friend Jane at Disney World. Luckily, Austine gets to miss some of Chelle's more outrageous antics, like the Sunday morning when she snuck out of Mom's new condominium, only to restage her show at St. Peter's, a local Roman Catholic church a third of a mile away. In the middle of the service, Chelle flings open the church doors to make her grand entrance. The eleven-o'clock Mass is under way, most pews filled, as Chelle strides, fully naked but with perfect aplomb, up the center aisle. Nearly to the altar, she spins around to face the shocked congregation. "You bastards," she snarls, "that's my husband you're worshipping."

Even though Chelle is not legally "dangerous to herself or others," we live in fear of her crossing that line. She is easily angered, although never violent. All we know is that she desperately needs help. After months of pleading, we finally present her with a non-negotiable proposal: she is going to the hospital. Elaine, Mom, and I pile into the car, and we breathe a sigh of relief when Chelle follows. We don't know if they'll admit her, or if she'll sign herself in voluntarily. We just know it makes sense to give her time to detach from the household for a while.

Twenty minutes later, Mom's car comes upon one particularly vivid landmark from their youth: the parking lot at the

Institute of Mental Health, the old brick building where on Saturdays Chelle had stood with her sisters waving up to our schizophrenic grandmother. For my mother, it must be a wrenching moment. But for Chelle it isn't bad at all, as she is too distracted to recognize the place. The rest of us say nothing, but we share the same thought. Is Chelle taking May's spot in the window of the old asylum? Is it Chelle's turn now to tilt her head forward, as May had done? Would Chelle now grow into the old gray lady behind the pane of madhouse glass?

In the end, Chelle surprises us all and signs herself in. The next day, during visiting hours, the place is clean and heated, but freaky and creepy as dozens of shabby, unkempt mental patients languish unattended. Some hold their heads between their knees; others lie on the floor, rock in chairs, or shuffle down the corridor cackling, a haze of cigarette smoke hanging above them. Long ago it became a cliché to say that psychiatric patients look like concentration camp victims, but as they shuffle past, their scrawny legs sticking out from their drab hospital gowns, no other image comes to mind.

In the unlocked room that Chelle shares with another patient, she is heavily medicated, speaking to us through dry lips no amount of water can make feel moist. She is polite but spaced out and distracted by her voices. When we leave, the putrid combination of disinfectant and smoke—a familiar mental-ward cocktail—stays with me. The atmosphere is the least of it, though. I had hoped Chelle would be properly looked after, naively believing that the hospital would prescribe whatever combination of drugs and therapies were needed to flush her out. I quickly learn that they are in the dark about schizophrenia. They don't know what causes it.

We have countless questions for Chelle's doctors, who

have ruled out physical disorders, such as hypoglycemia, which can mimic schizophrenia. Is schizophrenia a brain disease, as some postulate, or, as others believe, a confusional state of brain chemistry triggered by a genetic predisposition? And what about these voices? Are they a choice or a fact? Chelle's doctors can answer just a few questions, none of them noteworthy.

Whatever schizophrenia is, we seem bred for it. That much is obvious, while the doctors seem to have a neat hustle, masking ignorance with condescension. The meds do not eliminate the voices; they merely dim the volume, and there seems to be no attempt to address the root causes. Doctors are frustrated. This madness leaves no trace in X-rays or blood tests, nothing beyond a set of symptoms known diagnostically as "schizophrenia." So every day is the same, Chelle joining the others in line for their pills like peasants in the gruel queue, a situation that has no end in sight.

By and by we learn a little more. One of the most vexing things is that schizophrenia normally does not evolve slowly but comes in late teens or early adulthood like a thunderbolt, what doctors call "rapid onset." This we've seen on our own, that the condition is difficult to detect until it has progressed to full-blown psychosis. Apart from that, our quest for facts is met with blank stares. Despite intense study, biological causes remain largely a mystery. Serotonin, found in low levels in the depressed, appears to be overabundant in schizophrenics. Yet even that is not clear, and research is now shifting to glutamate receptors in the brain's prefrontal cortex.

When we come back a few days later for our second visit, Chelle is happy to see us, especially Seanna, her twin. Chelle is all drugged up on the antipsychotic Thorazine but still high on God. The drugs make her jittery, but she's content at first to stay as long as it takes to get help, joining the others doing the "Thorazine shuffle," puttering up and down the corridors in their sorry nightgowns. By the time we leave, the meds have worn off. Suddenly now Chelle appears frightened, her eyes a glancing plea for help. She pulls on Seanna's arm, begging her to take her away from here. It's a bright autumn day, and we stop to sit under a tree on the hospital grounds. I think of Grandma May, Uncle Robbie, Mary Egan, and now Chelle, and wonder why all this has to be. It's at least a relief, I think, that Austine, down in the Florida orange groves, is lucky she is not here to see this. As for Seanna, she is inconsolable about her twin.

As we leave the grounds, waving good-bye, I am dumbstruck. Nearly eight years separate Chelle and me, but I always felt a special bond with her. She was the big sister who always had time for Austine and me—"the babies," as she called us. On the beaches of Cape Cod and Narragansett Bay, while the rest worked on their summer tans, Chelle would spend hours with us making sand castles with moats and towers and parapets. We built grand castles for imaginary people to live in. Chelle would always have a fairy tale for us. This new Chelle seems light-years from my spade-and-bucket memories. Now she builds castles in the sky.

I go back to school to try to tuck back into my studies, but they don't seem necessary. It's hard to keep my head down. I can't fathom Chelle and I haven't heard from Austine in ages. This worries me. Why hasn't she called from Florida? Why is she so out of touch? In our family, when girls leave home, you come to expect the worst. Quietly, I suppose, I was bracing for the next pounce of the cat. Quietly it comes too.

CHAPTER FOUR

THE SECOND POUNCE

Mounds of snow glisten on the New England ground at night as Austine's plane touches down from Orlando. At the arrivals gate, my mother and I spot her easily, reassuringly. Austine's hair is shorter now, and frames her face like fur. She wears a white top and pale blue Capri-style slacks. As she steps closer, though, I sense something is wrong. From the way she walks, I can see that the old Austine has not landed. In her place is another young woman—shoulders hunched, body rigid, head bent forward. As she greets us, she is emotionless. I give her a hug, but she is stiff and resistant. She looks straight at me, forcing a smile, her face a dull mask. This cannot be Austine, but it is. She is like a light switched off, the madness apparently having carried her, pilot and passenger, into some dark oblivion. My heart sinks, my stomach drops, and I begin to cry inside.

Looking back, I realize there had been signs that this peculiar, late-blooming mental illness was developing in her. She sounded unfazed on the phone when I filled her in on getting Chelle hospitalized. I couldn't get a handle on her attitude and could only assume that she'd had enough of Chelle's drama—the reason she'd moved down to Orlando in the first place. I wanted to hear about Space Mountain and the rest of the fun down there at Disney, but Austine rarely called home, and when we reached her she had nothing to say. Now we see she is nothing like the confident nineteen-year-old who left home a year ago with plans to work at Disney. She didn't last long in the Magic Kingdom. All the while in Orlando, she must've been hearing voices. If we'd missed the clues, or were perhaps in denial about them, a phone call from her friend Jane had brought unmistakable focus to Austine's behavior. What Jane said had a familiar ring: Austine, she said, was "not well."

"Say what?"

"Austine," she said. "She is not doing very well at all. She's in this trance state."

Chelle and now Austine—two beautiful girls, child models, each with loads of charm and personality, who left home one day as young women, just as May had, and came home mad. It seems obvious that it's been passed down from our grandmother, who in turn had it passed down from her great-grandmother, Mary Egan, according to the family lore. Seeing Austine like this is a gasping, gut-wrenching thing—something that's still hard to reconcile. The fact of her affliction never retracts, a steady reminder of our mental frailty and an admonition against passing it on. Seeing her stuck there, haunted with a form of schizophrenia I had yet to encounter, one more frightening than all the rest, all I can think of is Edvard Munch's painting "The Scream."

It was a travesty with Chelle, but with Austine it's even worse. Whereas the three eldest girls were products of the 1950s and

'60s, Austine and I, born a year apart, were the younger clique among the children. Austine confided everything in me. Now she doesn't speak a word beyond a yes-or-no reply.

My earliest memory is of us side by side in our cribs. Austine climbs into my crib and shows me how to climb into hers. We cannot speak, but somehow we can splice into each other's perceptions. As little kids, we moved our mischief to my mother's walk-in closet, kitting ourselves up in her kimonos to stage our own little plays. We looked alike and were dressed alike, so were often mistaken for twins. We went to the same schools and summer camps. We took tennis, swimming, and dance lessons together, taught our dog tricks together. We scaled a fence and a neighbor's roof to reach our hiding place, where we smoked cigs and bitched to each other about parents, teachers, and the objects of our puppy-love crushes. We did everything together. She made my life twice as good.

Austine was extremely sociable, with a great gift for making friends and bringing people together. For added pleasure, she liked to mix them all up for some wild blends at parties: city kids thrown in with beach kids, mainly, but also the privileged types from the prep schools face-to-face with the edgier kids from the public and parochial schools. We had lots of friends: cool friends, nerdy friends, drunk friends, druggie friends, smart friends, athletic friends. They all adored Austine, the life of the party. You couldn't help loving this party girl.

I remember standing with her on the seawall at Narragansett Pier as teenagers. Looking out on the magnificent ocean tides, we dreamed of the possibilities. We were no more than fifteen and sixteen, and assumed the future would all be smooth sailing. Austine was going to be a fashion designer, meet the man of her dreams, and improvise from there. She wasn't determined to have it all; she just assumed it would all go our way.

As we stood at the seafront, she talked about each of us having lots of children who'd be close cousins and best friends. That was the plan. Maybe we were smoking too much pot at the time, but I don't think it would've mattered. I'm sure that wasn't the last time we looked out at that sea together, but it was the last time I remember doing so, because it was one of those rare instances when we talked about our futures. Standing on that seawall, we were a couple of adolescent best friends who were living large because we thought we had it all.

And now, just a few years later, Austine's quest for that good life has crash-landed, her future—like Chelle's before her—telegraphed to us days earlier via an all-too-familiar, and sadly understated, message: Austine was not doing well.

"Hi, Austine," Mom says. "Welcome home."

"Hi," she says meekly, gazing blankly, as if entranced.

"So how are you? How was Florida for you?"

Nothing, just a blank slate. Austine's whole affect has changed. She recognizes us, but that appears to be it. She does not seem to grasp our words. She is nearly catatonic; nothing we say seems to click. Each yes or no bears little relation to the question asked. No reaction.

My mother, at the airport, is speechless. She appears calm on the surface, but her devastation is unmistakable. Even as I go numb in my own state of shock, my mother's composure betrays an expression of complete fatalistic despair.

"Austine? What's wrong? What's going on? Austine, you're scaring me," I plead. "Austine?"

Austine looks annoyed with our questions crashing in; in her schizophrenic state, it must be like being asked for the most vital of answers in a way that's too vague and simple to understand. I ask too many questions, each of which has perhaps a million answers. For a moment, the three of us are silent.

As we leave the airport, I put my arm around Austine's hunched shoulders to let her know I understand, even if I don't. I understand only that Austine is in some sort of schizophrenic dream state, unable to register reality, locked away in a prison of psychosis, as unable to join with us as to be joined by us. Her mind—the very essence of her—has vanished like the little freckles that once speckled her nose. She has cognition, she has mental reflexes—it's just that they all seem to run on a closed circuit.

This new Austine is deeply strange. Whatever pictures she sees, whatever sounds she hears, they seem to grow more convincing as she entertains them. The tug of her voices is so strong she cannot resist. Whoever they are, whatever they are, they burst into her sound space from somewhere outside her skull.

On the ride home, she maintains her catatonic look. In the front seat of the car, she sits stiffly, chain-smoking Kool cigarettes, her gaze fixed straight ahead. For a moment she forces a forlorn shrug. Otherwise, Austine seems to virtually offer herself to her voices. I find it hard to look at Austine but make myself, the way you'd make yourself look at a car wreck. Another schizophrenic sister, this one stripped of every shred of her personality, splattered on the family windshield.

This is the worst. I've grown used to Chelle's illness over the last couple of years, but now Austine's insanity has struck like a big tiger, just two years after sinking its fangs into Chelle. I wonder if it has "picked" her, because who would choose this for herself? Two of Mom's five look to be genetically programmed for schizophrenia. The youngest, I wonder if I'm programmed too.

Austine and I were born within thirteen months of each other. She is Austine Patricia and I am Patrick Austin, and our lives are as entwined as our names. We loved each other in a unique, closest-sibling sort of way. We were always there for each other. Now the girl who used to be nothing but fun is suddenly lifeless, her once twinkling green eyes as flat and gray as slate. The sister most precious to me is being eviscerated by something I can't see or hear. What could be more sinister? Nothing seems real anymore.

Trying to read her face, I sense fear, confusion, and suspicion, as if her mind has caved in on itself. I glance over for any sign of joy, but there is none. This is hard to take. Austine's laughter used to ring high and happy through our house, her eyes dancing above her rose-colored lips. Now the madness has undone all those years of smiles and laughter, all memories of our happy days vaporized somewhere in the swamps of central Florida. She is traumatized by schizophrenia.

At home, when Mom finally speaks, her voice is calm and casual. Bizarrely, she takes pains to avoid laying any quick blame on schizophrenia. She says Austine must be "just feeling a bit low." Feeling low? The evidence for Austine's schizophrenia is every bit as convincing as it was for Michelle's. Barely an eyelash flickers on Austine's face, and my mother can only add that she's "going through one of life's rough patches."

Mom's response seems more than poorly considered. I am baffled to the point of anger by it. Schizophrenia in a second daughter may be shocking, but minimizing the madness was something for other mothers, not mine. Mom, of course, is trained in insanity and must have a pretty keen eye for it. Even if it's too alien to understand, it's too obvious to dismiss. Mom is an attorney, but when it comes to Austine she is deliberately overlooking the evidence—a reaction that continues to boggle. The triple-witching effect of seeing her mother, brother, and one daughter go mad may have worn her to a stub, yet Austine's condition has to be recognized for what it is. Hers may be a lower-wattage schizophrenia, less flamboyant than Chelle's, but as sure as eggs are eggs, *Austine is schizophrenic.* The word itself might as well be franked on her forehead. Schizophrenia has flooded the family's main vein like water from a swollen river.

In the coming weeks, I begin to understand that Mom isn't careworn. When Chelle went, Mom used up all her resources; when a second daughter was hoisted off the escalator, Mom could not cope. Behind the memory of her own mother's stolen beauty, behind Uncle Robbie's breakdown and then Chelle's religiously manic schizophrenia, Austine has leapt off the bridge with them. The savagery of schizophrenia seems to know no bounds. Once again Mom misgauged the strength of it in her maternal line. Mom either didn't see it coming back or didn't want to see it coming again, like the second fury of a hurricane after the calm of the eye has passed over.

Mom adored her baby girl. Now that she is gone, it's one too many cases of schizophrenia for Mom to handle. Mom's denial is a silent wail of anguish, a grief so deep that she has no words or tears, a mother's pain that is beyond all bearing. Poor Mom. Poor Austine. Poor Chelle. We all cherish a photograph of the two girls that graced the cover of the instruction booklet for an early-model Polaroid Land Camera, popularized in the late fifties and early sixties. Chelle is about twelve, Austine five or six. They are both in pigtails, both smiling for the camera. Chelle stands behind Austine, embracing her younger sister mischievously. Younger Austine is so serene, her nose freckled, her eyes quiet but happy.

There they are—a memory. I look at that photo and wonder: Why these two sisters and not the other two? Or why not me? Is there some throb of schizophrenic resonance, like one musical string answering another, that only Michelle and Austine can hear? The two child models look so perfect together in that Polaroid moment, so wholesome and full of the promise of youth. So bright a pair they seemed in that photo. What a loss. What blighted beauties.

Whenever I look at that old Polaroid, there's a strong attachment, a memory impossible to erase or replace. Having my own daughters might do the trick, but you never know when schizophrenia will turn up again. Could I bear the idea of looking into the bright young eyes of another child, knowing all the while that she might take the plunge? Could I be there to catch her, to pull her back from the brink?

Medically, there is nothing surprising about Austine's diagnosis: catatonic schizophrenia. As with Chelle, we're told that it would be a mistake to think anything can be done for her. For the next few weeks, I spend all my time with Austine, convinced that if anyone can bring her out of it, it's me. But schizophrenia is stuck like a block of ice on her head, and in that block is frozen every speck of the old Austine.

As kids, we had secret hiding places and secret meeting places, and shared every secret we had locked away. I want to walk with her again now and see what she sees. From what I can get out of Austine, and what I've learned so far about the delusions and hallucinations of schizophrenia, they are personal and particular, frequently featuring distorted images of dead people and loud, incessant voices whose shouts make it difficult to concentrate on what others are saying. I want to turn off her voices and reach into her head to remove her hallucinations one by one, like panels from our childhood slide-show toy. I want to insert a counterdream that ends her horror show.

I spend hours talking to her, but she just sits there smoking and fidgeting. I look closer and see her eyes flicker. Her head tilts, and there is something about the curl of her lip. But no, I am only having my own delusion. She just sits there, chain-smoking and fidgeting. As she struggles to speak, she seems distracted, while her face betrays an awful fear that never erases itself. Straining for a glimpse of her thought process, I see something just beyond the dull eyes. She seems to be pleading silently to some predatory personage for mercy. She seems certain of what she sees, so something must be there; it must be real to her. I light another cigarette, chain-smoking right along with her, but that brings us no closer. I cannot cross the chasm. Once so close, we now seem forever divided, all memories rolled up behind us.

Sweet Austine just sits all day in her darkened bedroom, speaking to no one, suffering what we cannot feel. From what I can gather, her mind, like Chelle's, is distracted by vague forms, changing shapes, disembodied voices. She feels under the spell of "something else," she says, a thing over which she says she has "no control."

There is not a span of even a few seconds when she is not trembling at some nightmarish vision. I try in vain to explain that it's all an illusion, a trick of the mind, and that she really has nothing to fear. I tell her that these phantoms have no connection to reality—that she is only seeing shadows. But it's no use: Austine's condition has complete authority over her, leaving her unable to have even a simple conversation.

Angry at this illness, I am also angry at Austine. However misplaced my feelings, I resent her for "choosing" to follow her hallucinations into this house of horrors, leaving me, her closest friend, at the outside door. As the days pass, Austine's illness forces an exclusion zone around her. I cannot intrude upon it or attack it, nor can I light the way out. After weeks of trying to coax her out, I reach the end of my rope. There's nothing I can do for her except light her cigs.

Before her onset, Austine never had a bad word for anyone. She was a giving soul, but this new quiet person would soon shock us all. It happened the following summer.

Chelle is out of the hospital on a weekend pass and we all go out to Cape Cod to a cottage belonging to Elaine's boyfriend. Upon our arrival at Truro Beach, just outside Provincetown, everyone but Austine is laughing and happy to be here; she, as usual, is silent and stiff.

I keep an eye on her, wondering why she's taking such a keen interest in the set of carving knives poking out of their storage block. Austine is transfixed by them, and it's clear to me she's planning something. Then, with uncharacteristic speed, she seizes a large knife from the block and lunges at Elaine's boyfriend, John. His back is turned, and a split second before Austine can plunge the blade into him, I tackle her, knocking her off balance. As the knife narrowly misses, we both hit the floor.

It is a shocking thing to witness—an attack entirely out of accord with Austine's sweet nature. Schizophrenia, we realize, has presented a whole new threat. What strange and distorted visions conjure such madness? What murderous voice or group of voices persuaded Austine to make the sudden movement? Austine's silence and the suggestion of voices behind it make a disturbing combination. What's next for us? we wonder. A macabre silent plot crept into her head. Will it creep back? Will Austine pull this again, on someone else? On one of her own siblings, even? It is an astonishing act that still gives me the willies, the heebie-jeebies, big time.

I take Austine out to the beach to talk things over, but she's unreachable as ever. From experience with Chelle and the others we know enough now about schizophrenia to understand that Austine is hallucinating badly. These voices, these auditory hallucinations, had somehow endowed her with the belief that John—a man she hardly knew—should die, and that she should be the one to kill him. Why, I ask her, would she wish to do this? She can't answer me. "I don't know," she says to each question I ask. In her state, she cannot muster more than a simple yes or no, as usual. Frustrated, I address the voices themselves. I demand that they show themselves, but they won't.

Back inside the cottage, we all quiz her for five or ten minutes. We are dumbfounded. Even John is more stunned than angry. I'm left wondering how to trace the impulse back through the mental passageway to where it began, to see how it was nearly carried out. Even if Austine could hold a discussion, she probably could never explain it. Because this is the most incomprehensible thing of all about schizophrenia: like Uncle Robbie with the slap, or May Sweeney with the teeth, or Chelle in the church, the knife attack from Austine was something that comes from a will seemingly beyond her own control.

Austine more so than the others seems to live under the spell of a whole band of voices whose raucous demands keep her narrowly confined until she lashes out. She never answers her voices audibly, as Chelle does in her chatty sort of way with her head friends. But in Austine's eyes, I can always see her losing a mental tug-of-war with the voices. Poor Austine. Chelle's voices are friend and foe; Austine's are all bad actors.

In the end, we cancel the weekend holiday, pile back into our cars, and head back to the complex of brick buildings at the Institute of Mental Health. Austine is the fourth family member to have her psychotic head examined here. She'll stay for just a few weeks and then transfer to a facility in Boston, but symbolically, at least, this is the end of the line. On her floor it's the same old scene: well-paid psychiatrists go from schizophrenic to schizophrenic, followed by nurses carrying Dixie cups filled with every kind of psychotropic drug. Austine drinks her Kool-Aid and says nothing.

CHAPTER FIVE

٭

TOO MUCH
FOR MOM

Stunning as the knife attack was, a graver tragedy had occurred six months earlier, just a few short weeks after Austine
had come home. It was January 6, on the Feast of the Epiphany,
a day the nuns called Little Christmas because Irish women are
given the day off to celebrate together. Mom had gone to Mass
as usual. Over the past couple of years, she had become a daily
communicant, attending early-morning services to help ease
her bitterness toward my father and, I think, to pray more
earnestly for her kids.

On that early January evening, Mom and Austine were sitting together at the dinner table. I can picture the two of them
facing each other, across the mahogany dining table, sharing
their Swanson TV dinners. No doubt Mom tries to strike up
some kind of exchange, but talking to schizophrenic Austine is
exhausting. In no time, you feel drained. On the dining room
table is a flowered centerpiece. Over it is the vast distance between them. As she sits there, making her fruitless overtures, I
picture Mom pausing briefly to recollect how many times

schizophrenia has deceived her. It is possible that the whole procession of schizophrenics flashes through Mom's mind—her own mother, May Sweeney; her mother's great-grandmother, Mary Egan; her brother Robbie; one daughter, Chelle; and now her baby girl, Austine, coming home like this, landing with crushing finality, detonating under ten tons of denial. It's possible they all click through Mom's mind, a full house of bad fortune, with the sane seemingly breeding the insane.

Wracked with regret, devastated by loss, my mother wrenched loose from her denial to confront the full brunt. She must have felt an aching pain in her head. A small burst of blood erupted in her brain. The aneurysm punctured an artery, and Mom died where she fell, more or less at Austine's feet.

Mom had seen one too many schizophrenics, too few remedies. No brain is built to cope with pain like this. In its own weird way, schizophrenia got her in the end too. My guess is that Austine never felt for a heartbeat or checked for a breath. Eventually she knocked at the home of the next-door neighbor, who had her dial Seanna up in Boston at her Beacon Hill apartment. "Hi, Seanna," Austine muttered. "Mom just died." Seanna, in turn, called me at college to break the news.

The wake is held at Skeffington's Funeral Home, where both sides of our family get buried. Dad is here, divorced from Mom but grief-stricken nonetheless. Nervous by disposition, he shuffles in and out of the viewing room, where Mom presides in her casket, nearly overwhelmed by wreaths and flowers. I run my hand over her head and kiss her cold brow. I wonder if she still exists in some other plane. Is what's behind death's door a somethingness or a nothingness? Is the grave all there is? Is the body it? Is death a consolation?

Mom lies in her coffin, a waxen mannequin of death, her eyes shut, her mouth neither smiling nor frowning, as I take my place again in the receiving line next to my four sisters. An endless line of mourners files past, offering condolences, while we try to hold it together. I'm all too aware of the lurking insanity: Chelle is all charged up to chatter, but at least she is no longer talking nonsense about her wedding to Jesus. Austine utters not a word, oblivious to the comfort offered by friends and relatives, her eyes fixed and motionless.

Chelle and Austine have been hit with the same disorder, yet they are damaged in different ways. How stark is the contrast between two schizophrenics so clearly unalike, Chelle with what's known as "positive" symptoms, Austine with the "negative" symptoms of social withdrawal. It's as if there's some stranger in Chelle who snuck into her while she was out in New York. Then there's another stranger in Austine, who replaced her down at Disney World.

If Chelle is downtown, as it were, then Austine's schizophrenia has led her way out to the suburbs of insanity. If Chelle is dumping Warren Beatty and dating Jesus Christ, then at least she's having a good time. Chelle still has her humor, if her meds are working, and even her sense of irony. They are a match of schizophrenic opposites, but I feel much worse for Austine. If Chelle can quite suddenly revert to paranoia, Austine never gets a reprieve.

My mother's wake is interminable, the length of each instant ticking past in slow motion. Though she is the dead one, I look over at Austine and think how close her catatonic state of mind puts her to death. Not just death, but something worse, as every twinkle, every smile, every little laugh that would be born is crushed by schizophrenia.

People cannot tell with Chelle. With Austine, most think

she is laid low by Mom's death; they do not see that she is schizophrenic. Only our very closest friends know that something more than grief is going on. Austine, especially, is lost to her condition. Elaine and Seanna maintain. I grow irritated, mainly by Austine, embarrassed that her stone gaze is giving us away. I hold my breath, clench my fists, and try to remain silent, fearing that I'll say something regrettable. I cannot make myself understood; I dwell on the past and think of what we did as kids, acting ridiculous and laughing at things no one else could comprehend. Chelle used to make sand castles and point out the Big Dipper to us. Austine used to ride bikes, dance, play sports, chase boys, shoot pool, tell jokes, laugh, cry. Now she says and does nothing, while Chelle is quietly muttering away to her invisible friends. Austine is stuck in the dead zone. Unable to muster a simple hello to anyone, she makes lazy nods at the well-wishers.

Finally, I lose it. "Austine," I bark, "why can't you just snap out of it?"

"I can't," she says, innocently, turning her helpless eyes toward me, her arms flopping at her sides, a look of sad resignation on her face. Of course she can't—the poor kid. Schizophrenia throbs in her head. She cannot just will herself to awaken from it; otherwise, she would. Her hallucinations are always there. Of course she would remove them if she could, but schizophrenia is like a total thought system for her. Chelle may vacillate between sanity and insanity, but schizophrenia is the world to Austine. She seems entranced by what she sees, an all-embracing beast that haunts her every waking second. In her world, I'm out of place.

I'm at a loss. All this bad stuff has happened in the span of a few short years—the bankruptcy, the divorce, the mental breakdown of half my sisters. And now, here at Skeffington's, it is as if we've slipped through some weird space-time wrinkle into a newer, even weirder reality. I can accept my mother's death, but the gone-and-not-dead are not so easily forgotten. My musings turn to fantasy: I imagine my mother alive and full of warmth, and Austine in her place, cold and in the casket. I wonder if it wouldn't be an act of charity to put Austine out of her misery. Her schizophrenia is like a rehearsal for death. If I had to live like that, I'd stab myself a hundred times. I think of sending Austine where Mom has gone, but I am not a killer. I wonder what Mom would say were she able to speak from her casket. *Now, Patrick, you know that we cannot play God. Your sister is not a horse gone mad in a barn, Patrick. She is not meant to be put down like a dog.*

I finish the death thought, although not entirely. I feel rotten for even thinking it, however briefly. Despair turns to guilt as I regard the family freak show. I clench my teeth, aching for the wake to end, but I have to hunker down, get through this. I keep shaking hands, taking condolences, thanking folks for coming. Only Elaine and Seanna understand now, and only Mom truly had an inkling from the get-go of what a misery this madness might make for us. Only Mom could see that sanity for us is like a cliff house built on sand. And now she's in the ground.

Back at home, gripped by death and pulverized by all this schizophrenia, I drank and with every angry breath cursed our meltdown. It was the beginning of a lost weekend that would last twenty-five years. There was no going back for Chelle and Austine. They were psychological invalids, schizophrenically disabled, and soon there'd be no going back for me.

I stayed in Boston with them for the next three years,

hacking it out as a cab driver, visiting Austine at her group house and Chelle at her latest mental hospital, one of many both shuttled through over the years. It was dispiriting. I was a young guy, but I felt angry. The situation was too dire. I grew tired of fighting for impossibilities. I saw myself as failing, but wanted to feel I'd tried. I felt I could do nothing, so I ran from Boston. I ran from Austine, mainly, not from Chelle.

I left Austine, a shuffling zombie, a wrecked, friendless mess, in her bleak world and moved to Washington, D.C. I straggled back for the odd Christmas visit, inevitably to find the pair steeped in their medicated fog. I gave up as the others took over. For ten years Austine would live with Dad in his South Boston apartment. Driving a cab himself now, the final rung on his downwardly mobile ladder of failure, Dad redeemed himself in his twilight years. For ten years he drove Austine with him everywhere in his taxi, and then he died too.

Friends grew up, got married. I dodged it. I was afraid to have kids only, like Mom, to have the schizophrenia sucker me in again for another one-two punch. Binge drinking was my way of going out of my own mind, like going crazy every night. I shook my head, downed the drinks, snorted and smoked and, yes, even shot the drugs. I abandoned myself, living for a while like an outlaw. I stumbled around, shot a lot of pool, quietly cursed the injustice of things. I was chasing women on the verge, pleading with them, appealing to them, testing their limits. It never lasted. I was hardly husband material. I was trouble. I lived recklessly, drifting in and out of journalism, all the while running in place, first in the District and then in London.

Drink made me forget about things in a way no therapist could. People swayed in the dark, lampposts caught me, and the demented sprites of schizophrenia flitted into view everywhere I went. In nameless cities they lived in crumpled heaps on flattened cardboard boxes, rummaging through the rubbish bins for food, the decrepit souls rising up for spare change like bodies floating up from the bog. I was drawn to the dispossessed while still craving the permanence of a normal family.

I was living in north London, still boozing, still coking, when one day I heard the click. Hangovers weren't just hangovers in my Islington flat; they were mini nervous breakdowns. Reality was a thin thread indeed. Monitoring my own sanity as a hypochondriac might take his pulse, I knew I was done. I could see my own crack-up coming, so I skidded to the crumbling shoulder.

For a year or two, I was the Charles Atlas of clean and sober. Soon enough I settled. I centered and began to wear life like a much looser garment. Living in London was fabulous. I was three years clean and nursing a sparkling water one day in an East End pub when I chanced to meet a British doctor. Madness came up, as it does, and the doctor dropped something about the discovery of the world's first gene link for schizophrenia. In Ireland, of all places. In Roscommon— home of my ancestors—of all places in Ireland.

This blew my mind. For so long everything about schizophrenia had been so murky, so hopeless, and now here was this chink of light. The doctor was on the level. Everything he said checked out later online. Dysbindin is a gene involved in the synapses, the points where one neuron connects itself to another, and blood samples taken from a few hundred schizophrenic families in Roscommon in the 1980s had led to the discovery, in 2002, of a chromosomal abnormality for the gene in a statistically significant number of schizophrenics. The research, published in the *American Journal of Human Genetics* and reported by the *New York Times,* had raised hopes that a cause might be found or a treatment devised. After years of desultory efforts and false claims of breakthroughs elsewhere, a team of Irish and U.S. researchers had made the first crack in the genetic code. Their research was solid gold, peer-reviewed, replicated in other studies, and would quickly be followed by the discovery of more susceptibility genes outside of Ireland. How had I missed it?

The Irish, a people known rightly or wrongly for having something of a head start on madness, are also known for tossing up the odd miracle or two. To me, this discovery was the equivalent of a medical miracle. It wasn't something that could magically transform my sisters, but it ignited my imagination, so I started asking questions again. The more I learned, the more I wanted to know why this cloud-shrouded mythic island off the west coast of Europe had been the breeding ground for a madness that is as spectacular as it is prevalent in our maternal line.

I was living in England, a short hop from Ireland, and the more I read, the more curious I became about the strong associations between schizophrenia, on the one hand, and famine, emigration, substance abuse, and older fathers on the other, factors so prominent in the peasant Irish experience. More and more I began to think of Ireland, just next door, as a place where I could go to pay a visit to our collective schizophrenic mind. It wasn't that I wanted to go to Ireland—I had to go to grasp how this fanged, hooded head might snake its way through our Roscommon bloodline. Live and learn, they say. Or die like Mom and forget all this madness altogether. For me, I felt, the choice was that stark.

PART II

THE
IRISH
ROOTS

CHAPTER SIX

BOG
OF
NO RETURN

The underground Cave of the Cat is my first incision because it's featured in tales of madness that stretch back for as long as there has been an oral history in Ireland. I am knocking around County Roscommon, beginning at the beginning, or at least as far back as the myths of madness go here. My ancestors were part of this twisted fairy tale. Given the hereditary force of the condition, there may be untold numbers of schizophrenics out there among ancestors going back thousands of years, long before the place was thick with "saints and scholars."

The Egans were the ones who spilled into the vast gene pool of people who fell from the Great Famine of the 1840s into the New World, at the time the largest migration of refugees in European history. It wasn't pretty. The British, who ruled here, surpassed everyone else in the nineteenth century with the scale of their cruelty, a campaign of human suffering so complete that it was difficult for the outside world to fathom.

This is where the Egans came from, so this—more so per-haps than any other place—is where answers may lie. From what little my grandfather said, and the small bits my mother added, it all started with the Egans of Cam-Kiltoom Parish in southern County Roscommon, now known only as Kiltoom. Where to begin? I have a name, Mary Egan. I have a Roscommon parish. And I have a mystery, schizophrenia. Mary Egan, I'm told, lived in these bogs, and went mad here before emigrating to America. Her schizophrenia was proba-bly passed down to May Sweeney, Uncle Robbie, Chelle, Austine, and the still unborn.

As a visitor, you can't help feeling an otherworldly sense of isolation here. What is it about this place that produced our madness? Was it just the hardships that ground Mary Egan down? Did Ireland's thick mist trick her eyes and ears with visions and voices? Or was her madness projected from more mysterious inner fissures? She was my mad grandmother's mad great-grandmother, I'm told, yet she left behind no DNA or paper trail, no tight forensic answers. She was what crime scene investigators call a "bone case." That's a great shame, be-cause mitochondrial DNA is passed down the maternal line. Mine would be identical to Mary Egan's.

Here in the bog land, history literally moves on the blan-ket of peat beneath my feet. In Mary Egan's time, in the 1840s, Roscommon was an impoverished county carved into more than twenty-seven thousand farms of about one acre each, mostly growing potatoes. Today the farms are bigger but the farmers fewer, with the county holding about a fifth of its pre-famine population of a quarter million. Left to the care of other historians, the story of the starvation on those farms has been well told elsewhere. Here the famine was especially hard-hitting, yet how it reshaped the psychological map is a more slippery inquiry.

Along the Shannon and Suck rivers, anglers fish in timeless snapshots of life. Shoals of dead fish float in the more polluted fingers of the rivers, once famous for their pike, bream, and perch in the sluggish sections and for their trout in the tributaries. There are some rolling hills, but much of the county is bog or flat terrain. The sheep fields, which lie on thin soil, are some of the best in Ireland because the limestone underlayer will bear any amount of wet weather in summer. Even by Ireland's standards, Roscommon is a wet place.

The bogs—formed by the accumulation of dead plant material, pollen and dust, and persistent rain when the forests were felled—is stripped for peat moss, the turf cut from the edges for cheap heating fuel. It's a landscape that was denuded of trees centuries ago as settlements expanded. The felling of large swaths of ancient forests made way for these farms, and still gives the place a bleak beauty in the steady drizzle. According to medieval maps of the area, this bog land was some of the most thickly forested acreage in Ireland. It was all woods, for the most part, until just northwest of here on the Magh Da Cheo (the Plain of Two Mists). No wonder the Druids worshipped the trees—so few were left standing. Between the rain and the hunger, it's hard to believe anyone could've had faith in a kindly creator.

In the cave's dark wetness it's not hard to imagine the fairies flying among the conical hats of the wizard priests and the poets, storytellers, singers, and diviners who were a part of everyday life. Pagan or Christian, Ireland has always conjured a magical, unseen otherworld that goes beyond the veil of the visible. A few hundred yards away are the burial mounds and passages of Cruchain (pronounced "CRU-ah-shan-eye"), a royal site back when fairy lore was at the core of Celtic belief, before Catholicism absorbed, but never fully replaced, paganism. This cave is connected—at least in myth—to Keshcorran, another cave some eighty miles away, with a squadron of fairies said to travel back and forth between them. Ireland abounds with supernatural tales of underground caves, and these are no exception.

I shout to awaken the fairies but hear only my own echo. These fairy stories have come down mostly in secondhand versions, but the proposition that fairies play a part in madness sounds like lunacy itself. The cave gets a mixed press locally. Christians call it Ireland's "hellmouth." Folklorists believe it was the mythical entrance to the netherworld of fairies who, they say, tumbled out of heaven and landed here on earth. Archaeologists believe that the cave was a royal site in pre-Christian Ireland, when the Druids claimed to draw supernatural power from fairies, including a curse of madness cast down upon generations, riding on a wisp of hair. The *Senchus Mor,* which contains the laws of Druidic Ireland, refers to the insane as those who fell under the spell of Fullon, a Druid who lived hundreds of years before Christ. The *dlui fulla,* or Fullon's wisp, was a ball of straw or grass or hair that had been blown into a madman's face.

Growing up, I knew nothing about all this stuff. To me fairies were always the angelic creatures with butterfly wings that had caught the fancy of Victorian artists in Britain. Irish accounts, real or imagined, tell a different story of menacing cats, grotesque dragons, triple-headed vultures, werewolves, goats with curling horns and a human voice, and a shape-shifting horse with yellow eyes and a wild mane. These creatures, the mere sight of which would send farmers diving into fields, were said to have wrecked the countryside.

The cave has an eerie sameness—a constant year-round temperature and dark stillness. Going in deeper, I feel I'm entering a forbidden tomb. With each step, I have a sense that I'm not supposed to be here—that this place holds secrets better left in darkness. The devil himself, sometimes portrayed as a cat in ancient Ireland, was thought to have held nocturnal orgies in this cave. It's said that "the devil knows more from being old than from being the devil," but what does he know about schizophrenia, and does he do his recruiting here? I see nothing—only a cloud of my own breath, visible in the flashlight, and the fleeting silhouette of my hobbitlike shadow thrown upon the cave wall. I feel silly, but the cave may be a good place for me to begin to look backward, and in that backward look to begin to fathom the madness.

The cave stretches for about fifty meters, closing in a narrow cone. I go to the end and back, but all is wet and blackness, apart from the carved initials on ancient lintel stones. The initials belong to Douglas Hyde, a Roscommon native son and Ireland's first president. A few yards in, a couple of dozen small stones form an inscription on the inverted V-shaped roof. The old runic-style letters—carved vertical lines from the early medieval alphabet called "ogham"—are also written on a doorway passage supported by lintels at the entrance. Old spoken Irish had no literature apart from these ogham words, which were used for magic and divination. These spell out the name of Orlam, the son of Maeve, the golden-haired queen of Connaught. Her name, which means she who is "mead," or she who intoxicates, links her to Shakespeare's queen of the fairies, Queen Mab, in *Romeo and Juliet,* the midwife of the fairies, the miniature creatures who drive her chariot, carved out of an empty hazelnut, across the noses of sleeping men to make them dream.

Maeve's home marks Roscommon as the center of Ireland's bygone matriarchy. She was the personification of feminine power in pagan Ireland, and the Irish Catholic fixation with the "holy virgin mother of God" probably owes something to its devotion to Maeve. The queen held court here, burning turf fires at the mouth of the cave as much for invocation as for light and heat. There was nothing puritanical about old Queen Maeve. In her royal raiment, she was said to have sexually exhausted thirty men a day here, "one man in another man's shadow," according to the *Tain Bo Cuailnge,* a great epic tale that recounts her struggle with Cuchulainn, the hero of Ulster and the most fearsome warrior in all of Celtic folklore. Cuchulainn himself was a famous madman. As he laid waste to Maeve's forces, he swirled into paroxysms of insanity all over the island.

It's the realm of myth, which suggests tall tales. Yet some of these stories survived because they were told and retold until they were taken as truth, and even as morality lessons. Myth was man's earliest form of psychology, a useful guide to the deeper meanings of life. Everything was divine at heart, nothing profane. To think in terms of myth was to be attuned to the spiritual dimensions of life.

Druidry never did die out entirely in Ireland. It shape-shifted through the centuries, thanks to storytelling. This was as it should be, because the Druids believed that the soul does not die, but rather its wisdom gets etched on each new lifetime. Apparently, the Druids did know a thing or two. Pythagoras claimed they held amazing magical knowledge. Connaught myths, which deal with clashes of forces of light and dark, normally involve a wounded hero's journey to the womb of that greatest of all earth goddesses, the ocean.

Rathcroghan, where the kings and queens of Connaught were inaugurated and buried, lies just outside the cave's entrance. It was the setting for the opening and bloody conclusion of the *Tain Bo Cuailnge*. It's a quiet archaeological complex now, just a bunch of earthen mounds on the road through Tulsk, according to the nearby visitors' center. Dioramas show how early in the first millennium it was a very active area. Archaeologists probing under the mounds, the so-called fairy forts, have found man-made ridges and circles that date from 3000 B.C. Here the largest fairy mound, ninety meters in diameter, was topped by a two-meter-high nipple. At this nipple, the Connacht kings were crowned by virtue of their marriage to Maeve, the great fertility goddess.

Like many archaic cultures, the Celts had some bizarre practices involving the head. They indulged in head-hunting and drank the blood of bulls to inspire dreams. Archaeologists finding heads separated from torsos in Celtic burial grounds on the European continent have fueled speculation about the Celtic "cult of the severed head." They believe the mad were feared, even after death. The head, the cauldron of insanity, might be detached and placed meters from the body, and the feet were sometimes burned to keep the dead from rising and walking back. Although head-hunting was not unique to the Celts, they believed you could control a person's afterlife through the use of his head. Skulls were cleaned out, decorated in gold leaf, and used for ritual libations or nailed to doorways in deference to ancestors.

———

In the cave there's nothing of what I've read or heard: no cats, no fairies flying airily, no cloven hoofprints in the mud here by Ireland's gates of hell, no dark cornerstone on which madness rests, no portal to the world where the minds of schizophrenics have gone. As with madness, blindness seems the way. Passing back along the cave wall, my heels sunk to the ankles in the thick muck, I squeeze through the meter-wide exit and into the Roscommon countryside. A spray of fireworks paints the night sky and bonfires burn on distant farmlands, a tradition dating back to pagan Ireland, when tribes gathered for the Samhain, the biggest feast day of the Celtic calendar. My hosts, sculptor and pagan scholar Davey Patton, the professor and his students, and the whiskey-sipping farmer, are here stoking imaginations with their own bonfire celebration.

Stories are swapped about this and that phantom fairy ghost. Opinions are nuanced as we poke the fire. Almost everyone is open to the idea of fairy abduction, though it's hard to pin anyone down in the pale moonlight. The professor says I need to channel a deep but possibly dormant sense of mystery. I play along out of respect. Long before there was a Halloween, the Samhain was the original "mischief night," when youngsters begged door-to-door for food and drink. In the midnight darkness, Irish kids might swipe a gate from its hinges. Today they still set candlelit pumpkins in windows to welcome harmless passed ancestors.

The fire burns, the old man stokes it, and a story lives on, like a hangover from the ancient past, about a grisly pagan practice of roasting cats over bonfires. Way back when, the fires were made of slaughtered cattle bones—thus *bonfire* derives from "bone fire." The piles of sacred peat-flamed cattle bones, lit each year on the last evening of October, burned on every hill in Ireland, a plea to the otherworld to keep the evil spirits at bay and to give thanks for the harvest. Dressing in costume dates from the belief that disguises can hide us from the visiting dead tonight. The reimported myth of the night of the living dead thrives in Ireland as Halloween, with kids dressed up as Simpsons and space aliens out collecting candy.

Unlike their ancient brethren, modern-day Druids no longer lay on curses or practice sacrifice. They believe in the communion of all living things and harmony between nature and human souls. Nor does the Catholic Church continue to rule with unquestioned authority. But mystic "vision" still hangs thick in the air, because the past was not so long ago in Ireland. The Great Famine of the 1840s, which sent my ancestors to Boston, was blamed by some on the fairies. After the fungus ran down potato stalks, destroying crops overnight, some farmers swore they saw legions of fairies waging war in the skies above their blighted fields. Given the scale of the famine, the bad legion apparently triumphed.

From bad health to failed crops, fairies explain the unexplainable. So people with a mental disability were said to be "away with the fairies" or "in the fairies." According to Irish folklore, fairies envy Christians and often possess them, but they are not purely evil because they aim to get back in heaven someday. Newspapers from the time are strewn with police accounts of suspected changelings being killed, usually by drowning, by parents trying to break the spell. Such cases shocked readers then, yet were dealt with leniently by courts whose magistrates accepted superstition as a mitigating factor.

Insanity is not something you do to yourself; it's something that's done to you. The sheer speed of its onset suggests that schizophrenics are not simply misguided by themselves. They appear to be guided by voices. Most of those who kept the lore alive were Catholic peasants. Apart from a few literary-minded Protestants who were interested in mysticism, the likes of William Butler Yeats and George Russell, the non-Catholics tended to dismiss it as the fairy nonsense of an ancient culture rich in superstition.

The Irish aren't ones to stand on ceremony, and so before I know it, the old farmer is pedaling off on his bicycle and the students are boarding their professor's Ford Transit van. I follow in my rental, driving past pumpkins lighting windows in farmhouses, by a dozen bonfires twinkling in distant fields. As I drive, I reflect on fairyland. Even if we can't see them, that doesn't mean fairies don't exist in another dimension. A classic tautology, but there it is.

And there I'll have to leave it. In Ireland, it's difficult to say where fact ends and myth begins, because so much is pseudo-history. Belief in fairy stories in one form or another is found all over the world, and one man's myth is always another man's gospel. But here in old Ireland, myths have a certain staying power.

Given the strong streak of mischievousness in the Irish, who knows what to believe? Despite the breakthrough in gene research, schizophrenia remains idiopathic, meaning there's no known underlying cause. It is conceivable, though far from obvious, that schizophrenics may be tapping into another dimension, a comprehension of some hidden realm perhaps. Fairies may be the local expression of the transcendental visions known only to mystics and madmen, the saints and schizophrenics of this green island. It's curious to me that the two basic species of fairies who inhabit the land resemble my sisters symptomatically. There are the "trooping fairies," who are an outgoing bunch, much like Chelle. And there are the introverted "solitary fairies," who resemble Austine. They are said to be found near hawthorn bushes and sacred stone circles and the "rath mounds" that sprinkle the pastures.

Sigmund Freud would have none of this. The renowned psychoanalyst, who famously said that the Irish were the only people who would not respond to psychotherapy, judged myths as hogwash, but he never denied their psychological power. Freud's onetime collaborator, Carl Jung, who also worked under Bleuler, saw myth as tethering man to a common spirit. To Jung, whose study on schizophrenia, *The Psychology of Dementia Praecox,* fostered years-long correspondence with Freud, fairies were images of the psyche (Greek for "spirit"). If science makes sense only of the outside world of the physical senses, he believed, then myth taps into the deepest inner wells of human psyche.

I'd lean toward Jung, if only because the family schizophrenia has taught me to credit less of what I see and hear to the senses. If only a tiny slice of the light spectrum is visible to the human eye, only a fraction of the sound spectrum audible to the human ear, then who knows what we're all missing. If fairy faith remains strong here in the Roscommon countryside, it must have something to do with the willingness of the Irish to toy with the notion—what Yeats, the grand poet-mystic of Irish letters, called "the vast and vague extravagance of the Celtic heart."

It was Yeats, more than anyone, who burnished the image of the romantic Irish dreamer who, with the soul of the poet, had never lost a sense of other worlds. This poetic other-world—in folklore an eternal place like heaven, where there's no unhappiness, sickness, or death—was to Yeats a real place, as real as our physical realm, and preferable in many ways as a place of refuge. Be that as it may, I have a hard time romanticizing madness. Because if this old cat cave really is a home of madness, then it is the darkest bowel of hell.

The next day is All Souls' Day, when the Roman Catholics get their own day to counterbalance the Samhain. They believe that this is the day when the living may intercede on behalf of the dead, rather than the other way around. It's also the day that St. Malachy, Ireland's first saint to be canonized by a pope, died. The prophet, who predicted the very day of his death in 1148, was said to be a healer of madwomen through prayer. Not very differently in the pagan times before him, witch doctors "cured" lunatics the same way that they cured mares of the parasitic disease farcy: by whispering spells and incantations in their ears.

I have no strict itinerary, just a vague sense of duty—to my sisters and to the unborn, at least—to take a fairly long glance back, to follow the leads as best I can. It's the thinnest of threads—the one that tethers the mind to reality—but here it begins for me, my eyes shifting from the string of cars in my rearview mirror back to the slow-moving tractor coming up quickly on the stretch of highway out in front of me.

The Irish literary giant Samuel Beckett said something about a man's fathoming the darkness only at his own peril. At the very least I am not prepared to brave a dark Irish winter. It's too cold, too gray, too soaked with rain now, but I'll be back in the better weather to have a thorough look around. It's not advisable for me to jump too soon. I've had an up-and-down time of it, so I try to take things as they come.

Looking into psychosis, you have to have the proper mental attitude.

There is an old Irish saying, "To know me, come live with me." I decide to take them up on it, for a few months at least. I hatch a plan to find a camper van back in London, and relaunch from there in the summertime.

⟨🌀⟩

CHAPTER SEVEN

LONDON
CALLING

Back in London, the friend whose flat I am sharing is nowhere to be found. Janet's mother tells me that she has had "an episode," and I can catch up with her at the local mental hospital. Down near the Thames River near Westminster, Janet has been "sectioned" for manic-depressive illness. Janet (this is her middle name) is a great friend, a gifted painter and photographer, a brilliant mimic whose sense of the absurd is as keen as her wit, and an all-around good egg. It's sad to find her like this, all drugged up on a drab psychiatric ward, a crumpled heap barely able to tie her shoelaces. "I was ready to go spray-paint Buckingham Palace," she manages, "so they shot me full of olanzapine."

What can I tell her, that she'll soon be back to her old self and we'll spray-paint the palace together? I suspect she'll come around once they fine-tune her medication, and she does. As rough as it is, bipolar mania is a mental-illness minnow next to schizophrenia; it's a mood disorder, not a psychosis, though it can and does reach psychosis in some. Manic-depressives can soar in the real world. For the schizophrenic, there's very little in life to do; for the manic, there's often too much. From what I can tell, schizophrenics can't park as easily in one reality because they cross so many. Those with bipolar disorder are just up and down in this one.

On Janet's psych ward I get to meet a few more schizophrenics. There's an Italian who holds a string of rosary beads and is obsessed with picking particles of dust off his clothes. There are two Romanian Gypsies, a Lithuanian, a Dane, and an Englishwoman named Lucy who is convinced that a Harvard psychiatrist has implanted chips in her brain. A young biologist, Lucy is planning to postpone her career for a temporary stint as a nun. "For a few months," she said. "I'll take my vows and sacrifice all sorts of things, and they'll call me Sister Lucy."

Shortly after this, Lucy manages to escape from the hospital and is last seen heading for Cornwall, in the south of England. Her plans are upended when she is arrested as a peeping Tom. "They put me in this hospital just for doing nothing," she tells us by telephone from another mental hospital. The only problem now is that invisible people are sewing razor blades under her skin and putting pulsing objects inside her body somehow.

My new acquaintances might seem like an odd coincidence, but throughout life I've had a weird affinity with off-kilter folks, as if my sisters' sufferings have placed me in stream with others like them. I've lost count of the number of schizophrenics I've known, who have moved, amused, confronted, compelled, puzzled, perplexed, and annoyed me. Some of the most appealing and provocative characters I've met have been schizophrenic, including a man who thought he could bounce radio waves off the atmosphere. There was a woman who claimed to have three children from six different men, including me. I once knew a schizophrenic who was sure that light rays were bending themselves into rubber, another who thought he was a giant turtle in a parking lot on Mars, another who felt that fish were swimming in his head, literally.

Wherever I've lived, I've made a point to meet the local schizophrenics in the neighborhood. In passing, whenever I can, I've tried to extend myself, but never without reserve or trepidation at first. The most extraordinary schizophrenic I've ever met was a plump, unshaven black man who, in the summer of 1995, stumbled into a Washington, D.C., blues club, Madam's Organ, with a weather-beaten suitcase in hand. He ordered a beer, shuffled his feet to the music, and started talking nonsense into his mug. He mumbled something about James Brown this and James Brown that. Then he popped open the side latches of his suitcase to reveal thousands of psychotropic pills, which overflowed and spilled out onto the bar. "You want some happy pills?" he asked. "I take 'em 'cause I'm schizo."

The stranger vanished into the crowd, then reappeared hours later onstage, where he somehow had talked the lead guitarist out of his instrument. And when he put his hands on that axe, fingering the fret board with a geography that was alien to the rest of us, magic happened. The whole place erupted for his brilliant version of James Brown's "The Payback," followed by Robert Johnson's "I Believe I'll Dust My Broom," not easy numbers for a sane man to play, and rarely with such mastery. When he finished and the crowd roared for more, he flashed a puzzled, gap-toothed smile and shimmied a bit, looking like he'd just been Tasered. Moments later, he was back at the bar talking nonsense to his beer foam again.

I bought him another and he told me his story. He said his name was Prentiss Richardson and he lived in a psychiatric unit at St. Elizabeth's Hospital, the nation's first large-scale, federally funded psychiatric hospital. Prentiss said he was out on a weekend pass. "I'm schizo," he continued. "I talk to myself. Talk to myself and talk to myself. Hear voices and talk back." We struck up a friendship. I gave him an old Fender Stratocaster I couldn't play. Eventually he formed a band called Weekend Pass. The band didn't last, mainly because Prentiss pawned his guitars as soon as he got them. "I don't know why," he told me. "It's the voices. They tell me to sell 'em."

In London I was looking for a camper van, and in the borough of Camden—known by the Irish as the Holy City, because so many of their immigrants have wound up there—I found a Scotsman at an informal market with a 1994 Nissan Vanette for sale. He was a tough and tattooed Glaswegian—a Celt, which boded well, I thought, for my journey. I liked the van's power and handling; it felt fast but heavy, like a police car. So we did the deal—2,100 pounds sterling—and I was away. At a friend's flat in nearby Kings Cross, we tore out the back section to accommodate my gear. Out went all the space-cramping cabinetry that held the gas cooker, the sink, and the tiny fridge. I'd be sleeping back there, my buddy Mark reminded me, and what I needed most was room to sprawl. I could make do with a cooler for a fridge and a small Sterno stove to cook on.

It was June, and I was eager to get out of London, but Janet was not doing well. She is a nature lover, and she and her mother and psychiatrist felt that a little outdoor living would do her some good. It made sense. A whole new field of ecopsychology has flowered around the commonsense notion that barren institutional settings can be crippling while nature is beneficial. Janet is five foot three but has a definite presence. On the surface she appears together and, at age forty-four, she looks more English soccer mom than recently sprung mental patient. Her story was not complex—just another wiggy tale of serotonin hormones out of balance. In many ways, she reminded me of my sister Chelle with her good-humored high energy, but she can also hiss at you if she gets irked. Still, the balm of a few days in nature, it was thought, might help her find her balance, and Mark might ease her edge. The mad Irish poet, who helped me overhaul the van, is a bit manic himself, though not clinically so, and is a wealth of insight into his own people. More to the point, he comes from the west of Ireland, and has a schizophrenic aunt here of his own. The plan was for Janet and Mark to come over for a week or two; I'd stay on when they headed back.

There's a good reason for Mark to live in London town. A tall, dark, and handsome (and decidedly heterosexual) Irishman, he is a bit of a dandy who has an alter ego, named Mandy, who likes to kit him up in women's clothing. Dandy Mandy stays in London, never coming out in Ireland. The old turf has come a long way in the last ten years, but it's not London's Camden Town. It still isn't ready for Mark's leggy, lingerie-clad alter ego. I have no problem with Mandy. In fact, I'm all for her in the way I'm all for Bugs Bunny cross-dressing just to mess with Elmer Fudd. Nothing against the "normal" people of the world, if there is such a thing, but I'm more at home with adventurous eccentrics. It's the repressed, guarded Fudds of the world, out to wreck the fun for the rest of us, I worry about. How do they roll when the going gets weird?

With the van in top form now, the three of us rode it like

we'd stolen it through the night to the ferry at Holyhead, three hours south of Liverpool. I'd booked our reservations for July 7, not knowing it was the one-year anniversary of the terrorist subway bombings in London.

It is an early Friday morning when we pilot the van onto the ferry amidst a fleet of sleek new RVs, some so pricey and elaborate they're like little palaces on wheels. Mark and Janet each have tents for themselves, as do I, but for my purposes, the Vanette should be mostly adequate. I have it packed tightly with my one-man tent, a go bag with dry clothes and a blanket, some canned food, dried fruit, jugs of drinking water, a halogen headlamp, a battery-operated VHF radio, a small video camera, a laptop computer, and a few good books.

On the ferry kids watch movies on a large screen, eat junk food, tease one another, and fall over seats. It's mostly Irish on board, but a fair few Danes and Brits as well. Of all the English dialects, nothing compares to the Irish tongue. I love the way they arch and lilt a phrase, the way their voices float on the top of the breath. The Brits, by contrast, can be a bit stiff and standoffish. I'm feeling a bit distant myself, slightly queasy as I do on boats, which brings me back to those long, nauseating childhood journeys with the hair spray and cigarette smoke making me throw up in the old beach wagon.

We've put to sea in rough conditions, and soon I can feel my gut groaning like a plunging humpback. Even in my queasiness, I can't help noticing the smiling Irish eyes. If there's one thing the Irish excel at, it's conversation. They have a good-humored courtesy, a willingness to please and be pleased, an easy flamboyance, and a sense of largesse in a world that sorely needs one. There's a gentle waywardness to discussions that allows anyone to come in. It's all a finely tuned balance, and it's all about having what they call "good craic," which sounds like "crack" but means good cheer.

Many Irish Americans are infatuated with their historical homeland. Not me. I was into American crack, and, having no nurtured sense of ethnicity, an American kid knowing the barest bones of Irish history, I'd puzzled over James Joyce. Mostly, though, I've enjoyed the genius of Rory Gallagher, the great Donegal-Cork blues rocker who drank himself to death, but also dug the Dubliners, Van Morrison, U2, and the immortal alkie soul of Shane MacGowan and the Pogues. Add to that a couple of soccer legends from the English premiership—George Best, of Belfast, and Roy Keane, a Corkman—and that about exhausts my list of modern Irish idols.

But the Irish grow on me quickly. Their natural warmth hit me on my last trip there, when a mother boarded a Dublin bus with her brood in tow. There must've been five or six children, boys and girls alike, swarming around her. Before I had a chance to free my seat, she smiled and plopped the smallest toddler onto my lap. As the young mother wiped noses and buttoned up coats, for a moment I felt like a father.

I'm not too worried about the crossing, but any large craft sailing into open water is always at risk. I wonder how far these big Irish hearts would stretch if the ferry went down here in the Irish Sea and we were all reaching for the same helicopter basket. The journey is speedy and, happily, uneventful, and within a couple of hours we are catching our first glimpses of land, vague snatches of a country seen through mist. Darkened mountains, if you can call them that, press menacingly against the horizon around Dublin, and beyond them the famous green fields and the mysterious, fog-shrouded lakes—more than eight hundred in all dotting an island that's only the size of Indiana.

South of Dublin, over the gardens of Wicklow, fast-moving clouds form a heavier garment against the sun. They vanish within minutes, opening like soft drapes to the mountaintops again. Beyond those mountains, green land slopes slowly in the southeast to sandy beaches lapped by gentle waves. Far out west, dramatic rock cliffs cut hundreds of feet high into crashing waters. It's all like looking down on a myth, a fantasy land. Such a small country—just 33,000 square miles—with Scotland and Wales the last redoubt of a nomadic Celtic people who galloped out to Spain in the south and parts of Poland and the Ukraine and the central plain of Turkey in the east. In the middle of it is County Roscommon, the easternmost county in Connaught, Ireland's western province. If I could unlock the mysteries of our schizophrenia anywhere, it would be there.

The view is stunning as the ferry coasts toward shore and the Great South Sea Wall that surrounds Dublin, the longest seawall in Europe. Behind it, short peaks rise out of the low bank of clouds like lunatics peering over the asylum wall. My stomach settles as the little figures who shift and move around on shore come into clearer view. As we alight from the ferry, Ireland looks perfectly normal on the spangled surface of things. It's not my ancestors' Ireland, however. Just a few decades ago it may have resembled the place where Mary Egan had lived, for better or for worse, until twenty-four. Now, with construction cranes everywhere, she might not recognize the place.

As ever in Ireland, it's all about land: a place so small can withstand only so much growth. But if the developers have their way, there will be no end to the boom. Whereas Ireland was once an affordable place with no opportunity, the global real estate market has transformed it into an unaffordable place with loads of opportunity. Even Tara Hill, archaeologically the richest sacred site in Europe, is having a four-lane toll road built through its valley, desecrating the bones of ancient ancestors.

As we arrive, newspaper headlines are noting the departure of Ireland's biggest cultural export: the messianic U2 front man, Bono, who may be on to something when he preaches about the profligacy of the rich and the poverty of the poor, is decamping the band's music-making empire to Holland for the tax advantages. Not much is made about U2 leaving, most likely because the band has lots of company. The Irish have gone thoroughly capitalistic. So many are parking their money abroad, positioning themselves even as the taboo thing, absentee landlords, in the global economy, it would be bad form for the press to bust Bono. Normally they don't let up on the poor guy for being a bit above himself.

As in America, the wealth of the wealthy shows no signs of abating. There's enough cheap money sloshing around that property speculation has been called the new pornography. For the fat cats, a posh Dublin hotel bar recently began offering 500-euro cocktails sprinkled with 23-karat gold flakes, but there's loads of wreckage in Ireland's fast lanes these days. In a nutshell, it's a fast-growing nation with loads of money, more single than married adults, many more new cars bringing ever more road deaths, and people, particularly lonely farmers, killing themselves in record numbers, making suicide the most common cause of death of young men in Ireland.

Suicide, sadly, is seen as the desperate resort of rural men who can no longer drive to the pub. Cut off from their traditional social outlet, bachelor farmers are spending more time alone. Considering the smell and the isolation, the poor money and long hours, especially during calving season, Irish farmers often are scorned as marriage material. For the bachelor farmer, the pub is a place of therapy, a social center to mix with mates, or just do the crossword. In the new Ireland, you can't even smoke. To keep the roads safe and the suicide rate down, the government is debating whether to drive its drunks to drink, literally, by shuttle-busing them to and from the new smoke-free pubs.

We are back as part of a historic pass, with fewer Irish leaving, many returning, and three times as many Americans coming in as Irish going to the States. Yet as the natives ape the American model for stressed-out living, in the overly lit aisles of the convenience-store franchises, it's as if history never happened. Slashing through Dublin's narrow Georgian streets, a speed demon riding our tail, I pull to the side to let him pass with all the other lane changers, the shoulder runners, the quick darters bobbing and weaving their way through traffic while yapping on their phones.

Through Dublin's narrow streets, the radio notes a rash of road deaths over the last two days, including two in Roscommon. Using the roads, apparently, is the most dangerous thing the Irish do every day. It's a nation of car wreckers, the ongoing carnage blamed on two things: boy racers taking blind bends in turbocharged Japanese sports cars, and older drunk bachelors lurching back from the pubs at night.

The Irish seem so alert—so switched on—that it's hard to fathom the madness that thrived here not long ago, as recently as the 1960s, when the madhouses were full. Since the famine era, they've made a robust comeback. It's another story out in some of the secluded pockets. As recently as the 1980s, a study of one Roscommon parish with 2,051 adults found that one of every forty-seven was actively psychotic—an alarming rate in any part of the world. Thirty-two matched the formal diagnostic symptoms of schizophrenia, a rate of 1.56 percent, compared with the 1 percent average elsewhere.

Punching the radio buttons, we land on an all-sports-talk-all-the-time station that's running an ad for a group that calls itself Schizophrenia Ireland. Mental illness "should not be faced alone," the announcer intones, offering a hotline number for anyone who fears he or a loved one may be afflicted. The ad seems to run most often on the sports-talk channel, possibly targeting the young Irish men who, for some reason, are at a slightly higher risk than their female counterparts for developing the disorder. I flick the station and the Gnarls Barkley summer chart topper, "Crazy," is on the air. For a moment, I wonder if I'm going mad.

Through Dublin, clouds of car exhaust billow around as traffic crawls toward the Dublin-Galway Road (the N6) that's the natural east-west highway first followed by the high kings of Connaught. I head west toward Roscommon, just beyond the Shannon River, to the far horizons of our insanity, to swim in stream with our genetic life cycle. The rays of the western sun, still high on a July afternoon, light up Ireland's green fields. They are achingly beautiful, marred only by the villages sprawled along the straight road. Each village is pretty much the same: service stations, shop fronts, five or six pubs, people ducking in and out of quick marts, talking about local families or stories in the news, and then we're out again to the countryside and the sunbeams that slant over the fields until the next village.

Mark is good fun, but as we cross Ireland on the N6

Janet, as a painter, is so struck by the beauty of the bluish-green fields that she is charged with a whole new voltage, an unstoppable surge of energy that leads me to think she's gone off her meds. It's good to see she's pulled out of her doldrums, but she doesn't have time to answer silly questions. I'm to keep out of her medical life, I'm told. Fair enough. She has her own agenda, a no-money-down plan to launch a chain of coffee shops to compete with O'Briens, the Starbucks of Ireland. I let it go. I am trying to be cool, calm, and collected.

It's impossible to get lost looking for the Shannon River. No other river on the planet is so large in proportion to the land mass it bisects. The Shannon is not just a river—it's an enormous delta that takes its name from the Irish word for hazelnut, legions of which would ripen and burst their purple juice into the water. In two hours I sense Roscommon's closeness, recognizable by the plumes of peat smoke that twist above the river's other side. When I detect the smell of burning peat, I know we are back in the omphalos of our schizophrenia, just between the Shannon and Suck rivers.

Just west of the Shannon, Roscommon was a psychological refuge of sorts for the so-called real Irish, a poverty-stricken people on the edge of the known world. Beyond Connaught, in the Atlantic Ocean, is where the old maps are marked "dragons." Texts purported to be a record of stories handed down orally (the earliest being *The Book of Invasions,* also known as *The Book of Conquests*) take us back to the first mythological settlers, a slave race from Greece known as the Fir Bolg (in the Irish language, "men of bags") who were defeated by a warrior race, the Tuatha De Danaan, who floated in from the west on clouds in the sky. In turn the Tuatha De

Danaan fell to the Milesians, according to *The Book of Invasions,* and sought refuge underground in caves, where some remain today as fairies.

Like most families here, mine were probably farmers and turf cutters—dried peat sod farmers, basically—who were cleared off their land to make way for larger grazing areas for the British gentry. They probably shifted between planting and grazing animals as food prices in English market towns fluctuated on the European continent. They lived here on the Shannon, that great vein that flows through countless generations, carrying first the early Milesians—the coastal inhabitants from Iberia, and particularly Spain, who arrived six thousand years ago—followed by Anglo-Saxons, Vikings, Normans, and all the subsequent settlers who came to be labeled Irish through the lure of this island. They came and stayed for the most part because Ireland was always a welcoming place, always able to subsume outside influence, until Oliver Cromwell arrived. To him, the western province of Connaught was a tidy prison for Irish peasants, a trap with the sea on one side and the big river on the other.

The English leader sowed terror as he went about confiscating the lands of Catholics east of the river. Following his "godly slaughter," he ordered the whole Catholic population to live west of the Shannon. "To hell or to Connaught" was his battle cry. Only the loveliest women were spared the trek—they were sent on as slaves to the plantations of Barbados. The old, the sick, and the dying began the journey into exile in the winter of 1654; the exodus took months. Today the only foreign invaders are plying these waterways in their Jet Skis and yachts, or stepping off their Shannon cruises to relax in the beer gardens that dot the shore.

Crossing the river, we zip down the ancient Bo Tain trail,

which follows the scenes of a legendary ancient battle between the forces of Connaught and Ulster. In it Queen Maeve, the last great symbol of the matriarchy of Ireland, attacks Tara, the new royal seat and the center of the new patriarchy. Tara wins out, and gradually the female goddess of Ireland becomes a hag, but the epic battle, likely a cattle war, was started over a mere bull. Apparently the Celts of legend were as petty as the Greek gods.

Heading north to Tulsk again, around a bend that leads to a tree-sheltered spot by the banks of the river Ogulla, we stop to see a life-sized statue of St. Patrick, the Welsh Christian who was taken into slavery by an Irish chieftain, escaped, and returned to drive the snakes from Ireland. Or so it's said. The problem is that there never were any snakes in Ireland. When the polar ice caps melted, submerging the causeway that connected Britain and Ireland, the snakes never made it to Ireland before the water rose. Never mind. It makes a good story. Gifts of pins and old clothing and rags and rosary beads adorn the saint. A strip of prayer cloth—a *clootie*—is tied to his finger. The cloth is believed to drive illnesses into itself.

Janet and Mark wait while I check out the shrine, which includes a glass goblet for visitors to drink from the stream that trickles into the well's fountain. The water is beautifully clear. The stream gurgles through the shrine, a water source for villagers who still hold this place in great reverence. Even some Catholics believe the fairy spirits flow with the gushing water to fill the springs of Ireland today—and that a land as rainy as Ireland must be blessed.

In the *Breviarium,* a biography written of him and preserved in the Book of Armagh, St. Patrick visits this spot during his seven-year stay in Connaught some fifteen hundred years ago. The patriot travels with his entourage from Elphin along a road west of the Cave of the Cat. They pass through pagan Ireland's royal burial site, the largest of a network of more than twelve hundred burial mounds throughout the island, and pitch camp near here. Then something extraordinary happens. Two royal princesses appear from the trees to bathe at the well. Surprised to see his entourage, the two princesses—Eithna the Fair and Fidelma the Ruddy, the high king's daughters—ask who these people are who have come into their home. "Who are ye, and whence do ye come? Are ye phantoms or fairies or friendly mortals?"

Patrick replies, "It would be better [if] you would adore and worship the one true God, whom we announce to you, than you would satisfy your curiosity by such vain questions."

Eithna asks, "Who is God?" and Patrick speaks of a God of pure love who is there for those who'd have a look.

She and Fidelma delight in hearing this description. They ask for and receive a second sight through which the door of heaven is opened to them. They ask to leave our world altogether, and for the light of love to speed them on their way. Patrick baptizes them both, blessing the girls with a snowwhite veil, which he drapes on their heads. Upon receiving communion from him, the two princesses die immediately, so keen are they to meet this new God of love. The ancient narrative adds, "They slept in death and they were placed on a couch, arrayed in white baptismal robes."

I toss a coin in the pool, sip from the goblet, and go inside the round wooden chapel. I pay a euro each for two votive candles, light one for Chelle and one for Austine, take a knee, and say my bit. I ask for healing, and for guidance through a far country. Before leaving, I get a third candle to light for all schizophrenics cowering in the dark arches and hidden door-ways of Dublin and Boston and everywhere in Ireland and America tonight. I place this last candle behind the first two, knowing that behind my two sisters there go countless schizo-phrenics. And behind each one of them, on the same sad road, there go countless more still.

CHAPTER EIGHT

BEWARE THE MOON

Heading south, hurtling down the N61 through the scruffy ditches of Roscommon, we search for a campsite just north of the town of Athlone, where we won't be able to hear the road. I know from my mother that our Egan ancestors were firmly settled in this part of Ireland, in the small parish of Kiltoom, known then as Cam-Kiltoom.

In Dublin and Cork, and even in Galway, on the country's west coast, the sight of shops and police stations had reassured nineteenth-century visitors that they were still on the edges of the civilized world. Here on these back lanes of south Roscommon, though, they were meeting a poor, raggedy race of peasant people gabbing away in a strange Gaelic tongue. Along with their Celtic cousins, the Scots and the Welsh, the Irish were the "others" of Europe, wearing kilts, uttering charms, and bouncing to jigs and reels whose hornpipe melodies take flight swiftly and hardly seem to land.

In Athlone—or *Ath Luain* in Irish, which means "the ford of the moon"—the Druid priests celebrated the night of the full moon as ancestors were honored and the cycle of life and death invoked, symbolized by the changing seasons. The Irish were not alone in their superstitions. Virtually every society had paintings and beliefs about shape-shifting werewolves and other animals. Similarly, the belief that the full moon creates lunacy in people was prevalent around the world. This too was myth. One small study, which found that schizophrenics act out during the full moon, has been thoroughly discredited by decades of studies around the world.

Yet even among the ancients, the Celts were the most sophisticated of moon worshippers. They produced the world's first map of the moon, carved into a rock in a prehistoric tomb at Knowth, in County Meath, about 4,500 years before Leonardo da Vinci followed. In their stone circles, beating drums of welcome to the waxing moon as it returned from the otherworld, they let the stars tell them when things would happen and the moon reveal the reasons why. They gathered at night because they depended on the darkness to see their central symbol of worship. In 1691, a visitor described their behavior on a full moon here: "When they first see the moon after the change, commonly they bow the knee and say the Lord's Prayer and then speak to the moon to 'leave us as whole and as sound as thou has found us.'" As recently as 1950 it was not uncommon to believe that those born during a "castrated moon" were born under a bad sign.

In the early moonlight we inspect various sites for a mile around the town and pick a caravan park on the big lake known as Lough Ree. As we settle in, history snuffles close. In the summer of 937, a huge naval battle was waged on this lake between the Viking forces of Dublin and Limerick. Two centuries later, the O'Connors established their kingship here, the last high kingship of Ireland. I begin to feel the motherland taking me into her bosom. On Goose Island in the lake, a cut-stone monument called Hodson's Pillar marks the country's geographic middle. Our ancestral psychosis, it turns out, is in Ireland's dead center.

Mark says the moonlight is Ireland's poet. It casts a luminescence on the lake, whose waves might have lapped the feet of Mary Egan as she stood near Quaker Island, where Queen Maeve had her castle. Moon worshippers from her cult lived on these islands. They believed in fairies and tree spirits; they thought our everyday world was a sort of unreality, a screen that covers the hidden presences. I have the same feeling about my vanished ancestors. I have no photos of them, nothing to go on except my mother's word that they fled the famine from Cam-Kiltoom parish and made it to Boston in 1847.

In a family full of mad ghosts, the oldest schizophrenic ghost can spook the most. She was Mary Egan, who, according to the stories handed down in my family, was May Sweeney's maternal great-grandmother. In my head I hold two images of her, one of a nice-looking young woman, sane and well put together, a black-haired Irish beauty with large blue eyes, another of an old hag in a shawl, her hair stringy beneath the hood that covers her head, a wonky eye drooping when she looks out from hunched shoulders.

It's Egans in general I'm chasing, but my ancestral Sweeneys were here too. Mad Druid King Sweeney, the hero of *Buile Suibhne,* a major work in the canon of medieval Irish literature, camped here on this lake. In the translation by Seamus Heaney, Ireland's latest Nobel Prize–winning poet, Sweeney hurtled over bare mountain and bog and "proceeded to Roscommon in Connaught," alighting on the banks of the river Suck, and then to the shores of Lough Ree. Mad Sweeney may have been a distant ancestor of May Sweeney, my beshawled, toothless grandmother, but I can follow only so many lines at once. A figure in Irish folklore from the infamous "clan of the battleaxe," Mad Sweeney was the personification of insanity for Ireland, occupying a claim so large that no one, not even Cuchulainn of *Tain Bo Cuailnge* fame, can touch him.

Not far from here, at the ancient monastic settlement of Clonmacnoise, monks battled their own inner demons until the Viking hordes came, sailing their fire ships up to loot along the Shannon and take the women. The Anglo-Normans followed, assimilating like the Viking invaders, adopting the language and famously becoming "more Irish than the Irish." Then came the English Tudors and a three-hundred-year campaign to obliterate Irish identity. The effort was nearly total, a mad social homicide to wipe out an already fragile culture.

British penal laws occupy a uniquely evil place in nineteenth-century European history. In other countries, laws were turned against minorities. In Ireland, they were used to try to wipe out the majority. Gaelic language, music, and literature were banned. The penalty for playing the bodhran (handheld drum) or uilean (Irish bagpipes) was death. Catholics were forbidden to buy land. Even saying Mass was illegal. Mass was said at night out in secret fields whose names—Priests Hollow or Mass Rock—still litter the Connaught landscape.

In the morning, the campsite feels like a wooded fairyland. Irish mosquitoes are about the size of small birds, but are oddly tame. When they do bite, they are thoughtful enough to not leave whopping welts on your skin the way tropical mosquitoes do. The flies resemble emeralds with their green eyes; lichen, which grows only in the purest air, covers the trees. There are no bears in Ireland, but radio reports warn—apocryphally, I hope—of a puma-sized black cat on the loose. Apart from that there's a Rottweiler here, chained to a big white RV, who howls along to the Elvis music blaring from the vehicle. Last night there were bats winging through the pine trees, and the magpies this morning are a noisy bunch. The swallows here like to fly at low altitudes, at disturbingly high speeds, in loops around the campground. There are woodpeckers in the trees, along with blackbirds, chaffinches, and thrushes. The baby robins that nest in abundance must be the world's friendliest, fluttering right into Janet's tent for bread crumbs. Janet knows everything about birds. Any minute I expect one of them to sit on her head.

There are oddballs in the caravan park too, and Janet's meeting them all. There's a black-haired boy of about ten who circles the field on a bicycle like a mad swallow, repeatedly announcing, "I can live without bars." Then there's an Austrian boy who's convinced he's Italian. His German-speaking parents explain in polite Tarzan English that the boy suffers from national identity disorder, a condition that has him believing he is from another culture entirely. No matter. They're both good kids and run me ragged playing soccer. I can tell the parents are happy for the break, as long as I don't get too close. I keep a safe distance, kicking the soccer ball back and forth.

Paddy Lenehan, an old farmer, runs this ten-acre site with his wife, Brigid. They are small and old like gnarled leprechauns. Paddy is a severe hunchback. Mark says he looks like "the incredible human tortoise." Stooped under his hump, his head clad in a Glengarry cap, listing onto his cane, Paddy moves through the campground at a uniform speed. He eyes me suspiciously when he spots my video camera, asking in a bossy tone what I think I'm "doing with that."

"Nothing much," I say, "just making a little home movie." Old Paddy seems interested, so I tell him a bit about our history and my consequent interest in Irish madness.

"D'-d'-d'-d'ye happen to know where they came from?" he asks.

"Just down the road, in old Cam-Kiltoom."

"Ah J-Jaysus, it was j-j-j-jammers here," he stutters, smiling enough to reveal the gaps in his yellowed teeth.

Indeed it was. By the time Mary Egan left, the fairies were capturing Ireland end to end. It was a heyday of insanity, a time when Ireland was said to be overflowing with madness. At the stub end of the nineteenth century, the editors of the *Journal of Mental Science* had written that "the tide of lunacy seems ever flowing." They were unsure why, exactly, but the authorities warned ominously that they would "wait in patience, as those who have gone before us have waited, for the turn, but it does not come. Each year we scan the high-water mark, and hope, but with only a half-hearted expectancy, that the maximum limit has been reached, but the flood still creeps upward with a wearisome, irritating persistence, and we look in vain for the ebbing. On a priori reasoning, if there were no other grounds for the conviction...if this process were to go on indefinitely, the insane must eventually outnumber the sane."

A lonely itinerant, the Irish lunatic was often sketched by artists as a bent old man with a cane, usually leading a dog along with a lantern. Some foresaw a landscape of them stretching to the horizon as lunacy spread quietly, darkly, insistently across the island nation. Ruling from Dublin Castle, the British dilated at length about the problem. Whatever was happening, it was widespread. By 1849, with as many as six thousand lunatics at large island-wide, Dr. Francis White, a doctor who held the post of inspector of lunatics in Ireland, said people were demanding explanations. White told Dublin Castle that so many mad were on the loose that they were becoming "the subject of most universal complaint, that the number of such lunatics has been multiplied, and the country burdened to a prodigious amount, because the poorer class of lunatics have been allowed to remain at large." Even in America, the increase was noted. By 1861, the *American Journal of Insanity* was reporting that Ireland's "increase in insanity is exciting much attention."

A moment later, Paddy's look shifts. A new poor thought is surfacing. He runs a gimlet eye over me. "D'-d'-d'ye know what I'm about to tell ye?" he asks, waving me off already.

"No," says I, "but I'm all ears."

"D-d-d-don't be looking into all of that here is what I'm telling ye."

"And why not?"

"Ye won't be m-m-makin' a holy show of us, asking silly questions with that camera. D'ye hear me?"

Yes, boss. I make a few despairing gestures. Even if the old tortoise gets tetchy, I can accommodate his nonsense. If he runs hot and cold, then he conforms to the contradictory image of the Irish as friendly and hostile, cheery and angry, happy and melancholic. Old Paddy apparently is no exception. There are two sides to him: he works tirelessly at keeping the campground spotless, but try getting your shampoo bottle back if you leave it behind in the shower. When I ask for it, Paddy goes all dumb, muttering under his shell, gliding off in his open-toe sandals to spear the next stray piece of rubbish. My hunch is he's nicking the shampoo and selling the bottles off somewhere. When I confront his wife with all that's missing—my shampoo, my voice recorder, a French woman's pearl necklace—the look of shame gives her husband away. She has a face that can't hold a lie, and I suspect that old Paddy's got more nerve than a bad tooth.

Not that they are short a penny. The caravan-park business is booming with a new French film, *Camping,* that's a box office hit. Critics are calling the retro-camping trend a "harking back to childhood," but sophisticated Parisians—whose only previous experience with anything resembling camping gear was sipping wine under a large tent at an outdoor wedding—are having the whole camping-in-rural-Ireland experience, right down to the mud and the insects and having to make coffee with milk that's about to go off. The campers come and they go. This week it's the French, English, Germans, and Danes. Some Germans are boozing away. A middle-aged Danish couple has two cute girls with the most amazing toys—a singing jump rope and a soccer ball that collapses into a Frisbee that looks like a flower. The next morning it's coffee in the French press and a thumping Irish breakfast—not quite the "full Irish," but scrambled eggs, a rash of bacon, and black pudding—that sets us up for the day.

It's a better-than-even-money bet the Egans tilled a potato patch. John, possibly the senior male member of his clan, may have got some more work on the bridge being built in Athlone. Right through 1843, there was dredging to do. On average, 263 men were employed daily during that final year before the famine hit. John may have found employment for years excavating the riverbed.

Like most Catholics, the Egans could not own land—at least there is no record of them as landowners. Anglo-Irish landlords owned thousands of stony acres and rented them out to hundreds of poor Irish peasant farmers.

Not knowing where to start looking, I go walking for hours in any direction. It's impossible to get too lost for too long in Ireland. The place is too small. In the tiny village of Knockcroghery, I find the remains of the old "tumbledowns," as the stone-house ruins are known, left standing as harsh reminders of what happened when the peasant farmers fell behind in their rents. Dwellings that were surrendered were knocked down to prevent reoccupation, the cruel sting in the tail from the British Crown. Today the tumbledowns are left as echoes of the famine that pushed so many peasant Irish souls to America—as testament to the suffering and the frantic flight from it.

Roscommon was a place engulfed in grief as the hardships hit. The failure of the potato crop in 1845 was the proximate cause, while the long-term one was the system of land ownership. The peasant Irish had no right of tenure, so no poor farmer stood a chance. Crops rotted, rents fell behind, and those who resisted eviction were dragged from their dwellings and flogged bloody. Left to cross the barren landscape, outcasts in their own land, a million Irish died of starvation, typhus, cholera, and dysentery in that mother of all Irish famines.

The county was in a seriously run-down state. Newspapers of the period reported that the roads were unpaved, grass grew in the streets, and rubbish went uncollected. By the autumn of 1846, as the full horror of the famine became clear, some 4,000 destitute locals turned up for an open-air meeting in nearby Moate to ask for relief. The British opened soup kitchens but refused to send food for fear it would corrupt the free market.

Nowhere was the "Irish genocide" worse than in Roscommon. The National Famine Museum, just north of here in Strokestown, stands as recognition of that historical fact. It wasn't a famine, technically, because *famine* implies an absence of food. The Irish didn't starve for lack of potatoes, they starved for lack of food generally, and there was plenty of that taken out by British guards and sold off to the rest of Europe. Feeding the Irish their own food would have been the loose change in England's pocket, but starvation was a neat answer to the age-old Irish problem.

Some of the devastation that redrew the mental map of Ireland remains visible to this day in the tumbledowns, but maternal malnutrition, which medical studies elsewhere have linked to a twofold increase in schizophrenia in offspring, has vanished. I wonder what the hardships had to do with the madness that moved out of Roscommon. Was all their misery somehow mixed into a recessive schizophrenic stew? Was Irish suffering bred into our DNA?

At the library in Roscommon town, the county seat, a couple of amateur genealogists have tied up the computer that searches for surnames. I give it a swerve and head out to find parking in the town's main square, where history and insanity collide again, the main square featuring the remains of an old asylum glowering down at me. The building still occupies a most commanding spot in the central square. Constructed in the early 1740s, it served as a prison for less than a century before being converted. Today, only the façade remains, housing what is part of a shopping center.

A bronze plaque on an old wall informs me that a certain

Lady Betty used to hang prisoners here in the eighteenth century, right in this square. The story goes that she was a poor widow who took a traveler in one evening, a smartly dressed stranger. During the night she decided to kill him for his money, only to discover he was her long-lost son, who'd returned to Roscommon after making his fortune. Betty was spared the gallows herself, but only after agreeing to become Ireland's last hangwoman. So crazed was she that she sketched macabre portraits of the heads she strung up. It's all good information, and I have to wonder about a place that would locate a lunatic asylum in the town square, to say nothing of the treatment of long-lost sons.

Back in the campground, as the sun sets, the black night throbs with insects. The next day the gloom lifts. The sun is warm, the air is cool, and I sit in a soft field enjoying myself, happy to be in Ireland, happy to be away from the world with no one, except for Mark and Janet back at the campsite, knowing my whereabouts. I oscillate between wanting to be alone and not wanting to be alone. I walk in old cemeteries but get bored. I head for the pub and get bored there too.

The next day I decide to get "lost" some more so I can ask unsuspecting locals for directions as a conversation starter. I find myself on a road called the Golden Mile that loops around a small hill and back to the main road. A half mile in I meet a white-haired woman—a widow, I presume—who introduces herself as Mrs. Dervin. She's in a sturdy white pair of trainers, blue shin-length skirt, and plain navy top, and her attitude seems as sensible as her outfit. I ask about a fairy mound standing between us. Also known as a fairy fort, the mounds found all over Ireland are where the mythic *sidhe* live, the mischievous wee folk said to intervene in the human world to bring good luck or bad.

"All the one fort, 'twas, half and half before the road was built, before they made a road to get people up from the village. They cut a road through the ring fort, which they shouldn't have done," she says.

She looks surprised when I tell her I'm chasing Egans. "See the ruins," she says, pointing to a rambling old stone tumbledown. "That was an Egan house, right there. And this was their land."

"No kidding."

"Yerra, she was a schoolteacher and he was a carpenter."

Looking out across the valley, Mrs. Dervin casts her memory back. "That was an Egan house. Those were many moons already, God knows, when I came here thirty-nine years ago. God rest them. I just wouldn't know what year that was. They left it to a neighbor and the neighbor sold it to us. The Morrises were the neighbors next door. They wouldn't know because there's old people in that house that's dead now, gone. Whether they'd have any connection with your Egan or not, I'm not able to tell you."

I ask about the property across the street. She says it's all one property and they never should have built the road there. There are more than thirty thousand fairy forts in Ireland, both earthen and stone, one for every square mile, on average, and woe betide anyone who tries to build on one. It's illegal without permission, which is never granted—a tradition that grew out of the fear that an evil curse would befall the builder.

"That's the biggest thing you can't do now. You can't remove the fairy fort—that's it. You can't cut a tree in it and you can't run a road through it. It has to be made natural."

"Who built the road then? Was it the Egans?"

"I'm not able to tell you now. But they should never have put it there. Thirty-nine years I'm here and it never changed one bit. Maybe that little bit of fence that way, that's it. But I'm a stranger here, from ten miles clear on the other side of Roscommon, so I wouldn't know."

The rural Irish are known for their insularity. Anyone whose grandparents were born in the next town is still an outsider, a "blow-in," as the Irish say. After thirty-nine years, Mrs. Dervin is still a blow-in here on her fifty-seven-acre farm. I walk with her over her property, and try to get some questions answered about area Egans. "Yerra," she says, looking me up and down. "You're not the first Yank to come looking for relations. Yer man Kelly comes from America," she says by way of instruction, "and I could name about twenty Kelly families for him, but I tell yer man, 'You'll have to go a bit further. You'll have to tell me their first name, and then you'll have to tell me what business you're going there on.' I don't want to be nosy or tell yer man Kelly his business, but every fifth house was a Kelly."

Ah, I have it now, Irish circumspection at its best. You hear the phrase "yer man" all the time, often used as a way of not bringing someone's name into the conversation, so as not to offend or divide loyalties, I suppose. Now I am seeing a more nuanced use of it. By making an example of Kelly—the moral of the story being what a moron yer man Kelly is—he gets the insult and I get the point. Mrs. Dervin has told me all she has to tell.

I like the old tumbledown, an eight-sided job with scrubs that push past a corrugated red tin half-roof. It's an Egan mystery, choked in vines, that hints at famine memories and the journey to the New World. The cottage holds history that wasn't all bad. In good times, families shared potatoes, salt pork, and cabbage, with a bit of bread and tea and maybe even a duck egg, all washed down with a quart of port. But the inferno of hatred that Cromwell lit, symbolized by the tumbledowns, burned deeply into the consciousness here. The Irish psyche was shaped by British terror, and the people trembled when the sheriffs came to dispossess them. The famine and the pestilence had pressed heaviest on the pauper population, the poor being among the first to lose their minds.

"Destitution itself was no infrequent cause of madness," according to a report from the inspector of lunatics, Dr. Francis White, who noted that the asylum population kept growing even as the famine emptied Ireland. "And in many instances," he said, "it would seem that insanity arising from starvation was a mere prelude to death."

The famine and pestilence had "visited the insane with peculiar severity. And perhaps, as a class, no portion of the community suffered more than the destitute, whether laboring simply under the aberration of mind, or a total deprivation of reason. At a period of aggravated misery, when individual life depended on individual exertions, or personal appeals to charity, it cannot be a matter of surprise that the unprotected lunatic or idiot, in whom physical debility is for the most part combined with mental imbecility, should be amongst the first to suffer," White wrote.

I can only guess if the Egans stood here and gazed upon the wreckage of their lopsided home. It has stood like this for 160 years now, longer in ruins than when it was whole. "It has to be left here," Mrs. Dervin tells me. "Yer man came, and he wanted the birds to nest in it, because you'll have to get planning permission to remove it." As it should be, she says, arguing both sides of the same question. "If they didn't have a law like that, wouldn't people build homes anywhere? They'd please themselves, well now, wouldn't they? Isn't that the truth of the thing?"

In the nearby village of Knockcroghery, I have lunch at the Widow Pat's. The oldest of a handful of village establishments, it's the only business spared by the Black and Tans, the ruthless Scottish thugs employed by the Crown to quash revolution in Ireland. The unconquerable Widow Pat's remains a gathering spot for locals, and I'm hoping to catch an old Irishman to fill me in on the madness. Ireland's old storytellers, or *seanchai* (pronounced "shana-key"), were once found telling stories on street corners. For the tossed coins of a passerby, the *seanchai* would recite tales, so I hope to find one myself. I imagine him with his pipe and his whiskey, leaning toward the hearth and telling me a tale of our lunatic ancestors, of their sorrows and sufferings, and of the gulfs of their anguish as he pokes the burnt bones of our schizophrenic kin.

It didn't turn out that way, exactly. Outside the pub an old farmer in Wellington boots and a lint-covered sports jacket identifies himself as Jim Murray. Jim knows a lot about everything, even if he looks wired to the moon, his red hair setting off piercing blue eyes, his purple face that looks like it's done some drinking in its day. He lets me in on where the common-sounding Irish surnames in my lineage tend to cluster. There are Traceys in Four Roads, Gradys in Carrowell, and Egans in Ratawaragh, he tells me. "Watch out for the Gradys," he says, winking, "they're fond of the jar."

Inside, as it is, only three of the bar's half-dozen customers are Irish, and only one seems happy to talk. The others are from Poland and Pakistan, which reflects Roscommon's new-found multiculturalism: inhabitants include Brazilians, Poles, Lithuanians, Estonians, Syrians, Pakistanis, Russians, and Filipinos. In fact, 12 percent of the hamlet of Roscommon (population 1,450) are Brazilians, many of them skilled butchers who are here to work in the slaughterhouses.

Brazilians must be the world's happiest people, always singing and dancing, so it's nice to see that they've brought along a touch of Rio. Now Roscommon farmers who wouldn't dream of leaving the dank pub are said to be clipping their nostril hairs and splashing on the after-shave, primping and preening to run with leggy Brazilian beauties. Some area pubs even sponsor carnival nights, where the bachelor farmer can be found putting a little samba in his jig.

Everyone in the world is all over the world now, but in old Ireland the clash of cultures can be jarring. There's a tongue-in-cheek item in the paper about a sixty-two-year-old farmer who caused a local fracas when he mistook a Pakistani street trader for Osama bin Laden. The Pakistani man told the local newspaper that he was "punched, bitten and held on the ground" in a headlock for twenty minutes while the farmer waited for the police to arrive. The farmer said he was in town to buy an angle grinder when he spotted a man he assumed was the world's most wanted terrorist. According to the *Roscommon Champion,* the old farmer told the police that his "nerves were at him" because he'd heard a rumor that "al Qaeda were planning an attack on Athlone" in retaliation for U.S. jets using Shannon Airport as a refueling point en route to Iraq.

Next door at Murray's pub, a tall old gentleman seems to have his wits about him, even as the barman continually refills his whiskey tumbler. Paddy O'Connaughton, wearing a smart green suit with his cap on the stool beside him, is a dude in the truest sense. "I'm eighty-four whether I like it or not," he says. "I could think back a lot, but the memories are getting scarce now."

Paddy says there was an Egan who might've been schizophrenic, a Peter Egan, who died just a few weeks ago, in fact. "He was at home for ages. He didn't leave his bedroom for years. His brother was a bit off too. His name was Paddy—Paddy the postman—and he was on the job over forty years. Paddy the post, he used to say anything that come to mind. He'd pass by, rain or snow, and say, 'Here, O'Connaughton, I hope it's a check, so you can wipe your arse with it.' His father was a Peter Egan too, and he fixed chimneys. There was another brother named Oddie and then a sister. She retreated into her house and never came out."

There was another sister, he says. A retired nurse, he thinks. It's coming to him now, but he can't quite remember her name. Still, I feel, the game is afoot. Far from some ancient storyteller spinning me a well-woven web, word of mouth from a few of the locals is slowly unraveling the skein. I am following a long road down unknown country lanes to a goal uncertain, but if there are Egans in the parish with schizophrenia in their line, I want to meet them. Whatever the outcome, it feels good finally to be backing this thing down, to be starting a conversation about something that isn't much talked about. What does not feel good is the need to ask personal questions, never a comfortable thing, particularly with country folk. Here as anywhere, families shroud their truths in a heavy fog of facts, half-truths, conflicting memories, and closely guarded secrets. In the poor areas of old Ireland, there was a simple reason to hide mental illness: a family history would have crimped your marriage prospects, grinding you into even deeper poverty.

That night I settle into the motherland. I dream of shaved severed heads. In my sleep I am rubbing the pregnant belly of a headless ex-girlfriend. In my tent, she is as calm as can be. I am relieved to wake up alone. It's a fine morning, shrouded with mist along the lakeside, as I go searching for clues again.

CHAPTER NINE

CHASING EGANS

Back in Roscommon town to check the library, I think of my happy childhood and wonder what it was like to grow up here. I walk down wet village streets, window-shopping under an umbrella as though I had kids of my own to buy stuff for. I think of corny things, like putting kids on carousel horses, teaching them how to tie knots and ride bikes, building tree houses, or going to see the Sox, the Celts, the Pats, or the Bruins. Then I catch my reflection in a shop window—the touches of gray, the age lines, the thinning hair, the softening middle that cries out for crunches.

I'm on the back nine for sure at forty-eight, my golden years gone, a string of missed opportunities behind me. I've known and loved women who could turn heads with the best of them. When they mentioned having kids, though, I could always hear that old cat prowling again. Never having my own was one way to get rid of this internal fear. There were three pregnancies, though none delivered. As rough as it sounds, there's no chance of schizophrenia developing at the end of adolescence if the unplanned conception is not brought to term. You'd think I'd have been more careful, because termination is never easy. But when you have an inner voice telling you what to do, sometimes you just have to listen.

The Internet cafés and cappuccino stalls take some of the rustic roughness out of Roscommon town. I wonder if I ever could have belonged here. Of course, with a little growth on my face, mud on my boots, and camp grime on my clothes, I don't feel too alien. In town an old lady I pass for the third time on the sidewalk stops and takes my arm. "I hope we meet in heaven," she says sweetly.

I hope so too.

Down in the hind end of town, old men mumble greetings outside Paddy Joe's barber shop. I remember how civil-rights activists in the American South used to make the black barber shop their first stop in town, and I figure I could learn a lot in the time it takes to get a trim. Inside, Paddy Joe's is packed with farmers on a rainy afternoon. Everyone is wearing dungarees tucked into mud-splattered Wellingtons, except one old gent whose black suit is immaculate, shoes highly polished. And then there's Paddy Joe. Sporting red cornrows, Paddy Joe, in his mid-forties, is a man of the world. He's traveled around, but could never dream of leaving Roscommon for long. "We have our spot of heaven here," he says, "and how could it be otherwise?"

Paddy Joe is one happy guy—maybe a little too happy. Life has its ups and downs, he says with a shrug, but for him it's all about maintaining a positive outlook. "Right here in Roscommon," he says, "we have everything we need." This barber shop serves as a case in point. The handful of farmers aren't just farmers. One was quite an athlete, another can fix anything and has a memory like a computer, and they all know the quickest way to get anywhere in a truck or a tractor. There's an old joke about small-town folk going to the barber shop to watch haircuts. It's true enough here. You get the idea they all come as much for the good *craic* as the cut.

With a smile that softens sharp observations, Paddy Joe dispenses sidewalk psychology with each head he cuts. All the *craic* today is about the Rossie Minors making it to the All-Ireland football finals for the first time since 1951. Gaelic football, which is different from both soccer and gridiron football, is all the rage. There's hurling and rugby and soccer here too, but the passion is Gaelic football. Matches, both local and intercounty, take place throughout the year. Every local is an expert, not least Paddy Joe. He bangs on and on about "the little Rossies going all the way," piling it on without mercy.

Paddy Joe has the place adorned with team photos. There's a peace sign on his cash register, a cross of St. Brigid, and pictures of Jesus and Mary. Watching him sculpt each head, I settle in for the ten-euro trim. In the big chair, I let slip I'm chasing Egans, mad Egans. Bingo. All the farmers start muttering at once. The one guy with the computer memory is as good as Google. "Check the hills of Ratawaragh," he says. "There's some in Kiltoom," says another, "but more up in Ratawaragh."

Mad is an acceptable word, but it's a snip too far when I use the word *schizophrenia*. Paddy Joe goes silent, then bursts into hearty laughter. "The whole world's nuts," he says. "Gel?"

"Go for it."

In the library I find a short history of the parish, written by a local man I reach easily on the telephone. We arrange to meet at Sunday Mass. When I get back to the camp, manic Janet is all over the place more than ever—skipping around the camp-grounds like a dust whirl, making friends a mile a minute with various couples, their children, and ten British bikers in leathers who come roaring in together on their Harleys, film-ing us as we film them on the video camera.

One moment she is chasing butterflies; the next she is speed-dialing London in a vain attempt to line up financing for her farmhouse or the island-wide chain of coffee houses she plans. Spending time in nature is thought to be as beneficial to mental health as adequate sleep and good nutrition, and I can see it is working better than expected. Janet has flown out of her depression, all right, but her euphoria is equally hard to handle. Getting a word in edgewise over the rush of her rapid-fire speech is like trying to get a drink out of a fire hose.

Janet is having flashbulb insights, many of them brilliant, about what a gem of a find Roscommon is. She chain-smokes cigarettes she rolls herself, and does not sleep a wink for days. Euphoria is difficult to compete with, so my quest has been thwarted. Instead, Janet has me driving from farmhouse to farmhouse on a mad, no-money-down errand with Roscom-mon real estate agents. Within a fortnight she crashes again and follows Mark back to London. I'll miss them both. They were my road dogs, the poet and the painter, and now they're gone. I'll miss the flights of their imaginations, their intelligence and humor, and their sense of the ridiculous, but I need to get the van rolling calmly and evenly with my own investigation.

Off a straight road that stretches up and down for four miles under a canopy of overarching trees, St. Brigid's church was the house of worship for my Egan forebears. Whoever they were, this is where they were last seen when, much like today, the lives of all the parish Catholics were knitted together beneath the surface of things. Ditto everyone's mother. To know a bit about one parish mother was to know a bit about them all. This Sunday the church holds a couple of hundred worshippers, mostly older folks, sporadically pewed. Today in Ireland not half the population goes to Mass even once a week, and they tend to be the older, rural folks. For younger adults, sleeping in on a Sunday morning seems to be the better deal. People clear throats, shift in their seats, grunt, and mutter prayers in hushed tones. An elderly woman beside me worships fervently, her face red with prayer, her thumbs stroking the beads of the rosary under her palm.

The priest recites biblical passages as easily familiar as the ones I'd learned as an altar boy. Under stained-glass windows and the stations of the cross, he reads the gospel in passionate tones, delivering a sermon on marital disobedience. This is why I ducked out of church in the first place, back when I was young and wild, because the belief in hell felt so psychologically unrewarding. I've always admired Jesus Christ as a natural man who saw the divine in everything, but mostly because he was the sort of guy who won his points with gentle parables, not rigid rules of conduct. Of course I'm a believer. Until we learn what these voices are made of—until science can tell us that—I'm tilting toward miracles.

Who doesn't like the general wisdom that the church imparts, such as "Do unto others as you would have them do unto you"? But more than ever the Roman Catholic Church is its own worst advertisement. The Vatican has taken a hiding for turning a blind eye to the fourteen thousand victims filing for redress against rapist priests in Ireland. Every part of the country has been hit, but the Ferns, a tiny diocese bordering counties Wexford and Wickford, rivals the massive Philadelphia and Boston dioceses for the scale of the abuse that took place in seminaries and church vestibules. No wonder they can't keep the flock under the ecclesiastical roof—it's unsafe there.

More to the point, in the Book of Deuteronomy, the Jews were warned that disobedience would lead the Lord "to smite you with madness and blindness and confusion of mind." Confusion of the mind, like the famine or anything else bad that happened, was seen by some as just rewards for those not under control of their religious and moral principles. For the most part it was treated as a gray area, since so many of the saints heard voices or saw phantoms. Besides, schizophrenia is hardly the stuff of Sunday homily, defying simplistic categories of good versus bad, or sin versus saving. I kneel in the modest majesty of St. Brigid's and try to fathom a few of the grievances that grip me. I can't help wondering if it's reasonable to love a giver of insanity.

I know it's rude to take potshots at religion unless it's your own, so let me rush in. A few priests, though not many, did starve to death during the famine, but the diocese itself was no place to go for comfort. From the Victorian era until recent times, it ran a Dickensian regime. If there were not enough landed men to marry, a girl was sent to live behind the walls of a nunnery. If she first found herself pregnant, she was a slattern, her child a bastard. If the child survived the pregnancy, the Church wouldn't baptize him, damning him, effectively, in a false God's name. If he died, the Church wouldn't bury him. As a rule, a child born out of wedlock could not be registered with the parish. Illegitimate stillborn babies were laid to rest in fairy mounds across the county line. These days, recuperation ceremonies are held in border villages to reclaim the remains, and a new sense of tolerance prevails.

When the service lets out, the pastor reassures me that God does not dispense madness to poor deserving souls. The Irish Catholic God has moved on. He's a kinder, gentler sort of higher power now. I'm not barking up the wrong tree, then, and my simple prayer for healing could be heard, passed on to God by the Holy Ghost himself. In any case, the Church is no longer the last word on God here. As old-line Catholicism ebbs, Ireland's vast treasure-house of mythological tradition is making a comeback. The wheel spins again and a more balanced set of views returns. I relinquish an Old Testament resentment, and ponder self-forgiveness.

In the fresh air, groups of bachelor farmers huddle across the street, smoking and looking like country bumpkins against a stone wall. They say the parish historian went thataway and I can still catch him. On the cell phone I do, and a half-mile down the road Willie Gacquin greets me smiling at the door of a modest, cream-colored home. He's portly and red-cheeked and as Irish-looking as Paddy's pig. In his well-appointed den, a rose-colored room with polished antiques, Willie plants himself in a comfortable armchair as I go for the edge of the sofa. "Sit, man," he says, his blue eyes clear as ice, his head balding, his face florid, near ruddy. "What can I do for you?"

"Just a little information."

Willie, a Roscommon high school teacher, has sympathy for my quest since he's been on one himself, writing a published history of the parish from its first appearance in the Church of Ireland records in 1749. He says the Egans were traditionally a Brehon family, meaning they were lawyers—

legal advisors to the ruling clans back when Ireland was a patchwork of kingdoms. The medieval Brehon laws, which governed Gaelic society right up until Elizabethan times, regarded schizophrenia as supernatural in origin. The laws had two categories of mental illness, the *mer* for the idiot or fool, and the *dasachtach* for the lunatic, often described as the victim of the magic wisp.

More recently, in Cromwell's wake, Ireland began to suffer a series of famines—in the years 1740, 1755, 1766, 1783, 1800, 1816, 1819, and 1822, to name several but not all. But An Gortar Mor, as he calls the Great Hunger, using the Irish, lasted longer, and hit much harder, because there was no export ban on Irish food. By the time it was over, he says, Cam-Kiltoom lost nearly a third of the parish. Willie shows me a photo of his dedication of a memorial stone to the 2,487 parish victims who died or emigrated, out of a pre-famine population of 9,000. "Nobody loved the land more than the millions who left," he says. Subsequent generations "have every right to come back."

Willie began tracking the families of Cam-Kiltoom decades ago as a hobby, picking up bits and pieces here and there, tripping through cemeteries filled with dark and hidden tombstones. Like me, he's intrigued by gravestones. His only complaint is the paucity of information that's on them. He spent years cross-referencing names with the parish register. He is *the* local authority, his wife, Carmel, assures me.

As Carmel serves sandwiches and tea, we begin with a review of what I know so far: that Mary Egan was married to John, that they came from here, and that she went insane in the middle of the Great Famine. She and John landed in the Boston slums, age twenty-four and twenty-seven, respectively, in May of 1847. She was already gone and passed her schizo-phrenic genes down to subsequent generations.

Willie shakes his head. So she would've been born in 1822 or 1823. Roman Catholicism was still officially banned back then, before the Catholic Emancipation, so anyone who was a priest was still technically guilty of high treason. For that reason, records of parishioners were sparsely kept. Where they exist, they rarely go back before 1850. "We're in luck, though," Willie says, emerging with his copy of the parish records. "Here the records predate the famine, going back to 1835."

As Willie thumbs his parish register, he finds a record of a couple of different Mary Egans from the time immediately preceding the famine. One from the parish was a younger woman who was baptized on May 30, 1840. Her parents were Bernard Egan and Mary Carrol and she had a brother named Patrick, who was born on March 29, 1837. "The trouble with these Egans," he says, "is there's no location of them," no townland in the parish to identify.

There was also Mary Gallagher Egan, whose daughter, Brigid, was baptized on December 18, 1835, so she was prob-ably born a day or two before, in Ratawaragh, a parish town-land about two miles away. Apart from Brigid, the parish register shows no other children for a Mary Egan, which would indicate that they emigrated. "But a woman could have had ten children and we wouldn't know necessarily," Willie points out, because there was no parish register before 1835 and even that may be incomplete. "One of them might have been yours. I think that's all we can say—they might have been."

Since my Mary would've been twelve or thirteen, it's

more likely Brigid was a sister, or a cousin. The name Brigid is as common as Mary in Ireland. Brigid was an important pagan fire deity whose feast day was adopted by later Christianity. The name means "exalted one" and was invoked by pregnant women worried about having a healthy newborn. Even in the Christian version, Brigid was said to be a daughter of a Druid who was raised on the milk of cows from the fairy otherworld. There was no Brigid listed on the passenger records of the ship that carried John and Mary to America. Whoever she was, I suspect she may have perished in the journey out of Ireland.

This is why I am not enamored of genealogy. I don't mind that Irish ancestry is largely a service packaged for the consumption of American tourists. What irks is that at some stage—for me, it's this stage—a gap appears in your factual understanding of who your ancestors were. I realized this going in. I knew that even in this computerized world of name searches, the most mundane details of lives lived 160 years ago can be as hard to unravel as the tangle in my grandma's knitting bag. Sooner or later if your people were peasant Irish, the trail goes cold, the search thwarted at a sudden turn. I feel lucky to have gone this far, but which Mary Egan was mine? It's a very common name, and I have no hard proof that either was.

Carmel says I sound like Bill Clinton. A tall brunette, she is lovely, even if she can't tell a New England accent from an Arkansan one. "Let me tell you," she cautions, "loads of people have turned away a Yank because they think they're coming for the money. Back in my mother's day, illegitimate children given up for adoption had to go to England. Now there's a new law they can come back to claim the farm."

Willie believes any coolness I encounter may be a symptom of something else, a misplaced guilt that may lurk deep in the Irish psyche. Not everyone who stayed behind opened their hearts to those who fled the famine. Many, he surmises, suffered a sort of survivor's guilt. Fear of spreading the contagion forced homeless families on their way out of Ireland to sleep in barns or freeze outside. Just west of here, Willie says, they found twin boys frozen dead in a field. The two boys were only eleven, their dead eyes a desperate plea for help when neighbors came upon them.

Back in the van I punch the radio looking for good blues, but it's nonstop Johnny Cash in Ireland. I head for the hills to try to meet some Egans firsthand. I'll have to tread lightly, given Carmel's caution. The insular, inward-looking nature of the Irish probably came with colonialism. Before that, the Irish were a seagoing race, traveling far and wide. Eighty-five years after independence, some of the older Irish folks are still a bit hidebound, some as weary of foreigners as any lost tribe in the rain forest. They have a healthy sense of hurt, and who can blame them? What the British did here was so warped and heartless that the penalty for forgetting looms large.

In Ratawaragh, two miles away, there are two Egan families living just past St. Ruth's guest house. No one is home at Ned Egan's white, ranch-style bungalow, apart from a handful of sheep in the front yard. I poke around and have a look in the window. It appears to be a bachelor's house, with an unmade bed just past the drawn curtains. I take the next right and the first place on the left is an older gabled house, the home of Martin Egan. I stop the van and a tall, dark-haired septuagenarian, who looks like Burt Lancaster, walks out to see me. As I roll down the window, blasting a gust of stale air into his face, his blue eyes are ablaze with life, his thick black hair tumbling to the side. I tell him with an easy casualness that I'm here chasing Egans. When he hears my American accent, he straps on a smile, welcoming me in with the typical friendliness that is the famous Irish warmth. "Come in for a cuppa tea," Ned, who is Martin's brother, says with a smile. "We'll have a month of talking."

As I jump the stone wall, leaving behind a footprint in a patch of lawn that starts to rise with water, Ned's eyes survey me with real curiosity. "Oh," he says, "you're a culchie." I suppose that he had expected me to take the long way around rather than leap into his garden.

"What's a culchie, then?"

"Oh, just a rough type of Irishman," he explains. A culchie, apparently, is a rural Irishman, just the opposite of a smooth-talking jackeen—a Dubliner trying to pull a fast one on naive farm folk. (Later I'd miss the seventeenth annual Culchie Festival, featuring more than five hundred guys competing in tractor racing, nappy changing, sandwich making, potato picking, and karaoke in a bid to be crowned Ireland's top culchie. The Culchie Olympics has bale-rolling events, horseshoe throwing, tire pulling, and nail driving. Contestants are mad, turning up on mopeds as nuns, priests, and Elvis.) Being a culchie does me no harm in Ned's eyes.

I gratefully accept the backhanded compliment, doing my best to convey the impression of a nice, polite Yank here to shake the Egan limb. An American accent usually means money, though the old van betrays me. But then, remembering what Carmel said about bastard sons coming back to claim the father's farm, I figure they are probably guys who look like me, in vehicles like mine.

A culchie himself, Ned still cuts a dash in his black suit. His thick black hair is touched with gray, but upon closer inspection his suit bears the grass stains and mud marks of the sheep farm. The brothers Egan are both six-footers, although Martin is a slightly taller, whiter-haired version of seventy-two-year-old Ned, who's the younger of the pair by a year. As Martin extends a hand, I give him the same pressure I receive and ease up quickly so as not to inflate myself. The handshake is overrated here. Americans overdo it, while the Irish tend to shirk the shake. When they do shake, it's done swiftly. The custom, with roots in Roman arm-wrestling, was introduced by the British. I wonder if the Irish ever got used to it. Despite their reputation for great personal warmth, they are not an overtly friendly people, certainly not tactile, never glad-handing. It's an arm's-length sort of friendliness, part of the unwritten code of culture here.

Sipping tea in muddy boots, Martin maintains the dignified aura of not wanting to say anything too revealing. I'm cautious at first, and dare not mention the schizophrenia unless and until I can determine if we're related. I've learned over the years that it's best not to broach the subject right away. Often when I do, it provokes a distinct chill, the way I felt when I first heard about it on that car ride from Uncle Robbie's. Often I'm asked if I too am schizophrenic. I appreciate the question, since madness does not always present any obvious physical manifestations, and the curious can only wonder further. It's not my place to make anyone feel uncomfortable.

Ned digs up the family papers, which show that his Mary Egan left Ireland to go to Australia, not America. The two gents have no information that Willie, the parish historian, did not have, and we quickly establish that we're not related. "An

Australian woman came here ten years ago, and her grand-mother was a Mary Egan," Martin says. "She went to Australia after marrying a man named Morris."

After an hour of talking, I take my leave, feeling discouraged. The tea was pleasant and the conversation cordial, but ultimately my visit was a waste of time, except as a necessary step in my process of elimination.

CHAPTER TEN

๖

DRIVEN
TO
BALLINASLOE

M_y halogen headlamp comes in handy for reading in the van, the perfect little caged-off alcove to get lost in literature. Too much time alone can start to feel like the razor's edge. I pass it reading Ken Bruen, a master noir stylist whose private detective (and former Galway cop) Jack Taylor had a partner here in neighboring Roscommon. In *The Guards,* Taylor is a poet-detective with a tortured soul who lands in the Ballinasloe mental hospital for a quick spin-dry after a run-in with a bottle of brandy sends him off on yet another bad bender. Checking out, Taylor calls it "the most infamous asylum in Ireland."

While the name of the place, the Connaught Lunatic Asylum, has changed to St. Brigid's, Ballinasloe is still the byword for the asylum if not the village itself, which is today a medium-sized Irish town of colorfully painted shop fronts not ten miles from here. "You'll drive your mudder to Ballinasloe" remains the lament of some careworn Irish mothers. To reach it, I follow the same back-country route Mary Egan might have walked or taken by horse cart along the Suck River, through the Suck Valley Way. It's a fine place to locate the bedlam for Ireland's poorest province, six acres of buildings surrounded by five acres of marshy ground, incapable of cultivation. Between the river and the bog, escape was well nigh impossible.

Although it's actually across the Roscommon border in County Galway, Ballinasloe was once part of the great O'Connor lordship, which included all of mushroom-shaped County Roscommon plus parts of Galway and Sligo. In ancient times the town was called Dunlo. But it earned the name Ballinasloe ("town of hostings") because the clan chieftains gathered here.

Later, Ballinasloe was described in the quaint terms of the nineteenth century. One contemporary scribe wrote that the Suck "purls and almost trots and becomes mirthful while passing the town, and is overlooked by such swells and tumulations of ground as very sensibly relieve the general monotony of its aspect." He compared the smaller river here to "its elder brother, the Shannon, the same slow, dark-flowing stream, gliding like a black snake through callows, moors and red bogs. Was it not very poetical in a Roscommon bard," he asked, "to call the punch-drinking squires dwelling on the banks of these sedgy streams 'the sons of Suck'?"

In *The Irish Sketch Book,* an account of his travels around Ireland, the English writer William Makepeace Thackeray, whose wife had gone insane, maintained that Ballinasloe had not a lot to recommend it, "except a church, and a magnificent lunatic asylum, that lies outside the town on the Dublin Road, and is as handsome and as stately as a palace. I think the beggars were more plenteous and more loathsome here than almost anywhere. To one hideous wretch I was obliged to give money to go away, which he did for a moment, only to protrude his horrible face directly afterwards half eaten away with disease. 'A penny for the sake of poor little Mery,' said another woman, who had a baby sleeping on her withered breast; and how can anyone who has a little Mery at home resist such an appeal?"

In Mary Egan's day the asylum opened on the Dublin–Galway Road in 1833, when she was just ten years old. Twenty-five years ago, it still had two thousand people; now it has only a couple of hundred, most of them elderly, the others having been moved to sheltered homes. Before Ireland sprouted county asylums, those unable to handle lunatics at home had few options. The physically unruly were sent to one of the almshouses, the precursors to poorhouses that were established by philanthropists. The closing of religious monasteries in the sixteenth and seventeenth centuries left enough lunatics uncared for that a network of mental asylums was built to meet demand. This would become the world's first national network of government asylums and a real drain on the public treasury.

The population had nearly tripled between 1780 and 1841, making Ireland one of Europe's most densely populated countries, and the poverty is difficult to exaggerate. Nearly half the population of 8.2 million—twice what it is now—lived in windowless, one-room mud huts. During this same period, the number of petitions for admission to insane asylums grew at an even faster pace. For those families able to afford it, however, private asylums were sought out. So many poor were on the loose that by 1830 a report of pauper lunatics noted the many complaints about "wandering lunatics" who had been "dispersed over the country in the most disgusting and wretched state."

When the asylum opened in Ballinasloe, it did much to relieve the local stress. Yet demand for services kept growing during the famine, and continued with a sevenfold increase over the next sixty-five years, even as the population fell by half from death and emigration. Censuses of Ireland's asylums, workhouses, and jails show an annual rise in the numbers of insane of 11 percent between 1833 and 1841 (years that preceded the famine), and an annual rise of 7 percent between 1843 and 1851 (a span of time that included the famine).

The new asylums were a big upgrade over the old *gaols,* the jailhouses that also housed the mad. Early accounts exist of poor souls locked up there, confined for weeks without benefit of exercise. The more physically unruly were manacled; some lost the use of their atrophied limbs. Often forced to sleep on cold, hard floors, often without bedding, they lived miserably. As the ranks of the insane swelled, more modern facilities had to be built. But before 1757, when St. Patrick's, the first insane asylum in Dublin, was opened, home care was bleak. As an alternative form of restraint, sometimes the family lunatic was kept in a four- or five-foot hole dug underneath the floorboards, or, worse, in the pit in the outhouse. The pit was kept shallow so he could not stand erect, making him easier to control. In those damp dungeons, beneath those rotting floorboards, untold numbers twisted into the mud of schizophrenic death.

———

Modern writers such as Michel Foucault, the late-twentieth-century French philosopher, historian, and activist, have foisted a grand myth on the world—that of the Great Confinement, of the sane being clapped away due to their inability to work. It is an intriguing theory, argued with eloquent assertions, but the evidence is thin here in Ireland. As difficult as it is for us to imagine, the historical record suggests that asylum beds were much coveted. A spot in a bedlam might seem like an odd windfall to us, but for the Irish in the 1840s it was an envied opportunity.

Even after Ballinasloe opened with beds for 150 patients in 1833, built at a cost of £27,000, workhouses for the poor still had so-called lunatic and idiot wards, and many more of them were forced on the jail and prison system. The crime rate had risen sharply in the midst of the famine, but innocent people were also pleading guilty to the crime of attacking bread shops just so they could be taken away and fed. Doing time in jail was called "doing the porridge," in reference to the unappetizing servings lashed up in jail. These meals, like the ones at asylums, consisted of "stirabout," made with oatmeal and milk.

The picture that emerges from these dusty pages of Irish history is, on the whole, one of a crowded little island whose asylums are full to bursting. Bemoaning "the sad evil of over-crowding these asylums," inspector of lunatics James Palmer reminded authorities that the new system of county and provincial asylums, built to house the truly insane, had no beds for criminals, much less the merely poor or worried well. The asylums, Palmer insisted, are not "the suitable places to be permanently occupied with a few pauper cases of harmless idiocy."

One asylum manager frets about a new and growing class of patients "whose cases held out no probable hope of recovery, thus throwing them as an incubus on the establishments into which they were admitted. Of patients of this description, we had at first, and repeatedly since, received a great number, several of whom still remain, and occupy the room that would be far better applied to the reception of many urgent and probably curable cases that are daily seeking for admission."

A petition from a woman of means for a place at Ballinasloe for her husband is revealing. So packed is the facility, she has to hire an attorney to pull a few strings. Her petition to His Excellency Lord Viscount Ebrington, then governor of Ireland under the British, describes how this woman "applied to some of the influential gentlemen of the neighborhood to have her husband put in the lunatic asylum at Ballinasloe, but unfortunately their application was useless, there being no vacancy at the time. It was, however, thought necessary to send him to the county jail, until such time as a vacancy occurred in the asylum."

One had to be significantly depressed or clearly psychotic to keep a bed. Even alcohol-induced psychosis, as widespread as it was among men, was not a condition that was eagerly treated. A physician described a Mr. Mathews, a chronic drunk, and how he lost his place, and makes this subtle point. The doctor had "frequent opportunities of examining Mr. Mathews and to this date never could examine any symptoms of insanity about him. I have no doubt that Mr. Mathews is excited by strong liquors or other means. From what I have heard from some of his immediate relatives, Mr. Mathews might again become insane."

In Ireland, there was little in the way of forced confinement. The records of the lunacy inspectors make clear that one had to be prima facie mentally ill to get a bed, and even that was no guarantee. Each individual was considered on his own merits, in light of the surrounding circumstances, before he could be declared a lunatic ward of the state. In most cases the medical authorities had little difficulty in satisfying themselves. Then as now, a patient suffering from a mood disorder such as bipolar mania was typically released sooner than one suffering from what was later called schizophrenia, which required longer-term—or even permanent—confinement. The law, then, was not much different from the law today. While a person had to be "dangerous to himself or others," he could only be confined—even against his will—on authority of an order signed by a friend or relative and certificates from two physicians describing the individual as of "unsound mind and a proper subject for confinement."

Long-term confinement was reserved for those who exhibited "peculiarities so decidedly different in some respects from all the others" that the medical authorities, in dealing with them, were baffled by varied symptoms. The patients were wild or extravagant, often bizarre in religious belief or otherwise, yet the doctors determined their mental states on a case-by-case basis. "In no case," said the lunacy inspectors, "did they decide that a patient was insane because his symptoms resembled, in a greater or less degree, those of other patients whom they have previously known."

Of course, there were no antipsychotic medications at the time. If, after observation, a patient appeared to be harmless, a plan of care was prescribed, including purgative medicines, shower baths, and, with the invention of electricity, shock treatments to the brain, then the cutting edge of treatment. If the patient responded, then the authorities would "frequently promote his liberation, if he have a comfortable home, or any friends disposed to receive and protect him and his property from injury." The person signing the order for a patient's confinement, normally a family member or friend, had the greatest say in whether to discharge, to their care, a patient who was still delusional. The commissioners stressed that they "have no right and never attempt" to interfere, despite their best instincts.

In the absence of friends or family, hearings were held by local court-appointed "masters in lunacy" to determine whether or not a person could, as a matter of law, be sectioned. Often it was a medical officer and clergyman who signed a certificate. In their observations, recorded in annual reports to their British governors at Dublin Castle, it was noted that the inclination toward madness often ran in families, as did drink. Of all causes, said Dr. Thomas Cary Osburne, who produced an 1827 report on lunatic paupers, "the frequent use of intoxicating liquors is the most prolific." Indeed, from ancient times, the Irish had distinguished between the madness of drunkenness *(meiscelenna)* and the madness of pure lunacy *(meisce merachta)*.

More muted voices saw religion as the cause, not cure. Acknowledging this, Dr. Osburne was careful not to blame the Church. "There is a generally received opinion that the insanity of several of our cases was caused by religious opinions," he wrote in his report. "Any single passion may be exerted to an excess production of mental derangement. It would therefore be extraordinary that religion, which has such great influence on mankind, should not occasionally produce it."

Two cases were noted, one presumably caused by "domestic misfortunes," the other by "drunkenness," and yet in both instances the hallucinations had been religious. Osburne argued that to blame religion would be to confuse cause and effect. "It would be folly here to say that religion was the cause of derangement, which, had it been cultivated, would have stayed the passions and administered consultation and support to the afflicted mind."

Ireland's new network of county asylums offered a slowly revolving door for those of unsound mind who, whether schizophrenic, bipolar, or suffering from some other mental disorder, were checked in and out. Many, it is true, returned after they were released, because their illness was recurrent. Most others who remained labored under delusions but were apparently harmless and generally well-behaved when supervised; when unattended, they were more likely to lapse into recurring patterns of madness. "The consequence of the premature discharge of a lunatic patient, however, is frequent relapse," the lunacy inspectors cautioned, "and as much as possible should be avoided."

It wasn't the worst thing. For the peasant Irish, the new madhouse at Ballinasloe was at least modern and well run. Eighteen new beds were put in during the two years prior to the famine, a second well was drilled on the grounds, and a new boiler was installed to provide warm water for baths and washing clothes. Steel bars were affixed to the window frames, which finally gave the living quarters some ventilation in the summertime. Winters, however, were always tough. The stoves that the inspectors had requested to heat and ventilate the damp cells never arrived. Bog turf, not coal, was burned for heat, patients crouching around anemic fires.

———

I kill the engine outside the hospital complex, which includes several run-down empty buildings, its grounds combining Victorian-era decrepitude with modern-day medical amenity. In that sense, it's not much different from others all over the world, just another sad stop on the schizophrenic road. Adjacent to the asylum grounds is an old cemetery where I can check for names on gravestones. Most are indecipherable. As best I can tell, none are Egans.

Who knows what swamp of lunacy gurgles up from here. Bordering the hospital, the boneyard's exclusion from the walled asylum grounds gives it a weird air of freedom, although I find myself uneasy walking over the corpses below, their headstones tilting from the clumpy grass mounds in thick disorder. Centuries of rain have eroded the only epitaphs to their lives. The sun throws a massive cloud shadow on their happy flower beds. The dead, like the once sane, live partly forgotten, partly on in memories.

Across the street, the asylum sits on marshy ground. The outward appearance of the massive peasant madhouse has changed little since the massive place was built 175 years ago. Nationwide, since the early 1960s, only a tenth as many people are in Irish mental hospitals as before. But the country still has one of the highest rates in Europe of voluntary detention. Through this gateway, a maw of Ireland's midwest mental health system is still entered. Inside the same main gate, the entrance is marked with numbers, and the main building itself is a lump of institutional gray. I turn left past the foyer and, seeing no one, bound up the stairs. Near the first landing, I meet a patient who looks fairly normal, a middle-aged man whose mouth is dry from meds. He says he's from the St. Luke's ward and is bored with watching TV, shooting pool, and attending group therapy. It's an amiable conversation, quickly intercepted by a plump, white-haired male nurse, who stops me and separates us.

Turned away, I can't find my way up into the old asylum, one possible passageway into Mary Egan's life. Downstairs, a helpful young lady introduces me to a set of old leather-bound record books, which prove to be water-damaged and largely illegible. If Mary Egan did stay here, then I'll never be able to confirm it. I do learn that the place was first built to accommodate 152 patients. A dozen years later, it housed 265 patients, with no room left to put new arrivals.

With money tight, some had suggested letting loose all the lunatics of nineteenth-century Ireland, but the inspectors feared for public safety. "In our own experience, we have known patients whose disorder has appeared to have abated, and who have been treated as harmless for a considerable time, but who, nevertheless, upon some sudden and apparently unprovoked impulse, and without betraying any preliminary violence or irritation, have attempted, and in some instances have effected, the destruction of themselves or others," a report of the inspectors of lunatics detailed.

Inspectors' reports also noted that, in their estimation, religious fanatics were the most dangerous. "In some cases of monomaniacs, a patient suffering under religious delusions (not apparently tending to any dangerous result), we have known repeated instances of their attempting and committing self-destruction, homicide, and acts of violence, owing to some imaginary sentence of condemnation, or under the influence of some imaginary voice or spirit."

Mary Egan would have been deloused immediately before seeing the governor of the asylum, thereby beginning the admission procedure. Just past the foyer and off the first corridor, in the governor's office, he sat behind a large desk, a portrait of Queen Victoria glaring down from behind him, a reminder to everyone about who was in charge (despite the madness that also ran in her inbred family). The governor would've had a warm fire burning, and next to the fire he would have had torches to light the way down the dark corridors.

There was something special about him. He had his salary and a businesslike staff, with nurses, wardkeepers, and servants all living on the grounds. One or two of them would have led Mary Egan down a passage with men and women housed in separate wings, treading in the footsteps of hundreds of other psychotics who had walked this same way to begin their incarceration. Gaslight filtered in to illuminate wards; in one of them, Mary Egan may have been nurtured in religious guidance by visiting Sisters of Mercy.

The staff were warned "never to use harsh or intemperate language to the patients, which may tend to irritate or disturb them; or to inflict any punishment or to subject them to any bodily restraint without express direction of the physician or moral governor."

Nor were they to mix too closely with the patients. "They shall not bring spirits or fermented liquors into the wards, either for themselves, for the use of the patients, or for persons who may come to visit them." If the staff was too lazy or inattentive, or if any patient escaped because of their negligence, a fine of one guinea was due. And if a second escape was made "within a short time thereafter, such nurses or keeper shall be dismissed."

By 1845, as the famine spread, the place became packed

with 318 patients. "If there was adequate accommodation for this additional number in the present asylum, there would be or (by right) there ought to be 468 patients in the institution," wrote White, who reckoned that the Irish were more prone than the English to madness. "I apprehend strongly," he testified to the House of Commons, "that when we are able to get more accurate statistical information respecting insanity, etc., than we have the means at present of acquiring, it will be found unfortunately that the ratio of lunacy to the general population will be greater in proportion here than in the sister country."

Many of the patients dressed in corduroy jackets and pantaloons, cardigan waistcoats lined with flannel, and Scotch caps. The women—except for thirty "very quiet" females who were "all incapable of being employed," White wrote—spent their days cleaning, mending clothing and bedding, and weaving coarse linens, while the men gardened, made mats, carried coal, and cleaned the wards. For their efforts, they received the barest minimum.

The men, who made up the vast majority, were mostly farmers. White said many of them were "a very difficult matter" because "independently of the maladies under which these unhappy persons are suffering, they are of the most uncultivated and illiterate class of society, whose attention cannot be engaged, or the current of their desponding thoughts diverted to such objects as might, under more favorable circumstances, be chosen for their mental improvement and recreation."

Not everyone was disturbed. The sole issue for one man was that his mind and body weren't reconciled to the same gender. White described this patient as "a remarkable instance of an adult male patient in this division, who, from an early period of life, feigned himself a female, who dresses alike and whose general habits and manner partake altogether of the female character. He presents a very grotesque appearance, on first entrance into the day room, seeing him sitting amongst a group of men on the floor, just like a woman."

The first ward was home to twenty-four "violent cases" of insanity who were left to themselves as much as possible. "Some of the ticking and the bedding were not of so clean and good a description as I found in other parts of the house," the inspector noted. "The matron said it was impossible to have them otherwise, owing to the filthy habits of some of the inmates. I suggested the propriety of having pieces of strong oil cloth placed under the sheeting, in order to keep the beds dry."

With fifty-two more lunatics in the Connaught *gaol* and fifty-five in the workhouses, the British were feeling the pinch. By 1844 there were some twenty-one hundred under treatment in Ireland, yet the inspectors still fretted over "a considerable number of lunatic poor throughout the country, who are totally unprovided for, and who, from the unprotected state in which they are allowed to remain, [might] become highly dangerous to society."

Throughout Ireland, the story of one county or provincial asylum mimicked another. They were all overcrowded. Demands for admission always exceeded accommodation. Ballinasloe, serving the peasant province of Connaught, was one of the tightest. In the cold, wet climate of Ireland, inside the rubble walls, Ireland's earliest institutionalized schizophrenics huddled and heard voices together.

Of course, it was important to make some provision to keep the physically ill from dying. In a report back to Britain,

Lord Henry John Temple Palmerston begged Parliament, if it pleased their lordships, for "stoves to heat and ventilate several damp cells, and also the use of coal instead of turf, as the latter did not diffuse sufficient heat." Request denied, the record shows.

CHAPTER ELEVEN

🌀

GRACE
OF THE
GARGLE

Back at the campsite, another night descends. The air is pure, the sky full of stars. The silver edge of the pale crescent moon looks like a thin grin that's not sure if it's ready to smile. Without much trouble I can see the low moon from my prone position in the camper van, much the way my ancestors did from their small cabins. It's deathly silent as the families settle in, the only sound being the whispering of the leaves, the ticking of my watch, and the endless chatter I can script in my head when all goes quiet.

In the morning, the summer combination of moist and dry air has formed thick, puffy clouds that hang in the lazy blue sky. Not far away a father in a monster mask chases his excited children around the grounds. One is a three-year-old boy named Simon who laughs hysterically, his dad distracting him from fretting about the fairy goblins (he calls them "doblins") in the woods. I'd let Simon know he has nothing to worry about, that the doblins are down at my end of the caravan park, with me under the Scotch pines.

The park, I realize, is again filled with couples and happy families and me. There are laughing children and sun-bathed family get-togethers that boast good food and good times. A pregnant Northern Irish woman has a T-shirt pulled taut over her ample belly. She says she prefers the RV to a hotel because she has trouble climbing stairs. Her partner catches her around the waist and nibbles on her ear. They seem as easygoing with each other as old grandparents. I'm happy for them, but it's hard sometimes to identify with perfect families.

I try not to dwell on it. Fish sizzles in pans soaked with oil, and I think about some of the guys I grew up with. I could be trapped in a suburban home somewhere, stuck in a dead-end job. I might've gone that route if I hadn't dodged the bullet, sparing myself the anxieties that lurk under landscaped American lawns, the wear and tear of partnerships that strain to stay together, the uncertainties of broken dreams and shattered fairy tales. Being single somehow feels more dignified. I have my own time, no one to answer to. But the degree to which I am enthralled by other families can be maddening.

Bachelorhood almost by definition makes you an outsider, forced to spend vast tracts of your time alone. I am the lone man in the old van—always a bit dodgy—and my backstory would only scare the other campers witless. I don't want to explain myself or tell them why I'm not hitting tourist attractions such as the Blarney Stone. I don't want to entertain them with my true-life ghost stories and have them feel sorry for me. I don't want to tell about my family and then be unable to say much else about what ails them. I reveal no more than necessary about why the whole breeding thing leaves me cold.

Alone in the van, trying to read, I see the little Irish urchin faces with their wayward hair peeking and pouting out the RV windows. Inside lights glow like warm hearths. I feel hollow, my thoughts running to my sisters back home. The amount of second-guessing I can do, the scenarios I can write in my head, are endless. What if Dad wasn't a drinker? What if Mom wasn't quite so detached? What if we hadn't done drugs? Self-recriminations can bog a guy down. So much easier to blame errant genes woven through generations of famine and hard-drinking old farmer fathers and the whole émigré journey. Either way, I'll always have schizophrenia between me and the world. Like some sad dog at my ankles, it does not master me but is always there, nudging and reminding me that people who are in your life can suddenly disappear. You never get over the loss, and you never get used to it either.

A friend suggested my journey is a form of penance, stemming from some long-buried survivor's guilt. If anything, I've been avoiding my duties for years, running from Boston, or at least spending as little time there as possible. If anything, I do see my quest as a ritualized occasion of my own necessity. Like a funeral cortege for a fallen head of state, it's a contemplation of a somber image, a chance to ponder the empty saddles and report to the next generation. I suppose that it is an amends, in the sense of forgiving the past to free the future.

Feeling lonely, and my mind wanders up to Sean's pub, a good place to go with all the happy Irish gathering for music and drinking. Or to the nearby Hodson Bay Hotel for a hot bath and a Guinness under the silver of the moon above the lake. It's a tricky thing, this business of alcoholism. Every American tourist has seen the postcard of the Irishman by the moor with his gentle pint. That image calls to me, as does the music and the companionship. I want my pint and I want it triple-hopped. I want the creamy head, the wheat, the barley, all brewed together with the hops and yeast.

My dark side loves it when I think this way. Part of the anguish is my desire to belong to something bigger than myself. Although deep in my mind I know booze and drugs are bad for me, another darker part of my mind tells me I deserve just one on a midsummer's Irish night. For me it's inconceivable, but the nut of it is that the very thing that remonstrates against my recovery—that tells me I don't have alcoholism and it's okay to drink—is my mind. And it's my double-bind mind I must convince that drink is my doom. Like a dog, I go round and round chasing my tail until I decide to turn it over to some power of the universe greater than myself. I know for sure that there's no problem in my life that isn't made worse by drink.

Checking my motives, I decide to get in the van and zip down to Sean's for a quick look-see. The place makes the claim to be Ireland's oldest pub, and with great music. Who could pass it up? A short drive, the old boozer sits across the road from a twelfth-century Norman fortress. Friends talk and drink outside. An old man hacks and coughs up sputum like he's gonna die. The claim to be Ireland's oldest is more than an article of faith. Inside the place the large barman points to the framed certificate from Guinness World Records on the wall opposite. The pub does, in fact, date back to A.D. 900.

As ancient as it is, its warm glow must've welcomed my ancestors in too. It is, in fact, everything you could want in an Irish pub. Nobody's too bothered by Ireland's pub smoking ban. Sean's is narrow and low-ceilinged, the floor covered in sawdust and slanted so water can flow back into the river when floods recede. It's crowded with drinkers listening to good contemporary Celtic music. Given its site, across from the medieval fortress, its history is an easy conversation piece. It was here to this castle that the forces of King James, the last hope for a Catholic monarch in Britain, had retreated following the Battle of the Boyne, which turned out to be the very last hope of the Irish for a Catholic monarch.

The Irish like to say that "Guinness is good for you," that "Guinness gives you strength." Whiskey too. *Ishkabaha,* Irish for whiskey, literally means "water of life," but in my case it's a death wish. Alcoholism runs on both sides, right down to me. My father had it, and on my mother's side, our insane side, severe alcoholism had four of my five uncles by the throat. Mom had warned me about this. As she told it, her brothers went through hell, shivering and shaking and flinging themselves on the floor in fits, a bundle of neurotic tics and seizures in the throes of withdrawal.

My uncles on our crazy side heard voices too—not the voices of the superego, the first-person voices we all hear, but the same third-person voices that speak to schizophrenics. My alkie uncles saw things too—snakes crawling all over the floor and water rushing in to flood the rooms of the sanatorium. From what Mom had said, one was haunted by visions of upside-down hounds snarling in his face, and the walls of his room morphing into hedgerows with swarms of rats rushing at him. Excessive drinking had induced alcohol-related dementia, a state of mind not unlike schizophrenia.

Like my own father and generations of Irish Catholic drinkers before them, four of my mother's five brothers took the pledge, as it was known, swearing on the Holy Bible to keep sober. Time was in Ireland when the pledge or the sanatorium was your only way to beat the booze. Times have changed. Nowadays there are rehabs and twelve-step programs galore for guys like us to talk about our feelings, whatever the obsession, and I check in less often than I probably should.

As I drive to Sean's, the obsession begins as a wisp of a thought that it's always happy hour somewhere in the world. It's 10:00 P.M. here in Athlone. By this time in Boston, five hours behind, I could be deep into happy-hour obliteration. I may never have reached the point of my uncles' psychosis, but I did flirt with it. I wasn't seeing leprechauns on the street at 9:00 A.M. I wasn't pouring it on my Wheaties. I couldn't stop once I'd started, but when the hard stuff was all gone, I knew how to detox down on beer.

There's no denying that in the campsite, alone at night sometimes, the booze still beckons. It doesn't grip me the way it once did; it just tugs at my sleeve. Like a schizophrenic who never got all the speakers connected, I hear my demons. *Come on, man, just one quick one,* they lie, and I can be out on the lash for days. Twenty years after we buried her, my mother proved right: it was quit drinking or die. No wonder they call it mother's ruin.

One slippery bit is that I still find great pubs like Sean's, and when I go in I still have the feeling of entering a holy ground of sorts. And it is, indeed, Ireland's oldest boozer—a place where my ancestors might have drunk, a place where their miseries might have mingled in the alchemy of alcoholism. I feel a vague sense of pagan alcoholic awe, a euphoric recall from the dark caverns of my own days of yore. I know those black riders of death, the dementors, are in those whiskey tumblers.

Sean's is filled with sad-eyed singers and writers with tales of woe still to tell. Ireland's bookshelves heave under the weight of memoirs that make *Angela's Ashes* read like the vicar's tea party. It's a recent industry here, the tombs of tales of drunkenness and repressive cruelty, of angst and rain—always with lots and lots of rain. I'd known silver-tongued Irishmen in Boston and more recently in London, in the Camden and Kilburn areas where families had flocked to rebuild the bombed-out capital after World War II. Drinking was assumed to be in the genes, as much a part of their makeup as the stories they told. They'd come from an oral culture and they got used to telling tales—and telling them well—in the confession box from the age of seven.

Sean's is that perfect place, complete with music roaring and drinks being ordered, a big Irish knees-up. I try not to be too obvious as I take in the gorgeous redhead shaking her shamrocks at the end of the bar to the Waterboys' hit "Whole of the Moon," Scottish Celtic soul at its best. She is a clock stopper, and her blue eyes lure me like a friendly smile. She says her name is Grace. She starts off nice, then turns on me, blaming me for Bush. "You thought you were so great when you were invading Iraq, but you ain't so high and mighty now," she says, her red hair suddenly setting her tongue alight.

I agree, for the record, but I've lived for six years in Europe now, so I'm also aware of the vogue these days of deriding Americans, even a blue-state Yank like me. I've traveled enough before and after September 11 to know how despised we are now. I switch topics and Grace has some slurred enthusiasm for my genealogical quest. When I let slip that I'm looking into my ancestral psychosis, though, she looks askance. I've seen this look before, on the old tortoise Lenehan and others. It's the look that says you've crossed a line. The Irish guard this border savagely because they are never too far from the fear that another insult to their proud race is ready to land. The rural Irish, especially, still feel a heavy lump of shame about their misery, coupled with great pride about their survival. They do not find madness riotously amusing. Of course, neither do I.

"And why would *you* be wanting to know?" Grace asks.

I'm getting this question so often now, I never have to think to muster an answer. "I'm doing fieldwork on my ancestors' mental state," I tell her. "Sort of camping out existentially among the bones of my mad ancestors, trying to inhabit their universe, so I can send a time capsule to the next generation."

Grace sighs for my benefit and swings her frame around. Again, missing the point, she takes offense. "So you are here to stir the shit, are ya?"

"No, I have my reasons. I'm merely looking for the truth," I say, elaborating now on my theory about the abiding influence of misery on mental health, and how I suspect that the suffering here might predispose us to a hereditary schizophrenia nurtured here. "Ireland is my cracked looking glass," I explain. Given the facts of my family, where else would I go to look at the nature of madness and its delicate dance with nurture?

Nobody pretends not to know what I'm talking about, but I'm not winning fast friends here. In a sense I am taken, I suppose, as just another invader. I am not what the Irish prefer, another dim but nice American tourist sporting an expensive camera and loads of money to blow on faux Irish theme pubs and golf courses. The Irish keep a lid on things; they close the circle, taught to never wash their dirty linen in public. Just who do I think I am? All booze and bad manners, Grace reminds me that I'm "only from America, a country that knows nothin' about being Irish."

Easy, Celtic tiger. I understand that the Irish have a strong
sense of national pride, that they want the respect they feel
they deserve, particularly after losing it for so long under the
British. I feel sorry for the old peasant Irish, sorry they lived
under such tyranny, sorry they were starved to death or drank
themselves into oblivion, sorry they had to endure the coffin
ships to America and the slums of New York or Boston, and
sorry that so many of their minds gave out like falling towers.
"But that was then and this is now, and you all seem to be doing just fine nowadays. Besides, Grace, and with all due respect, your ancestors are as dead as mine."

The Irish aren't always civilized, despite all of their new-
found grandeur, but in this case it's a mixed blessing, because
where would I take the woman if she wanted me? Back to re-
deploy the torn-out seat cushions in my hygienically chal-
lenged home on wheels? I've got zero to offer in the way of
material comforts, but this is the price I pay for the feckless life
I've led. Grace, as it turns out, is not the woman. Ireland is not
the place. And I am not the man. Which is fine because nothing rouses my inner alkie as powerfully as a beautiful drinker.
Nothing else ignites the kind of chemistry that can't be bot-
tled, like nitro kissing glycerin. I know this game. I've been
here before, and the outcome is all too predictable: irreconcil-
able similarities. I quietly remind myself that I am a reformed
drunk who spends his mornings sipping antioxidant-filled
green tea in fresh Irish fields, not sleeping off the night before
with some frilly fertility goddess.

Grace gets another remark off—it eludes me—and tells me
where to go as I walk away. As I pay up, leaving her brooding
and intense at the bar, a friendly Dubliner pipes up and leads me
to a table for two, where he apologizes for his countrywoman.
"She gets regularly paralytic on the gargle," he confides.

He says his name is Madigan and his people are batty too. "Get it?"

"Ah, no."

"We're the Madigans," he repeats himself, more slowly this time. "The 'mad Egans.'"

"Ah, I see now. Good one, guv."

I listen politely as Madigan feels the need to bring me up to speed on current affairs, as if by virtue of being American I hadn't noticed that the world was going to hell in a hand-basket. I nod dumbly, just wanting to play my "American guy" part with as much genuine humility as enthusiasm. As the old saw goes, be sincere, even if you've gotta fake it. "The Irish are a people who know what it's like to live under the boot of military occupation," Madigan explains. "But it's worse than that. This Irish-Americanism—it was something our fathers could tolerate, but we can't stick it. Our generation all thought, Plastic Paddies, fooken idjits. What do *you* know about being Irish?"

"Fair dues," I say, and I mean it. I have heard it said before that the Irish get more Irish the farther they get from Ireland. Not I. "No Plastic Paddy worries here, mate. Include me out. I despise the lot of you."

Madigan goes on in his political vein as if he's missed my insult, which is just as well. As he talks, I pretend to listen, but find myself mesmerized by the merriment around us and by the barman creaming pints over Madigan's shoulder. Something tells me I'm not long for the place. We shake on it and the old Timmy Thomas tune "Why Can't We Live Together" blares from the radio as I get the van started. It was one of Austine's favorites, and it's easy to see why. The organ's deliberate offbeat nails the on-again, off-again way of the world. It's pure genius and perfectly captures my out-of-sync relationship with the Irish.

No matter. I hit my pillow safe at home in the warmness of the camper van, drifting off with a peculiar factoid I'd read in the press about Irish love and marriage: that apparently they're having more sex more often than ever these days. I heave my knees to my chest and curl up in a ball of thwarted desire. Good God, I must be Irish. Or at least a fallen Catholic. Freud would be proud—I've sublimated my sexual desires. But what did that old coke fiend know?

Waking before sunup, I hear cows mooing, look at the blue glow of my watch, feel miserable about the harsh words with Grace. Why did she have to come off like an angry Viking? Part of me wishes I'd laid off her, another regrets not giving her the good tongue-lashing she deserved. All in all, I'm just happy to be back in the campsite with all the dull but nice Continental tourists. Outside, the rain starts falling in great buckets into lush green fields. It's a good day for driving to Dublin, to beat the bushes there a bit. First I need a good breakfast joint. But it's too early, so I scarf the last piece of un-rotten fruit in the cooler and motor out of the caravan park in the predawn darkness. I push the dial past talk shows and traffic reports, finally settle on soul, and head out again on the mad highway.

ⓢ

CHAPTER TWELVE

A
CELTIC
WALKABOUT

As the mist burns off, I make a quick detour into the heart of mythic Ireland. If Hodson Bay marks the geographic middle of Ireland, Uisneach Hill, some twenty miles southeast, just over the Westmeath county line, marks the island's psychogeographic center. Like Stonehenge, this noted archaeological site played host to prehistoric sun goddess worshippers and the blind bards and harpists who wandered the land freely, singing for their supper. The great Gaelic tribes all gathered here for their May fair festival, the Beltaine, seeking to bring their lives into harmony with the divine cosmos, and here they returned each year again.

Uisneach Hill is just past Moate, a small rural village that's now home to Michael Jackson, who popped up here sometime after being acquitted of child molestation charges to work on his comeback album with Will.i.am of the Black Eyed Peas. Later I discovered that *Access Hollywood,* the tabloid TV show, had aired a segment showing Jackson's studio, calling it "the middle of no-man's-land, Ireland." Immediately the press spread rumors that Wacko Jacko was planning a Neverland-style leprechaun park for this lonely outpost. Austine would love this. We grew up on the Jackson 5. She could dance like Jacko himself. Ask anyone who knew her before the change. Memories are like moonbeams, as they say. We do with them what we wish. Austine could bump and slide with the best of them.

The town has a shop, a pub, and a one-pump gas station. From the roadside, parked on a bend, I can see the famous limestone boulder—five meters in height—tilting on the lip of an enormous green embankment. As recently as the 1930s the locals dubbed it the Rock of the Cat because it appears poised to pounce. To the early Fir Bolg people, it was the *Umbilicus Hibernia,* or Ireland's navel or mother stone. Later it became known as *Aill na Mireann,* the Stone of Divisions, because it marks the point where Ireland's four provinces converge to form a sacred site that represents the mythic middle or fifth province, a province of the mind.

Just as the Japanese had the way of the gods, the Irish had fairies, gnomes, elves, and angels who were the stewards of each place, according to the *Metrical Dindshenchas,* or Lore of Places. An old Norse word that translates loosely as "tooth stories," the *Dindshenchas,* which dates from the eleventh, twelfth, and thirteenth centuries, follows a group of pilgrims going from peak to Irish peak, each symbolizing a tooth of God. The pilgrims follow rivers, streams, and springs through the meadows, mountains, and sacred woods of Ireland in a pattern that starts and ends here at this hill at the time of the annual *oenach,* or gathering.

This was the place, mentioned in the *Dindshenchas,* where thousands thronged each year for the first "mystic fire" of the Beltaine. The Druids arrived in caravans from all over Ireland, always bearing gifts in a procession led by the constant beat of the bodhran. First came the guides in yellow robes and ruby tunics, followed by the lower priests in saffron and green, then the bards playing lutes and drums, and finally the arch-Druids circling the cat-like boulder, their heads cloaked in velvet hoods and conical hats. The caravans moved in a clockwise pattern—the same pattern, found on gold discs, that was central to the Irish long before the Celts settled here. They pitched tents and played sports and gathered for prayers in the open air, believing that God was too great to be worshipped under a roof that blocks the sun.

On Beltaine Eve, every household fire in Ireland was extinguished before the hearth was relit again here as the island reemerged from darkness. The fire was sacred, representing the sun and therefore the spirit of God, just as within each man is hidden the flame of the divine self. It was a sort of Burning Man of ancient Ireland where the massive flame of the fire temple had lasted once for seven straight years. Indeed, today's tribe of "rainbow children" still gather here for the odd hippie festival. It wasn't all sweetness and light back in the day, though. When one Druid group decided to stop paying tribute to Midhe, the foster son of the sun goddess, he gathered them in a house near this hill. There they knelt and, at point of blades, offered their tongues to be sliced out.

All that stands between me and the rock is a herd of black-and-white-spotted cows I easily evade. I climb the hill and lean against the old cat stone until my pulse slows down. I had wanted to come here also because James Joyce himself set a chapter here in *Finnegans Wake,* the greatest unreadable novel ever written. *Finnegans Wake* was influenced by his discourse with his last child, his schizophrenic daughter, Lucia. When her father was fifty, in March 1932, Lucia had a full-blown onset. A promising dancer, the young woman torched her aunt's Wicklow house, wandered the streets of Dublin for a week, and was sent to Evian to take the waters on Lake Geneva. Lucia never recovered. Diagnosed with schizophrenia in 1935, she was hospitalized until her death in 1982.

Joyce and his wife, Nora Barnacle, searched in vain for ways to make their schizophrenic daughter well, but ultimately it was Lucia—dancing around him as he wrote, talking nonsense about sending telegrams to the dead—who influenced her father's novel and his pseudoscientific notions of the occult. To Joyce the otherworld was both an end and a beginning, just as this hill was to the Druids, just as *Finnegans Wake* ends with an incomplete phrase ("along the") flowing back into the opening words of the novel ("river-run").

Against the cat stone, I can almost hear the beat of the bodhran, a drum that in one form or another is used by shamans and healers all over the world because it has the primal, skin-on-skin thump of a heartbeat. Just by walking clockwise around the old boulder, I take my place in the ancient drama, a Celtic walkabout, known as a *midhe,* in which answers are revealed in the pursuit of a purer, if more elusive, truth, on a trek that spans the breadth of Ireland, beginning and ending here. I hadn't planned it, but here I put a vague plan into action. I'd go to Dublin, then loop to Dingle looking for the mythical healing well my mother mentioned, then circle back to make a final stab at finding the other Egans surviving in the area from pre-famine Cam-Kiltoom.

In going clockwise, I'd be on my own *midhe,* moving with the untutored intuition of an everyday traveler who might whisper some random knowledge to the next generation. It's an auspicious start. Halfway back to the van, a herd of black-and-white bullocks on the loose from a farmer's pen decide otherwise. As they gallop, I leg it. Doing the 200-yard dash in what must be world-record time, I reach the small metal fence with seconds to spare. Within the half hour I'm back on the Slighe Mhor, the island's great east-west road. In a bumbling sort of way, I feel I have the scent again. Heading back toward Dublin, though, my grand *midhe* notion drops away as fast as the van becomes enmeshed in traffic.

For the next two hours my Ireland again becomes a series of through-the-windshield highway scenes—sky and farms and fields and villages and communities held together by churches, pubs, athletic clubs, and village shops. By midafternoon, not far from Rush-Lusk, a commuter-belt town north of Dublin, I find the North Beach Caravan Park set between a stretch of sandy beach and the low-slung trailers that blend into a vast suburban wasteland.

The grounds have an easy ebb and flow of campers coming and going, many from a popular windsurfing spot on one side of the peninsula. It's a sprawling place and also has the best rates around—10 euros per person per night—drawing in about three hundred vehicles on weekends in the height of the summer music festival season. That's a far cry from the 17 euros the tortoise was jacking me for back in Roscommon. If the lives of many Irish have been improved by prosperity, good. I just wish they hadn't run the price of campsites up so high. Driven by necessity rather than luxury, I'm doing the no-frills tour and so warm to the place with the lowest rates immediately.

Mrs. McNally, who owns and runs the North Beach Caravan Park, has the gruff-but-friendly mien of a Dub who's seen it all coming and going here. Standing on the porch of her bungalow, small but stout, she seems a match for any man. Her eyes are blue and wide-spaced and strangely like my mother's. Mrs. McNally keeps them peeled for anything unusual in the North Dublin Bay. "Nothing today," she says. "Just two small boats waiting for the razor fish."

If camping and all its glories come cheaper here, my guess is that money is no longer an issue for Mrs. McNally. The widow's vast stretch of oceanfront property, between Dublin and the airport, is a pot of pure gold. She is content, and why shouldn't she be? She has it all right here: oceanfront on a bay as beautiful as you'll find. If she isn't coining it the way the tortoise is, my guess is that she's a property millionaire many times over. She knows she can sell anytime and forget the old Ireland that, she says, is vanishing before her eyes.

"No," she says, "Ireland's changed. It's not the same, even in this village. You'd go up and I'd know everybody in the village. You'd get your goods and pay at the end of the week. Now you don't know who's serving you, and you have to count your money. It's not right. There's still parts of Ireland where you can go and it hasn't changed, but they'll be gone soon too. You pays your money and that's that."

Each day I visit the bungalow to "pays me money" and get a dose of Mrs. McNally's no-nonsense charm. It's an outlook that stands on its own, taking no stock in glitz or glamour, but I'm always halfway conscious that I'm not from these parts. She says she has a long and storied family history, but I never can tease it out of her. I don't press her. It's just not the done thing in Ireland. What's past is never truly past on a small island that casts such long shadows.

For the next few days it rains so hard that being inside the van, which overlooks the beach and gets whipped by wet squalls every night, is like sleeping in a kettle drum. Waves surge on the beach. Doors bang open on big RVs. The wind howls like a banshee. Goth teenagers trying to get away from their parents mill outside the shower stalls, hair dyed green and pink and red. As the rain clears on day three, younger children chase one another out of a pack. Time for my first plunge in the Irish Sea. I swim away from shore, wondering what lurks below. Great white sharks are cruising in the waters around Ireland, overfishing having depleted their deep-sea dinner grounds, sending them closer to shore for food. The simple bass line from the *Jaws* soundtrack still haunts, ever reminding me that one bite is all it takes.

It's a few short miles from camp to the Rush-Lusk stop to catch Dublin's energy-efficient DART train, which snakes south around the bay into the city center. On my crowded car I revert to urban behavior, avoiding all eye contact—easy enough to do with my nose buried in the armpit of the businessman standing beside me on the commuter train. Every third person is tapping on the laptop, sending the instant messages, downloading the latest video ringtones to the newest video iPod or phone. There's the one guy on his phone—isn't there always?—letting us all in on how slaughtered his cheap date got last night: "Six pints and she was a complete mentaller," he shouts, laughing approvingly.

I'll spend a week drifting around Dublin, which looks magical as the clouds go pink. I'm in no hurry here, enjoying the randomness of never taking the same route twice. Until now I didn't notice how much Roscommon was getting me down. People there move at a lope, and I don't miss the cow-dotted scenery either. By contrast, Dublin is abustle, its walkways a riot of distracting beauties. Things have changed much for the better here. Plundered in 1176, burned in 1398, Dublin has survived it all. For the longest time, life had been a hard-core slog for so many Dubliners. In 1348 there was the Black Death, a bubonic plague whose victims were buried in mass graves in a section still known as Blackpitts. Over the next three hundred years, the plague visited on a regular basis. Then came the famine times.

Mary Egan was here at least once, on her way from Roscommon to Eden Quay, in the pre-antibiotic days when boils, scabies, eczema, and dandruff were common sights, the filthy streets putrid from horseshit everywhere. Far more cases of madness presumably arose from the delirium that accompanies almost any infectious disease. Hawkers squawked wares from street corners, like the West African street traders do today. The clip-clop of horses was a constant. These days it's the odd horse-drawn cart that's a curious sight in the city center, muffling the swoosh of car traffic.

Minutes from the station, I cut through Trinity College, Ireland's oldest university, to see the *Book of Kells,* the world's most beautiful manuscript, then scope out the parks and side streets for schizophrenics. For the first time ever, it's much harder to distinguish urban schizophrenics from the Bluetooth technology crowd in hands-free mobile phone conversations with their own invisible friends. Schizophrenics who slip through the cracks these days sleep with the homeless Poles in Phoenix Park, or somehow find their way to a clean bed in the St. Vincent de Paul's night shelter.

On the north side of the college I find the National Library, where they have the official records of the British administration, supplemented by the lunacy inspectors' reports to Parliament. Outside the library on Kildare Street—where Joyce and Yeats, the two biggest literary titans in a country stacked with them, first met—you'd have to be dead not to feel the ghosts. Apart from their genius, both men had clinical madness running in their families. Yeats' sister Lollie suffered from a lifelong mood disorder. Joyce, of course, had his schizophrenic daughter, Lucia, whose aunt Dilly also had spent eighteen months in an asylum.

To Joyce, Dublin's river Liffey was the goddess Anna Livia Plurabelle, a symbol of the life-giving feminine spirit of renewal. He tapped the psychic climates of Dublin as no one else, seeing reality itself as an act of the imagination. Longing for something lost or abandoned, his Dubliners moved through these streets as the streets moved through them, between modern and ancient, so that "a street full of traffic is also a panorama of prehistoric places and animals."

Reviled by his countrymen, the heavy-drinking writer had a wife who stuck by him despite "his necessity to write those books no one can understand." Reading *Ulysses,* his masterwork, I understand when Joyce cuts to the existential heart of the matter: "Every life is many days, day after day. We walk through ourselves, meeting robbers, ghosts, giants, old men, young men, wives, widows, brothers-in-love. But always meeting ourselves."

Dublin was a much different place when he knew it, a city of gaslights and horse-drawn carriages. The great squares and gorgeous Georgian houses are here still in the faded elegance that blends with the curbside cafés and bookshops. On Dame Street, workers pad in and out of office buildings. Blobs of people in nice clothes drink in pubs. Pigeons fly and flutter down to rubbish bins. A homeless man sleeping on the streets produces a ringing phone from his grubby coat, beneath his even grubbier sleeping bag. An old cat slinks out of an alley, licks his chops, and sneers.

Down by the river—on the refurbished Liffey Boardwalk, which was supposed to be a tourist haven—the drug dealers make scant effort to conceal their trade. I observe their habits along the river and in the laneways near it. Every day is pretty much the same for high people in low places. In the morning, the heroin addicts come out for their get-well-again shots, drifting off to the Land of Nod. By afternoon there are packets of crack for sale. Amidst shoppers and exhaust-spewing traffic, one man dishes smack and coke while his colleague takes euro notes.

At the National Archives, located in a district just outside the city walls in the Liberties section, Brian Donnelly, who specializes in hospital records, says the books are "in pretty bad nick," and he's not wrong. Donnelly places a delicate record book on a large white pillow to keep it from falling apart further. It's a fair bet that the local lockup, the *gaol,* was a frequent first stop on the ascent to the asylum. I find loads of Egan and Sweeney mentions in the sets of large, leather-bound convict reference books, but these are among the commonest of Irish surnames. There's a James Egan from Roscommon, sentenced in 1837, and many Sweeneys from Cork and Mayo and Donegal who fell afoul of the law too.

Occasionally, a volume lists the county lunatics, each presented with few details beyond brief notes. A typical notation is the lunatic "having been discovered and apprehended under circumstances denoting derangement of mind." There's no Mary Egan as a convict, but this James Egan from Roscommon, a convict whose wife, Mary, was not all there, intrigues me. James Egan was sentenced on February 27, 1837, to three months in prison for fighting at the Ballinasloe Horse Fair, within the shadow of the Connaught Lunatic Asylum, back in my forebears' neck of the woods. There is a petition from attorney Arthur O'Brien requesting that Egan be released early because he had "already made restitution," had "suffered sufficient confinement," and his wife, Mary Egan, had been "unwell."

The lunatics themselves are not listed by name in the old convict records, but simply as a "Roscommon lunatic" or a "Galway lunatic."

"Such kindly terms," says another reference librarian.

"Yes, sir, but who were they?"

"Who knows," he says. "Just a bunch of nut cases, really."

I let the slur on schizophrenics slide. I might be punching out of my weight class again. He's a lightweight like the tortoise, but I remember this is Dublin, the only city in the world that has an amateur boxing stadium, so I don't want to be duking it out here all alone. In the convict record books, an item on one Roscommon man catches my eye. It notes that he "stands charged before us with having been discovered and apprehended under circumstances denoting a derangement of mind." The entry calls him "an outrageous lunatic" who should be kept "in safe custody until legally discharged to a lunatic asylum."

Beyond the convict and lunatic records, the archives hold the earliest maps of Ireland. One of the few good things the British left behind in Ireland was a first-rate set of maps, mindful of the need to survey every inch of their neighboring colony. Set up in 1823 to update land valuations for tax purposes, the Ordnance Survey Office began work the following year. By 1846 the entire island had been mapped at a scale of six inches to the mile—the first country to be mapped to such detail. Even better, the academics employed as field officers by the Place Names and Antiquities section tracked down as much information as possible on the antiquities the surveyors were encountering in their travels. These antiquarians laid the groundwork for the archaeologists who came in behind them. To this day, archaeologists use the maps as a primary source of information.

Sure enough, in an 1841 index of parishes for Ireland, there is a place called Glannagualt in one reference. It's listed in the parish of Kilgobban as having three houses with twenty-eight permanent residents, fifteen men and thirteen women. In the letters of the surveyors, contained in two bound volumes, are the handwritten notes of John O'Donovan, the great antiquarian who did most of the mapping work with his sets of tripods, also collecting the stories of the locals and their *seanchais,* planting the seeds that inspired the Celtic Revival decades later. Locals told O'Donovan that the well at Glannagualt—known as Tobar na-n Gelt—was called "the well of the naked lunatics."

O'Donovan himself describes "a spring well of pure water with small rivulets running from it and covered with watercress, of which it is said the mad people who come to this glen eat abundantly which along with drinking of this water is effectual in removing their malady." He writes, "This glen comprehends the townlands Doonore North, Doonore South and *Glanna-gualt.* It is a beautiful deep valley with a stream running thru' the centre of it and was covered with wood of old. The inhabitants affirm that many people (from some cause unknown) recourse to this valley and by drinking of the water and eating watercress they return whole. Of such instance they quote many: among them a woman named Mary who in 1823 came into it entirely naked and mad and after some time spent in it returned quite sensible. Many others also until the present year (1840) a man named Sullivan wandered into it, spent three days there and returned sound. Thus from the great number of naked persons frequenting it, it was called *'Glan na a gelth,'* or the glen of the naked."

In his Ordnance Survey Letters that accompanied his maps, O'Donovan confirmed that the Gleanna-a-Galt was in the parish of Kilgobban, in the northwest corner of the town-land of Doonore South. He wrote that it was "still believed by the natives that all madmen feel a yearning to make it to this valley."

Bingo! For me it's a proud moment, since here is the car-tological proof of what my mother had said way back when. To Kilgobban, in Munster's Kingdom of Kerry, out on the Dingle Peninsula, I'll go, chasing my mother's myth. I doubt most schizophrenics just wandered way out there. In Kerry, they were dropped there by families with horse-drawn carts. Left to fend for themselves, the lunatics roving down the Dingle were pushed toward the Gleanna-a-Galt, the glen of the *galt,* the valley of the mad, which could have grown in leg-end as a place where the insane could find respite. I feel drawn there too. Even if the water has no special powers, I like the idea of a place at the ends of the earth where the mad could come together.

It's a good day of fieldwork. As the DART jerks north out of the city center and back up to the van at Rush-Lusk station, I feel a sense of accomplishment. The next morning, in the warm camper by the ocean, I wake to the call of seagulls. On the beach, the sun glints off the sea. The waves are small, the water icy cold. I want to find the valley, but there's more work to do in Dublin.

CHAPTER THIRTEEN

֍

GRAND
OLD
MEN

O ne of my jobs as a camper is to fetch water. I am doing this when I notice a rangy man, bearded and unkempt, who earlier blew into the camping ground alone, driving a battered, rusted hulk of a car. Pitching his tent not thirty yards from my van, he is cursing with a frenetic anger rarely heard outside a psych ward. For the space of a day I watch him from a distance. He doesn't have much—a tent, a sleeping bag, a frying pan, and a tea kettle, which is pretty much everything he needs to conduct his camping life without recourse to the outside world. He has no trouble pitching camp, but he never actually settles, pacing anxiously in the area of his army-green nylon pup tent, which, curiously, has several hand-painted grenades on the outside of it.

The next morning I stroll over, near enough to detect the softer vowels of a Northern Irish accent. He is not a young man; my guess is he won't see sixty again. He is dressed in earth tones and has thick shocks of gray hair, a stubborn set to his chin, large side chops, and a line of furrowed anger that splits his forehead. There's no sign of drugs or alcohol, but he is as mad as a bag of cats, his loud shouts echoing from his tent. The poor guy. Either he is screaming at his voices or he is striding across the campground for tête-à-têtes with the telephone pole.

I feel bad about violating the politics of peeping, engaging in a kind of voyeurism, except that I was here first. How can I ignore him? I can't. My eyes are out on stalks. I hadn't met a true schizophrenic in Ireland yet, but I'm not surprised that one would happen along in Dublin. In Ireland, as America, schizophrenics are strewn across the map of small towns and rural backwaters, but it's the big cities that own them. More than ever, Ireland's schizophrenic community belongs to Dublin.

There are hundreds of other campers on the five-acre site, yet the schizophrenic man pitches his camp next to mine. This confirms my theory that there's never a need to go far to find a schizophrenic. One in a hundred hears the call, so society is shot through with them. You have to keep an eye out, but if you just stay put, and look around, sooner or later one will find you, particularly in the city. With nearly three million in America, there's enough to replace the entire population of Miami. In Ireland's population, there's some thirty-five thousand to forty thousand in all.

My man here seems to get on okay, cooking for himself and cleaning his plates in the shack that houses the kitchen facilities. Every few minutes he engages in loud, furious battle with his voices. As he shouts, I jot down his side of the conversation: "Nothin' but a whore... The noise has to stop... The whole truth... Nothing but a whore... You say you'll leave the river... You're just a fucking cow... Fucking asshole never pulls together... Are you all done with her... She's a revolting... Don't ask me how... I told you then... You're disgusting to me ... You left-wing scum ... You're disgusting with all your filth."

Nothing can stop the invasion of his combative voices. Of course, no one tries, though Mrs. McNally does have a quiet word about his language, and he complies. The Irish happen to be colorful cursers, not at all prudish about the *f*-word, but there's a limit. "I told yer man he'd said enough. There's children about."

Mrs. McNally gazes out to sea and regards the schizophrenic man good-humoredly. "You know he ain't all there," she says. "But he seems pretty harmless." She doesn't bat an eye. It's all the normal state of affairs. "Sure he's crazy as bejaysus, but there's nothing new in that. There's one here every year," she says. "Every year without fail, we get one like him."

There was the one here two years ago who was, in Mrs. McNally's words, "another holy terror in the way he stunk. Yes, we had one all right, a French one. He didn't drink or smoke but he used to go down to Dublin to beg on O'Connell Street. You could tell he was smart and well-educated, but he used to piss himself and my husband had to give him some shoes. Every year will ya get one or two of 'em. And every year we always say, 'Who's it gonna be this year?'"

Squatting outside his tent, the schizophrenic man has simmered down for now. He is in the doldrums, which may not be a bad thing, but he is still a staggering spectacle, his facial tics the outward signs of the voices that kickbox in his head. He is the vilest-looking geezer I've seen so far in Ireland—no mean feat—and just the type of "schizo" society has been taught to fear. Looking up, he seems harmless enough, so I decide to take the chance to introduce myself. My greeting is of little consequence. Stroking his stubble, he nods. When he moves his mouth as if to speak, he has no words.

Downtown in Dublin again, I walk east toward the sea along the Grand Canal to find Dr. Dermot Walsh at his office at the Health Research Board. Courtly and relaxed, the white-haired scientist bears some resemblance to the leprechauns of lore, with blue eyes, a high forehead, and eyebrows as untamed as the Roscommon landscape. He has that unmistakable Irish twinkle, all right, but he is so at ease, so clearheaded, that I wonder if he has the recessive genes for madness. I feel a stir of expectation at what Ireland's grand old man of schizophrenia research might say. An epidemiologist whose work, with Dr. Kenneth Kendler, an American, led to the discovery of the first-ever schizophrenia-gene link, Walsh reveals that questions of causes and cures still tax him. Despite his press, and all the excitement about the abnormality in the dysbindin gene, he is nonplussed. "Yes," he says of the gene marker, "that's our discovery. But it's quite clear that its effect, like some other genes that have been since discovered, is quite small and you will only get this effect in a small proportion of individuals. How it works and how it operates is another day's work. We don't know much about that."

Attempts to understand the genetic roots of schizophrenia had gone back to the birth of modern psychiatry. Early studies confirmed the impression that it ran in families, followed by adoption and twin studies that indicated that genetic factors made a very strong contribution. Finally, the Irish Study of High-Density Schizophrenia Families, in July 2002, produced the first evidence of a gene that is expressed in neurons in many areas of the mouse and human brains.

Walsh folds his hands and speaks in a soft, measured voice. He says that we all have the gene, but dysbindin in some schizophrenics shows "some breakdown in its normal mechanism of action." By itself, Walsh stresses, the gene is likely to be shown to have small effect and account for only a modest bit of the genetic risk.

Epidemiological studies of schizophrenia are not an easy read. In most cases, you'd need to be a brain surgeon to penetrate the technical genre, and the Roscommon Family Study that started the Irish research is no exception. Roscommon was picked by Walsh as one of three places to start compiling so-called psychiatric case registers in 1973. The most westerly of the three counties, and the poorest, Roscommon is where the team selected 258 cases of schizophrenia—all that could be found—from the Roscommon County case register, and produced a matched sample of Roscommon residents who had not been diagnosed as schizophrenic. Twenty-two families in the sample had two schizophrenics; one of the families had three.

Contact was made by calling unannounced at homes. Face-to-face interviews were then conducted with cooperative schizophrenics and their first-degree relatives—parents, full siblings, and children sixteen years or older. Blood samples were taken. No big discoveries were made, but the research was promising enough for Walsh and Kendler, a psychiatric geneticist now based at Virginia Commonwealth University, to commence work on the wider Irish Schizophrenia Study.

Working in New York at the time, Kendler had seen Walsh's research and had become interested in the epidemiological, genetic, and biological aspects of schizophrenia. At that point, the research was expanded to every psychiatric hospital in Ireland and Northern Ireland, except for the war zone of downtown Belfast. Again, teams of social workers were trained to elicit details and take blood from those patients prediagnosed as schizophrenic. It was that work, a continuation of the Roscommon research, that led to the identification of the gene that plays a role in the disorder. More specifically, it was DNA from those blood samples that led to the discovery. Coming full circle, it was in the original Roscommon sample that the errant gene was found.

Since then, replication efforts have been published from nine samples in five reports, and several more genes have been associated with schizophrenia in Germany, Ireland, and Scotland. All of the work confirms that schizophrenia is the effect of many genes, each neither necessary nor sufficient to cause the disorder alone.

Walsh had the idea that blood samples should be taken long before he received the funding to do so. Back in the late 1950s, he explains, there had been growing concern at the number of people in Irish psychiatric hospitals, which at that time was about twenty-one thousand. Per capita, the number of Irish confined to asylums was higher than in any other Western European country—about seven per thousand. In other words, 0.7 percent of the entire Irish population, which at the time was 2.8 million, were hospitalized with one form of mental illness or another. In the west of Ireland, the proportion in some areas averaged 1.3 percent of the population.

Says Walsh: "Because of the concern about the peasant population of Ireland's rural western counties being heavily institutionalized, and because there was a feeling that Irish psychiatric hospitals were not up to scratch in terms of either the quality of service delivered to patients or the quality of the buildings that housed them, in the early 1960s the Irish government decided to look at the situation more closely."

In 1961, a Commission of Inquiry on Mental Illness was established to study the situation with regard to psychiatry and mental hospitals and to make recommendations for improvement. The commission, which had about twenty-five members across several disciplines, including several psychiatric experts from the United Kingdom, was hampered by a lack of data. In its first major report, published in 1966, it revealed that the only data available were those in the annual reports of the Inspectors of Mental Hospitals, a panel that's the modern-day equivalent of the nineteenth century's Office of the Inspector of Lunatics—and the information was pretty thin anyway. The commission suggested that a Medical Social Research Board be set up as the appropriate body to widen the investigation into why there appeared to be more mental illness in Ireland than elsewhere, and why there were so many hospitalized for it. Walsh was recruited to head up the mental health section, "which was a euphemism," he recalls, "because there wasn't any mental health section. There was just me."

One of the first things he did to try to gather hard data was to set up a national inpatient reporting system on the number of people going in and out of mental institutions. In setting up the case registers, they tracked their medical, social, and demographic characteristics through surveys conducted at inpatient facilities. These were records of anyone who had contact with any form of psychiatric care, not just inpatient care.

Because it wasn't feasible to cover all of Ireland with these case registers, they settled on three areas that seemed to represent the spread of socio-economic development in Ireland. "We picked an amalgam county in Leinster County, which was South Kildare-Carlow, a relatively affluent community at that time," Walsh says. "Another area, County Westmeath, was selected for the midlands. And finally," he says, "County Roscommon, representing the western, rather impoverished part of the country at that time." Walsh published his findings in international journals on what the case registers allowed him to say about schizophrenia, which, he says, "was very little indeed."

Then, in the early 1980s, he received a phone call from Kendler. The American subsequently wrote to Walsh detailing his interests and inquired about the possibility of formal collaboration. Irish and American research teams exchanged visits and, says Walsh, "it was decided that because we had this valuable data bank in Roscommon, that's where we would start. Out of that discussion grew a proposal for funding from the National Institute of Mental Health for further epidemiological studies in Roscommon."

The study was approved and funded, and the Roscommon Family Study was born. All the interviews that were conducted were strictly anonymous. "We never got names," Walsh explains. "Everything was confidential, and based on the case register of anyone who had contact with any psychiatric service—inpatient or outpatient—in the 1980s."

The study went on for years and received some $50 million in funding from the United States, a largesse not otherwise available in a small country like Ireland. Fieldworkers (Irish psychiatrists and social scientists with mental health backgrounds) were trained specifically to discern whether a person had the symptoms of schizophrenia, according to the best scientific knowledge of the time. "The problem was that a lot of people who might be called schizophrenic were, in fact, not schizophrenic," Walsh remembers.

To separate the schizophrenics from others who were mentally ill, Walsh instructed his fieldworkers to use the *Diagnostic and Statistical Manual of Mental Disorders,* which set out the symptoms necessary to make a diagnosis of schizophrenia. "And that's what these people were looking for, by using these instruments. They were asking people very simply if they heard voices, if they had ideas that God was talking to them, difficulties in thinking, their thoughts sticking out of their heads, this sort of stuff."

The variant of the dysbindin gene is known to be widespread throughout the brain and to play a role in the speed of information processing. But the Irish research, together with the work of geneticists worldwide, has demolished the long-held myth that clinical insanity, or even schizophrenia, is a genetic trait that favors the Irish. The Irish are no more prone to abnormal dysbindin than any other race. A companion fallacy, also discredited, was that the people of the west of Ireland, which had been hit with the world's highest rates of asylum admissions, were preternaturally prone to insanity. The story, first popularized a century and a half ago, when Irish immigrants began filling up American lunatic asylums in disproportionate numbers, resurfaced in the 1990s on the Internet with the work of, among others, Dr. E. Fuller Torrey, a veteran researcher and prolific author, once crowned by the *Washington Post* as the most famous psychiatrist in America.

Torrey was merely writing about the prevalence of madness in Ireland long ago and in some remaining pockets in Roscommon more recently. In *The Invisible Plague: The Rise of Mental Illness from 1750 to the Present,* published in 2001, he shows how widespread mental illness was first noticed in Europe some three hundred years ago, and how it stood out in Ireland. Noting that the satirist Jonathan Swift had bequeathed his fortune to establish St. Patrick's in Ireland, which opened as the world's first national mental institution in 1757, Torrey concluded that madness "was increasing everywhere in the Western world, but there was something different about *baile,* the Gaelic madness. Whatever was happening elsewhere was happening more frequently in Ireland."

Torrey, like all researchers, was stumped about the nineteenth-century causes. But he believed that "something unusual happened in Ireland to cause a sharp increase in insanity, a shifting geographical pattern, and a more recent moderation of incidence so that it is no longer unusually high. Rather than simply dismissing such patterns because they do not conform to social or political expectations, they should be studied for clues to the causation of insanity. As part of his generous legacy, Jonathan Swift would most certainly have wanted it that way."

While the standard explanation is that schizophrenia is the outcome of a genetic vulnerability triggered by psychological trauma, Torrey had developed an intriguing viral hypothesis, arguing that most cases of schizophrenia were caused by such infectious diseases as toxoplasmosis, a parasitic illness passed to a fetus via the mother's exposure to cats. Vast mountains of research point squarely at predisposing genes in combination with infectious agents, and Walsh himself is certain that schizophrenia is manifested in several genes, perhaps as many as fifteen, that interact with one another; at the same time, he believes such nongenetic factors as prenatal malnutrition may contribute to the cause. What triggers the predisposition, however, remains the great mystery. We all have about twenty-five thousand genes. None encode for things like "hallucinations" or "psychotic breaks." Some, like dysbindin, have a slightly increased probability of manifesting themselves in psychotic breaks. These are the genes that don't operate as well in life's fast lane, apparently.

In recent years a consensus has been forming around an "evolutionary theory" of schizophrenia that traces it back five million years ago to a short hominid in the genus *Australopithecus*. As a result of a fatty diet, our brains doubled in size and split in half, basically. Genetically speaking, schizophrenia may be a miswiring in man's most fundamental form of communication—left-brain/right-brain communication—and a harkening back to a state of mind that prevailed before the first curtain opened on earliest man. Tim Crow, a highly regarded U.K. psychiatrist, believes that schizophrenia may be the evolutionary price that man pays for left-brain language specialization, because during episodes of psychosis the right hemisphere of the brain is activated at the expense of left-brain activity. Walsh notes that the research, while promising, has failed to further confirm this theory. Neuroimaging may yet tell us how specific brain circuits are involved in hallucination.

There is strong anecdotal evidence that the high rate of insanity that swept over Ireland in the nineteenth century, and well into the twentieth, was a demographic feature—one that seemed to have much to do with the life of the country's impoverished peasantry. Seen in these terms, the issue is no longer one of race: proclaiming that the Irish were madder than most really means that they probably suffered more than others, and may have seen a flare-up that was a historical blip. All societies live on cultural myths, and one of Ireland's is that its people are somewhat batty. On its lighter side it feeds an image of whimsy that doesn't hurt the tourist trade, but schizophrenia has nothing to do with any personal qualities of the Irish. It transcends all cultures.

Famine conditions may have thrown rates of mental

illness into high gear, though there's no way to go back in time to tell. Similarly, efforts to establish whether schizophrenia was more strongly hereditary in the west of nineteenth-century Ireland, more so than elsewhere, are confounded by a host of unknown demographic variables, not least of which was the exodus itself.

"Migration was, particularly in the nineteenth century and the early part of the twentieth century, such a prominent feature of Irish life that many people have looked at whether the Irish who left were mentally healthier than the Irish who stayed behind," Walsh says. "So far there has been no simple answer. You would expect, all things being equal, that 'better' people would migrate rather than those who are happy to stick around, but it isn't a simple matter. There were gender differences, too. Women, by and large, tended to migrate more readily than men. Sometimes men held themselves back because they had a small farm to look after, which was probably barely viable."

Walsh is not being falsely modest in saying that the discovery of the first gene link, while shifting research forward in a major way, is nothing compared to the challenge of understanding how psychiatric genes interact with one another and, even more baffling, how life's circumstances can raise the odds that perfectly normal-seeming people such as my sisters will develop symptoms. As often happens in science, the discoveries have raised more questions than answers.

In the 1990s, there was a great deal of excitement about what molecular genetics might be able to tell us about hereditary or genetic contributions not just to schizophrenia but to all major mental illnesses. Already, giant strides had been made in research into rather simple diseases such as Huntington's, cystic fibrosis, and so on. Each of those diseases was genetically quite simple in that there was a single gene that was responsible for carrying the disorder. "Naturally, there developed an aura of expectation and hope that these methods, which have become much more sophisticated in terms of genetic analysis, genetic association, and all the rest of the techniques which were being applied, would be very revealing for schizophrenia as well. Or so we hoped," Walsh recalls.

"We knew at the outset that they were not dealing with diseases that were genetically simple in the old Mendelian sense," he says. "Nevertheless, there was a great deal of enthusiasm and so on in relation to all of that. I think it's probably fair to say now that some of those aspirations at least, or the extent of those aspirations of what genetics would reveal, have been somewhat disappointing. While we have identified a number of genes which do make contributions to schizophrenia, we think, and to other disorders as well, it is quite clear that the contribution that any one individual gene makes is quite small and quite limited. So to put it in ordinary plain language, there doesn't seem to be any easy genetic understanding of what causes schizophrenia."

While his work confirms that a family history remains the most reliable predictor of whether a person will get it, the role played by environmental factors—such as emigration, substance abuse, famine, and older fathers—may make an equal impact. It's nature *and* nurture, which covers the map but does little to narrow it down. We are all products of our past, our heredity, and our environment. "The observation is still pretty robust," Walsh concludes, "that there is a major familial aspect to this major mental disorder. How it expresses itself genetically is still unclear—and even more so environmentally."

Again, Walsh is more awestruck by the flow of circumstance and incident in one's life that makes up the whole choreography of human psychology. "Of course, it's not just genes," he says. "There are environmental factors as well—again, about which we know very little—but we have suspicions about this or that or the other. But overall, it's probably true to say that our understanding of the origins of schizophrenia is still quite limited."

I ask Walsh what he's learned about religious delusions. "One of my sisters had it in her head that she was marrying Jesus. Would you know why?"

"No, we don't. We don't know anything about why people should have these experiences."

I have to say, I feel deflated after meeting Walsh. Here is a man who has objectively observed and evaluated schizophrenia from every possible epidemiological angle in the fact-based world. Far from zooming ahead, the research is merely inching along. "There is a certain contrast between perhaps the naive enthusiasm that floated around in the eighties and in the early nineties and out of that, I think, a more sober, reflective attitude to matters—the realization that it's not going to be that simple," he told me.

That does not mean to say the medical approach does not have intrinsic value. But what happens to a schizophrenic is so far off the scale of ordinary human understanding that not even the best science can shine much of a light on it. Even here in Ireland, where some of the most groundbreaking work has been done, the evidence for what causes schizophrenia is as thin as the shadows cast through the clouds. From the bogs of science, the lives of future generations may be reclaimed, but not in this generation. Walsh cannot even state as fact that schizophrenia is expressive of an underlying psychological problem. "It's going to take much longer, and it's going to be a more thorny pathway than we originally thought," he says. "Not perhaps in the lifetime of any of the current investigators, even the youngest ones."

"And not in the lifetime of my sisters then?"

"I'm afraid not."

CHAPTER FOURTEEN

🌀

NO
GILDING
LILIES

In the morning I'm showering when I hear my man come rushing into the men's room. I can't see him, but I listen carefully to the angry, one-sided conversation going on. When I last saw him yesterday, his clunky gait was squishing his boots into the rainy summer muck around his tent. Now from the shower I wonder what he's getting up to out there. Naked in the stall, I have every reason to worry. Schizophrenia is a cruel machine—who knows what his voices are telling him. When a man like this is agitated, there are no rules. Savage acts of violence can erupt from out of nowhere.

Old concerns corkscrew up my spine. I flash on Austine raising the knife against John on the Cape, burying any doubts I might've had at the time about the power of voices in tantrum to turn violent. Predictions of which schizophrenics may become violent and when are no better than chance. Prior violence is the single best harbinger, but few factors that predict violence are malleable. It's the unpredictability of the acts of violence that separates the schizophrenic from the herd.

Their voices torment them, and some of those tormented individuals can go suddenly berserk, doing what they would not otherwise do. In the last year alone in Ireland, 1,257 psychiatric nurses were stabbed, bitten, kicked, punched, and assaulted with syringes, fire extinguishers, pool cues, chairs, and crutches. How many of the assaulters were schizophrenic is anyone's guess. Like the bite of the great white, all it takes is once. Persecutory ideation is the most frequent "positive" psychotic symptom that increases risk. "Negative" psychotic symptoms—such as the social withdrawal of Austine—actually lower the risk of acting on thoughts of hurting someone.

As my water times out and I hear his toilet flush, the closing-in-on-me sense of my man rises up in the small hairs on my arms. I am not eager to get out with him standing around either, so I drop my last euro into the coin slot to buy three more minutes of water. When I finally come out, wrapped in a towel, he is gone. I'm alone, shaving at one of a half-dozen white sinks that line the wall, when he comes rushing back in. He squares off in the mirror two bowls over and goes to work on his hands with a soapy facecloth. He looks like an aging car mechanic, greasy and sinewy, his gray hair a scraggly nest, his eyes dark, his lip curled back as he cups water onto his face. It's all fairly ordinary until he jerks his fly open and pulls out his manhood. He whips it out and there it is— raw and uncircumcised. Ignoring me, he soaps himself, splashing water onto his old boy and toweling off with no hint of self-consciousness. I should be shocked, but I'm not.

In the days that follow, what Dr. Walsh had to say begins to sink in. I'm over the crest to another vanquished hope that feels harder and meaner this time. I can't get angry with Walsh.

Having done the best work out there, he's a man to be admired. But anger always needs an object to hate, and I prefer to hate science itself. Ten years ago we still felt that science was limitless and that we were on the verge of making great strides. As space-age kids, we all felt that DNA was a rocket full of possibilities. The future is unimpressive, we now can say. Science can look back thirteen billion years to the birth of the universe, but it still can't hear the voices in my sisters' heads. Some things take more than a lifetime to know, and it may be that I'll never learn the nature of this dark thing that mugs us. Walsh and his colleagues have shone a light as far as anyone. Beyond that, there's the voices from beyond. "Here be dragons" said the medieval maps of the edge of Ireland, declaring the limits of human knowledge. Here be schizophrenia, straining the bounds of science still.

Online, I find mention of a series of discussions, billed as the Depression Dialogues, that's being held in the Dublin area, courtesy of the Institute of Psychosocial Medicine. Among other things, the folks running this program claim to be on the verge of finding effective treatment regimens. On a starry night they are gathering in a town house down in Sandycove on Dublin Bay. Forty or fifty people sit on auditorium chairs to listen to what Dr. Michael Corry, a psychiatrist, has to say about what he calls "non-ordinary states of consciousness." Several New Age-y types round out a mix of young and older adults. Corry and colleague Áine Tubridy, a psychotherapist, each say a few words of welcome and then open the floor for sharing. Or conversation. Or understanding and empathy.

As Corry speaks, the gathered go from squirming in their seats to peppering the pair with questions. The conventional medical wisdom is that schizophrenia is some sort of physical disease, and that hallucinations are tied up with the brain's signals to the eyes and ears. But there is a counternotion on offer here, namely that every schizophrenic's true self—the psyche, or soul—is in trouble. Corry says depression is one thing, but the trauma of developing schizophrenia places it "at the far end of the sanity-insanity spectrum. As a result, this nonordinary state gets a very bad press. It's like a country no one wants to visit."

One man makes the oft-told point that *schizophrenia,* the Greek word for "split mind," is a misnomer that does not begin to describe the set of symptoms. We live by names, the symbols for every discrete thing that we need to identify. I use the word myself for convenience, even though it never quite captures the cold darkness where the voices scream. All the arbitrary names that man bestows—madness, insanity, psychosis, lunacy, schizophrenia—must be meaningless to those who hear voices.

Corry leads the discussion, making the argument that if any other profession faced such a horrendous failure rate, its practitioners would be hauled into court on malpractice. He and Tubridy believe that medications are overprescribed and that genes alone do not ignite the mysterious, end-of-adolescence schizophrenic spark. If anything, they are even more pessimistic than Walsh about a genetic answer anytime soon. The focus here is more on acceptance of the schizophrenic as is. It's noted that the schizophrenic's access to multiple realities is a core experience of religious figures and tribal shamans alike.

In their book *Going Mad: Understanding Mental Illness,* a superb layperson's primer on what we now know about insanity, Tubridy and Corry make the point in plain language. "Walk into any Irish pub as a tourist and you will get a typical impression of Irish drinkers. You know absolutely nothing about the millions of variables that have gone into the composition of each individual drinker. Their background is a blank. If you were to get to know each one individually, you would know that they are more dissimilar from each other than similar. The same is true of your so-called typical schizophrenic. Having said that, schizophrenics have in common many shared characteristics, just like the drinkers."

What they do have in common is the hearing of voices and an inability to explain how these voices have them feeling. "It's a 'had to be there' situation. They may be seeing things, hearing things they are unable to convey to others," they say, likening the schizophrenic experience to a dream state. "When we dream, we see things, hear things, smell and touch things. We can even have sex with people we have never met. Our partner in bed beside us hasn't a clue about our experience. Without being too simplistic, we emerge from our psychotic dream state when the morning alarm goes off. But the schizophrenic experiences his or her dreams in a state of waking consciousness, bombarded by stimuli from within. Their internal images, how they process them and their matching behaviors close sufferers off from the outside world."

So the schizophrenic, according to this view, is in a walking, waking dream state. No wonder communication is so often disordered and nonsensical. The doctors use phrases such as "word salad" and "pressure of speech" to describe the fusillade of disorganized gibberish that bombards the schizophrenic.

The two place more store in the work of "energy therapists" than they do in sophisticated gene sequencing and MRI scans. There isn't a squeak of cynicism at the suggestion that schizophrenia is treatable through the undoing of blocks and imbalances in one's aura, the theory being that a schizophrenic has ungrounded energy, a condition that was possibly set in the womb and during the first year of life, even though the symptoms do not manifest until adolescence. It's an opinion that places this group outside the mainstream medical view that schizophrenia is an organic brain disease. But doctors are hardly of one mind when it comes to schizophrenia. Corry and Tubridy see psychotropic drugs doing little or nothing to address the underlying disorder. They believe the drugs are no more than a software patch. When one man vents against the stigma attached to taking pills, however, he is reassured that the meds are something of a necessity. "This depression has a life of its own," he says. "Thank God for the tablets."

Another person likes the Buddhist view that the world is an outside projection of an inward condition, akin to virtual-reality simulations such as Second Life, so when I am driving through Ireland I am literally driving through my own mind. It makes sense that the universe adjusts itself to your view of it. If Homer Simpson is useless and stupid, this view goes, then it's because he sees the world as useless and stupid. And by the same token, I don't really have schizophrenic sisters. They're all in my mind, I guess.

Here the favored treatment is acupuncture and holotropic breathwork. The idea is that a healthy, well-breathing person is firing with all seven major chakras open. In the give-and-take, I sit there trying to gauge my susceptibility to fad therapies. Investigating schizophrenia requires a certain suspension of belief. Hopelessness gives rise to faith in theories untested by science. Deeper meanings are read into questionable treatments to make sense of the incomprehensible. It's not that Corry and Tubridy discount conventional psychiatry; it's that they see it as a fairly narrow corridor, as do I. Here it all feels less scientific, more poetic. Only in Ireland are the scientists and the poets in the same department.

In psychiatric circles, it wasn't long ago that disregard for the voices seemed to be a prerequisite, to the eternal frustration of the countless millions who have heard them. Corry and Tubridy are at the first barricades of a revolution in psychiatry, one that is beginning to take the mysterious voices seriously. Through their patients, psychiatry is finally turning its stethoscope to the unfathomable abyss. Were Carl Jung alive today, I think he'd appreciate the whole psychospiritual viewpoint here, an approach that finds a home among the studies of schizophrenic religious visions in scientific journals over the past few years. To this school, schizophrenia is a condition of the soul. The psyche (originally a Greek word for "spirit") becomes split off from the conscious personality and speaks autonomously in the form of disembodied voices.

As Corry sprinkles his fairy dust, I wonder if the schizophrenic isn't a natural mystic, a mind with insights beyond the normal space-time compass. Questions and answers range over hypnotism and hypnotherapy to channeling, reiki, and past-life regression. Interesting stuff, but the whole muddle distills no more wisdom on my part. I try to be tolerant, but if we're all energy, then why don't I have any? What's next, a lecture on the zodiac signs of schizophrenia?

I used to wonder if insanity was a "choice" made passively, an off-the-cliff choice of no choosing, like releasing the steering wheel going down the road. Chelle once said it was. "Beats working in a large office with lots of fluorescent lights," she observed. When she made her remark, I understood. As R. D. Laing famously said, "Insanity is a sane response to an insane world." Still, I'll always wonder if Chelle's "choice" would have been different if Dad's movie-star expectations of her had not been so high. And what of Austine? I'll never believe that schizophrenia came as she requested it. What blind twists and turnings would lead her to choose her fate? Isn't sanity, like sobriety or good physical health, its own reward?

On Blessington Street in a downmarket section of Dublin, in the offices of Schizophrenia Ireland, a receptionist directs me to a chair in a modest conference room. There I find the group's director, John Saunders, who is tall and bald with rounded features, and Pat Seager, assistant director, who is middle-aged, like Saunders, with ginger hair and finer, sharper features.

Seager points out that many Irish were admitted to asylums with lunacy only to find later that their symptoms were caused by epilepsy, viral encephalitis, cerebral syphilis, a brain tumor, or alcohol-aggravated dementia. Intoxication delirium and withdrawal with delirium tremors can cause symptoms of insanity of a short duration. Only alcohol-induced dementia, commonly known as "wet brain," is of a lasting nature. In the nineteenth century, overuse of bromides was a frequent cause of psychosis. But alcoholics in the past had constituted a small portion of individuals in psychiatric hospitals.

Typhoid fever, an epidemic during the famine, is well known to cause madness. Of all the infectious diseases that cause sudden but transient insanity, typhoid tops the list, followed by pneumonia, malaria, smallpox, measles, diphtheria, tuberculosis, whooping cough, dysentery, leprosy, and gonorrhea. Apart from schizophrenia and bipolar mania, temporal lobe epilepsy is the most common form of insanity. One study has shown symptoms of schizophrenia in 17 percent of the cases.

It's good information, but like my meeting with the others, it all feels more like stones turned over than ones put in place. I learn from them that medication is only partially effective, and the toll taken by severe side effects of the medication attests to the ravages of trying to recode your mental self pharmacologically. Cognitive therapy works wonders for depression, anxiety, trauma, and eating disorders but has been considerably less effective with schizophrenia. Saunders takes issue with "the practice of almost bombarding people with medication." Medication pays off for only one in three or four schizophrenics, he says. "It can't work as a miracle cure, like taking something for a headache or an antibiotic for an infection," Seager adds. "It works partially for somewhere between 20 and 25 percent. And therefore the other fact is that it doesn't work for many more."

Schizophrenia Ireland coalesced in the 1970s as an informal gathering of families of schizophrenics being treated at the Cluain Mhuire outpatient center in Dublin. Once a private psychiatric hospital for women, it was developed as an outpatient center by the government with help from the Brothers of St. John of God. Dr. Walsh himself was a consultant psychiatrist at Cluain Mhuire, and also among those who felt that sharing concerns might be a way to engender mutual support. Informal monthly gatherings were held, and in the summer of 1975, with eleven in attendance, the organization held its first formal meeting. Some families were inspired by the groups, others a bit hesitant. When attendance was small and flagging, some were more worried about the situation within their own families, understandably, and less interested in weaving friendships among others similarly devastated.

During these early years, the glue that held the group together was Owen Mooney. The smiling, white-haired father of a schizophrenic child, Mooney had a merry manner that made him the perfect guiding light. In his death notice, he was described as one of "nature's gentlemen." It was Mooney who rallied families to come together, though he took care not to dispense psychiatric advice. "We leave that to the professionals," he said. "We do not nail our flag to any treatment mast or support any particular cure."

The association used James Joycean themes to amplify its message. It produced *The Lucia Anthology: A New Song to Sing,* a selection of prose and poetry (named in honor of Joyce's daughter) written by people with schizophrenia. In October 1979 it held its first national conference, in Dublin. By 1980, it had five regular meetings going in the Dublin area, and one apiece in Sligo and Cork. Slowly, its meetings grew to a few dozen throughout the country, proliferating to fifty-six support groups, a mix of group meetings for family members and other meetings for individuals who have "self-experience with schizophrenia," as they prefer to call it. As fast as they've expanded, there's still tremendous room for growth. There are an estimated 9,000 people in the psychiatric hospital population with self-experience, with another 1,800 being treated in the community, out of a population of 35,000 to 40,000 schizophrenics in Ireland. Including family members, as many as 175,000 people are in some way affected.

Schizophrenia Ireland, with its multipronged "bio-social-psycho" approach, deserves credit for beginning to dent the social problem. Seager and Saunders are also happy to trace the social trajectory that led to so many individuals being treated for mental illness in Ireland over the past 250 to 300 years, traipsing through the familiar history of British oppression, grinding poverty, bad potato harvests, famine, more British troops, more steady psychological degeneration. It wasn't just the homeless, penniless outcasts, they point out. Schizophrenia has been an equal-opportunity illness, striking all layers of society.

They are both well informed, conversant with the wide-ranging views of others on the subject. Correlation is not causation, as every social scientist knows, but the four most common links to populations of schizophrenics worldwide are emigration, famine, substance abuse, and older fathers. Historically, the Irish were firing on all four cylinders, possibly redlining rates among children and grandchildren. Widespread malnutrition, the movement of large numbers of people, and substance abuse are easy to pull onto the scale. Schizophrenia occurs worldwide in about 1 percent of the population, but in individuals who endured fetal malnutrition, the risk may be as high as 2.3 percent. Alcohol and drug abuse raise the risk by a third.

Severe nutritional deficiencies of thiamin (vitamin B_1) and vitamin B_{12} can cause delirium, mania, hallucinations, or catatonia. Under conditions of famine and emigration, one would expect to find nutritional deficiencies that could have produced symptoms of insanity. Nor can primogeniture, which tended to produce older fathers, a risk factor, be ruled out as a culprit. It's a bit of a puzzler—late paternity—yet studies have found that the odds of developing schizophrenia rise 30 percent with each ten-year climb in paternal age, due to more mutations in sperm. In old Ireland, men tended to marry very late, and women were married off at a very young age.

Or to get rid of them, women were sent to the convent, the younger brothers to the priesthood, while the oldest son was left the farm. As a result, it was not uncommon for men to be forty before they married. A man marrying into a family with three or four daughters "could be any age and be suitable," says Seager. "He could be fifty marrying a fifteen-year-old."

Sometimes cousins were married to keep the farm in the family. "Consanguinity" is the polite way of phrasing it, and it was a fact of life in peasant Ireland. Intermarriage was more common in the post-famine era. "The chances of meeting a second, third, or fourth cousin increased as time went on," says Saunders. "It's a fair pattern of what went on up to the twentieth century." So while pockets in the rural south and west were known to exist, there's no evidence to suggest any general prevalence of consanguinity in Ireland. Still, asked to investigate the "difficult and vexed" question of madness in the aftermath of the famine, the medical superintendents of the asylums of Ireland had blamed the rising prevalence on abuse of alcohol, bad diet, and consanguineous marriages, which, they noted, were found "in certain secluded valleys in the west and south of Ireland where inter-marriage is common."

This echoed what lunacy inspectors had concluded decades earlier. As Inspector White had written in 1849, "Insanity in all its forms can be traced, and even through degrees of relationship, to the practice of intermarriage which prevails in some districts from a desire of the parties to perpetuate the tenure of land or other property amongst the immediate kindred."

While the Church frowned on marriages between first or second cousins, because that seemed to lead to mental retardation and deformities, marrying a third cousin was not unusual with a Church dispensation. Nor was first- and second-cousin marriage on the sly unheard of. Britain's strict land system, which squeezed the Irish off their farms, pretty much guaranteed more intermarriage. Even so, an effort was made to marry at least one county across in Connaught, so that a man from Roscommon might favor a woman from Mayo rather than Leitrim. "Go east for a woman, go west for a horse," was the saying, and it was hard to argue with.

In fact, there is no rise in the risk of schizophrenia through "inbreeding." What raises rates significantly is when two people with schizophrenia have a child. That situation poses a risk of 40 to 45 percent that the child will develop the condition. If only one parent has schizophrenia, the risk of the child developing it is only one in ten. Saunders says the nod from the Church was just the done thing, but it did not raise rates except where schizophrenics bred with other schizophrenics, a phenomenon known as "assortative mating."

He's friendly enough, while Seager is the harder one, holding her energy inward. Steer her toward topics she doesn't wish to cover and she crisply puts you in your place. I had been hoping to attend one of their group meetings or weekend retreats for family members of schizophrenics. In the newsletter, the boat cruises and yoga retreats for the relatives' groups looked like fun. When I broach it, the pair share concerned glances. "It wouldn't be appropriate," Seager says stiffly.

I'm taken aback. Apparently it's a very buttoned-up schizophrenia scene here in Ireland. I've hit the tombstone-like silence, the classic Irish freeze-out from behind clenched teeth. I feel the undercurrent of resistance much stronger in Seager than Saunders. It's true that the Irish sense of place excludes those whose parents were not born here. That's where they draw the line. It counts for nothing that I am an

Irish American seeking my own truth, as every man must. One more request meets more concerned glances. More silence. More earnest chin stroking. More eyebrows arched. The line drawn again. I am welcome to attend their upcoming biennial conference, being held this year in Athlone, but not the relatives' groups. Aware that I'm on fragile turf, I drop it. Composing myself, I nod mutely, an island of resentment all to myself. I feel like saying "Thanks a lot," but I chomp down, not wanting to touch a nerve. I pretend not to care, but inside my heart is beating like a rabbit's, embarrassed that I've misfired.

The Irish feel proud about their distinctive Irishness, but Ireland has fast become a society with "others" in it like me. It was a shame not to see their hospitality extended. Apparently all that radio talk about not facing mental illness alone did not apply to an Irish American writer, but I wouldn't have been so eager had those thirty-second spots not drawn me in. After that, things felt sort of awkward. No group hugs here. Why gild the Irish lily?

CHAPTER FIFTEEN

LORD
OF THE
GLEN

Seeing the sun, hearing the roar of the sea outside the van, I notice a few early-rising campers gathering outside tents and trailers, talking in small bunches, but there's no sign of my schizophrenic man. "He's moved on," Mrs. McNally says, cracking a rare smile. "Last night."

"Where to?"

"Can't say, wouldn't know."

I spare her the briefing on the sink incident; it's not a story to share with an older woman. I take my man's absence as the cue to go myself. In jig time I am out on the road again, chasing down the Dingle well of the mad naked lunatics. Did my man go there? Like some old cat, did he feel the nocturnal call of the valley of the mad? Or has he crawled off to another margin, some other lagoon?

Looping out of Dublin, it's liberating to be running the gauntlet again. Driving must be in my American bloodstream—a primal, shark-like urge to keep moving, all the while waiting for some answer for my sisters. Schooled on

Kerouac, I know why Sal Paradise had to go on the road, and why the only people for him were "the mad ones, the ones who are mad to live, mad to talk, mad to be saved." I see why Sal had to pray that "somewhere along the line the pearl would be handed to me."

By noon I'm in the Glendalough Valley, an ancient settlement of monasteries that helped keep culture alive when Europe sank into the Dark Ages. You can see why the holy men were drawn here. The whole glen is a paradise of feral goats and red squirrels, peregrine falcons and dragonflies mating in midair delight. Only a few centuries earlier Ireland had been a pagan land, its people worshipping a pantheon of gods. Now they were taking to Christianity in numbers so vast that a poor hermit was hard pressed to find a spot of solitude. Sooner or later another hermit would happen along, and communities of monks were born, ascetics who made masterpieces like the *Book of Kells* in the silence of their scriptoria.

Tumbling through the Wicklow Mountains, I zig inland, taking the Wicklow Gap through Hollywood and Moone to Carlow, then southeast again, zagging through the salt marsh and mud flats to the sea. At St. John of God's seminary, I find a trail that leads to the beach, a stretch of sand that spools out like silk along the surf. Up by the dunes there's a quiet cave with the ashes of a recent campfire. Apparently people still come here to get away from it all, to sleep as the hermits and the prehistoric peoples slept, building fires and napping on the dry sand at the entrance. It feels feral camping here on the coast. In the alcove of the cave, away from the winds that knit the sands into smooth mounds around me, I huff a joint I scored on the Liffey and sleep, for once, like a baby. I know it breaks my sobriety, but it beats a drink. When I dried out, I was told I'd be a "sober drunk." The "sober" part of that prognosis isn't always easy to live up to, but then the "drunk" part is a disaster to climb down from. Today I miss a step.

In the morning there are nuns walking the beach in long black habits between the weeds and driftwood tossed up by tides. Up behind me the land is dabbed with white cottages with thatched roofs. These are real thatched cottages, not the kind built in 1993 to look like the real thing. There are small potato farms, a graveyard by a fairy mound, and a group of bicyclists bivouacked in colorful tents on a pillow of holly, bracken, brambles, and woodruff. Geese have flown here from Greenland via Iceland, making the journey to these warm dunes in just eight hours. Wexford sells itself as "the sunniest county in Ireland," which is a bit like billing yourself as the world's tallest midget.

Fields and farmhouses fall away from the inlet as I strike westward. Across from an old famine graveyard in Duncarvan that's worth a look, I stop for lunch at the Seanachai Pub and cross into County Cork near the sea at Youghal, a "bustling town" where Gregory Peck filmed *Moby Dick*. Cromwell sailed from here, never to see Irish shores again. Youghal beats the Irish out of Ballinasloe for colorful shop fronts. The story goes that when Queen Victoria died, in 1901, the word came down from Dublin Castle that everyone should paint their doors black as a gesture of mourning. Instead the people of Youghal did their doors in the most vibrant palette of reds and greens, going all-out with the gilt lettering and huge overflowing flower baskets that hang to this day.

Sweeney was a big name in Cork. Unlike the mad Egans, I'm told, the paternal side of May Sweeney's people survived the famine here, sailing to Boston during the land wars of the

1870s. In their time the asylum here was bursting with lunatics. Conditions were so overcrowded that the construction of a new asylum was deemed "a matter of the utmost importance." In 1844, a lunatics inspector warned of "the worst consequences [that] might be expected from the assembly of such numbers of irresponsible beings."

Cork has a lunatic history every bit as rich as Roscommon's. There's one story of a Captain S. who was committed to the old asylum after murdering seven of his crew at sea. A day or two after leaving Barbados for the return voyage home to Cork, he accused two of his mates of stirring the others to mutiny. During the crossing he barely slept, and for the last two nights stormed about in a frenzied state, a brace of pistols and a cutlass at his side.

In sight of the Cork coast at last, Captain S. had seven of eight mates tied up and shot. An eighth mate who fled into the hold was wounded just as another boat's crew boarded and overpowered the captain. Captain S. was described by doctors as a religious fanatic, subject to "maniacal paroxysms, the forerunner of which is an excess of piety, with a recurrence to the phraseology of his former profession. He is still impressed with the belief that the crew meditated mutiny upon his death."

Another schizophrenic sailor, a fisherman also from Cork, slit his own throat in the crowded asylum. He was described by Dr. Osburne as "a well-liked man" until then, an ex-fisherman who had become gripped with the idea that he was a fish. His case was "marked by the whimsical illusion of his being introduced to the world in the form of a salmon, and caught by some fisherman off Kinsale. He generally appeared thoughtful and gloomy when alone, but became cheerful when spoken to. His favorite subject was the 'otherworld,' expressing much anxiety to know how he could get there, and what his occupation would be." After seven years of treatment, the fisherman was found one morning dead, "hanging by a strip of his blanket to an old mop nail."

A third asylum death that year was a beggar by trade who lost thirty guineas, "became distracted, and in this state was brought to the asylum," according to Dr. Osburne. "His restlessness was excessive, running up to every person to make inquiries about his loss. In perpetual motion by day, he seldom slept by night, wailing and holding conversations with imaginary beings. He became daily weaker, and died of complete exhaustion."

Through Clonakilty and Skibbereen and West Cork, the views, true to hype, are arresting. Ireland gets more rural here, meaning all the familiar totems of village life—the fish 'n chip shops, churches, cemeteries, pubs, schools, and athletic clubs—are fewer and farther between. I tend to visit the stone circles and famine graveyards on my way out to Dingle. In the Kingdom of Kerry alone there are more than a hundred stone circles on my map, and cliffside scenery unparalleled anywhere in Europe—some would say in all the world.

Dodging oncoming tour buses the size of Norman fortresses, I slow for a sharp curve and lose the rear of the van, which starts skidding sideways toward the cliff edge. I manage to pull out of it, and take the Ring of Kerry back inland and north again, through the McGillicuddy Reeks to the Dingle Peninsula, another desolate place where jolly red-cheeked people wave at the sight of a passing car. I'd expected a breezy run down a series of narrow green roads; instead, I'm stuck on some of the most treacherous miles in Ireland, riding my brakes down a road so tortuous that in winter it's closed to horses. A driver on my bumper is flashing headlights at me, but it's hard to stop fast on the wet and slippery surface of a road so twisted that it ought to be committed. As I pull to the left and the car overtakes me, I lean out my window to see a woman flipping me off, shouting, "Ya big idjit!"

Going by two maps—an Ordnance Survey Map and a Rand McNally road map—I'm a little confused. I see Gleanna-a-Galt on the survey map, but if you're looking for it on the road map, you might as well be navigating by the stars. There's no sign of it. In its place there appears to be a village called Foilatrisnig as I follow the old track bed of the Tralee and Dingle Railway. Could it be the name has changed? I wonder as I putter up and down thirty miles of narrow-gauge railway. The line, now closed, had threaded its way up and over the Gleanna-a-Galt and down through Dingle, hauling loads of cattle and Beamish Stout. The most westerly railway in Europe, the Dingle opened in 1888 and ran its steepest miles from Camp to Gleanna-a-Galt. Now a tourist railway, the line's last train chugged out of the mountainside in 1953.

"Ah, the Gleanna-a-Galt," a shop clerk in Camp tells me. "It's the curing point for those who are known to be mad. The road's quite narrow and bendy, but if you go up you'll see the sign. It's supposed to say Gleanna-a-Galt, but the sign says Foilatrisnig instead."

"Huh, that's curious. Why is it called Foilatrisnig now?"

"Beats me. It's right down the road."

By now I've learned that "right down the road" in Ireland does not mean a little way—it means a long way down the road into whole new territory. "That's the shortest way then?"

"Are you walking or driving?" the clerk asks, sensing my confusion.

"Huh, driving, of course."

"Grand," she says. "Then that's the shortest way."

As I go out the door, stupefied, she calls me back. "Here," she says, slipping me a phone number. "Brigit O'Connor lives by it. She'll have the whole history. From her father she has the lore."

At the crest of the hill a sign says "Foilatrisnig." This must be it. I park the van and go out for a stretch. Any farther west and I'd be in Boston. Looking across the wide valley and out to the sea, it's hard to imagine a better setting for a lunatic population to gather. This is where Ireland's schizophrenics and manic-depressives were drawn when the world didn't want them, or so goes the lore. I have a quiet reverie: as the moon rises and the night shadow falls across the valley, they come in kilts and pantaloons, tramping up and over the lip of the hill. Into the valley they swarm, on foot and by donkey cart, hearing their voices and answering the call of the Gleanna-a-Galt.

Dropping into the valley, I see a small timber sign that says "Glen a Galt" on the green grass by the well, just visible from the roadside. This is the glen, and I am psyched. It's like being in the place in the fable, the well Mom told me about as a kid, right after I'd first heard the big word *schizophrenia*. Thinking back on that ride—and me being here now—is like dreaming a dream of seeing this place. I go low and scoop two bottles of water, one for Chelle and another for Austine, cap them, and stick them in the van, a fumbling and feeble attempt to do something for my sisters.

Can't say I don't like the idea of the place. It's been said that science tries to make complicated things simple, and myth tries to make simple things complicated, but in the case of schizophrenia it seems to be the other way around. Science still misses the mark in seeking out clear lines of answers to schizophrenia. This path takes me in between the lines for no less simple truths. What's simpler than bottling the gift of water, the essence of life itself, for my sisters?

Down the small dirt road a hundred yards is the pint-sized house of Brigit O'Connor. At the door of her cottage, I meet a woman about my age, friendly and talkative. "Yes," she says, "the sign says 'Foilatrisnig.' Do you know what happens? There's a lovely area down there and it's called the Cliff of the Free, or Foilatrisnig, and it's above this river, this lovely river, as you can see, which flows down, but what happens here in Ireland is the department officials who live up in Dublin, they pick a spot and they put a name on it. Without having any knowledge of Gleanna-a-Galt, they never bothered putting up the sign. So we're actually addressing that ourselves now."

Brigit says that her family, like mine by coincidence, was from Roscommon. "We could be cousins. Rory O'Connor of the O'Connor-Dons fled here too," she says, alluding to the Roscommon descendants the O'Connors, one of the oldest families in Europe—the kings of Connaught and the high kings of Ireland. "My father, as an O'Connor, was interested in the history of the area, and he told me a lot, I suppose, the whole background to this madness theory, and the well and that. Mostly it would be in the pre-hospital days for people suffering from mental illness. When people would have gone to the herbal remedies as such."

In the days before her father, her great-grandfather, a Thomas O'Connor, would churn his milk into butter here. To Tralee or Cork he then drove his butter by horse and cart, and it was not unusual to see him returning to the well with a few lost souls. They all hoisted pints of stout and became fond friends. In his spirit, Brigit is carrying on the family tradition of partying by the well. Each year, she says, friends toss a party here.

"I remember people mostly coming," she says. "They'd keep arriving, like yourself, usually unannounced because at that time we had no phone. And my father was always here. He'd be feeding the hay and he'd just give up his afternoon and he'd get talking to these people. And they would come back the next year and the next year. He created loads of friends. He was totally available, morning, noon, or night. If someone arrived at the door and he was in the middle of his dinner, he'd just get up and go off with them, you know. He just loved the whole concept. He liked being the lord of the glen, the hero of the valley."

Brigit rattles all this off in a flash. She is blond and somewhat studious-looking but good fun too, with an easy, ready laugh. She has lived here for most of her life, apart from five years in Dublin. Three years ago she lost her father, and with him any of the valley lore that he hadn't passed on to her. They were as close as a dad and a daughter could be, but she maintains a bright demeanor even when talking about him, as if he's still here with us. Her mood is infectious.

About fifty strides from the well—down a little dirt path known as a boreen—we come upon a fairy mound. She doesn't climb over the weedy dunghill but walks around it the way an archaeologist might. When I tell her about my mother's tale about a healing well for the insane in Ireland, her face lights up. "Sweeney, oh, God, that's interesting. Mad Sweeney came here, and was in Roscommon, the deranged Druid king. Here," says Brigit, "he lived for a year and a day in a tree overlooking the well. He drank cow milk from a stone and crossed at Fool's Crossing by the fairy fort and lived in the trees until he was sane again. Some think Mad Sweeney was Merlin the Magician."

We marvel at the shape of the fairy mound. It's not much bigger than a man and the opening is nearly all filled in now. Brigit expects ancient people would have slept in it when they were here drinking from the well. "And as I say, the history behind it, people came here to get a cure if they were depressed or whatever. Like in those days people didn't have much transport. And my great-grandfather would take the milk to be churned into butter. And instead of bringing it to Tralee or Dingle, they had to bring it to Cork. And they felt nothing about traveling up and down in his horse and cart, so he drove regularly in his horse and cart with his butter.

"And on one occasion, what happened at that time, people were coming regularly to the well. And on this day that this man was coming to the well, my grandfather was driving the cows. No, actually it'd be my great-grandfather, it's going back that far. But he encountered this man, and the man was a little bit off the beam, and they had a struggle. Afterwards, anyway, they went to the well and he drank the water and he stayed for a while, up above in me own house."

The well is a bit overgrown now, "but the good thing is, Patrick, it never dries," she says, walking me back to it. "Winter or summer, that well never dries. The finest summer of this year, the fine weather we've had this year, and that well hasn't dried."

"Is that unusual, for a well not to dry?"

"Not really, but some wells do dry up. It is unusual in some ways because it's not a huge river or anything. It's just like a stream. The fact that it doesn't dry up also means, I suppose, that it's meant to keep running. But definitely it's an unusual story associated with it and I think, like, there must be an element of truth in it, because, I think, things don't get handed down if they're not the truth. You know, it's like in life, you'll hear a lot of things, but at the end of the day this has managed to come down even right through the centuries."

Truth is a mirror more than a fact, and I am enjoying Brigit's version of it. I know how things get handed down too. The river that flows from the Cliff of the Free into the Valley of the Mad feeds a well that cures the mad. It makes for a nice story, a redemptive fairy tale, and I'm content to accept that miracles might spring from water that never goes dry. Maybe it's Brigit's good spirit, but my visit feels like a pivot point. I've been to the well to do my bit for the sisters, to fetch two bottles. I'll at least leave Ireland with the water.

I follow Brigit and listen until she's used up her supply of Gleanna-a-Galt stories. There's the one about the king of France coming here at the time of the Battle of Ventry Harbor. "My father used to say that—that they lost their reason—and it was a very magical way to describe it. And that he came here, and drank the waters, and was cured."

The lore comes down from generations of O'Connors living here in the valley since the early 1800s. "Not in this house, mind you, but in and around the valley. My grandfather was born in the old house in 1882, so that was during the time of the landlords."

A hundred years later, in the mid-1980s, the soil was tested. "Some persons came here with a scientific background. They came here and they took a sample of the water and tested the soil. Took it off, got it analyzed, and they said there was a very high content of lithium in the soil."

"Lithium?"

"Yes, which is used in the treatment of manic depression. So there may be something to do with the soil. And quite a few people would come—they'd just come now and ask me where it was and I'd tell them. And even now they come from Cork and from Kerry way, and like you from Roscommon and from Boston, they come for the water. There must be something to it."

Driving out of the valley that evening, motoring around the nether regions of Ireland with my well water in tow, I feel my drum beats in time with the Irish now. At least I'm done pushing the boulder up the hill.

CHAPTER SIXTEEN

🌀

THE
PEARL OF
GALWAY

Bouncing down through Dingle again on my final jaunt back to Roscommon, the van swerves as wind gusts hit it sideways. Just then the phone rings with news from the Hearing Voices Network that a workshop is on in Galway. Shifting course slightly, I head for the Paranoia Workshop, as it's billed, in the city of Tribes, just west of Roscommon. My only question is, will I be followed?

This ought to be interesting. For the longest time, conventional psychiatry has not known what to do with the voices, so doctors tend to treat schizophrenic brains like biochemical labs, overprescribing medication to try to quiet them. The Hearing Voices Network takes a more tolerant approach, seeing meds as a fairly crude instrument. Founded by Dutch psychiatrist Marius Romme in response to a patient's disappointment with conventional psychiatry, this self-help network (along with Resonance, a similar group in the Netherlands) counts thousands of European voice-hearers as members.

Before Romme came along, psychiatrists typically discouraged schizophrenics from talking about their voices; by contrast, more and more in psychiatry, and especially in Europe, the approach is to engage the voices by asking what they have to say. Romme's research into the history of voice-hearers found that a millennium ago some were seen as special, even revered as shamans, for reaching transcendental states of consciousness. In today's world, it's the social stigma, on top of the voices, that schizophrenics find so hellish.

In Connemara, a sea-swept countryside and one of the moodiest beauty spots in Ireland, I pitch a tent at the water's edge—about as far west as it gets in Europe. Just south of here, down a rugged Galway lane, is where Guglielmo Marconi installed his famous aerials, locating them where no land mass could interfere with transatlantic radio signals. In the morning, it's an interference of another kind: a cow pokes her nose in my tent. By afternoon I'm watching the water rush down by the Spanish Arch, feeding bread to swans, taking in the sights.

Christopher Columbus worshipped here at the Cathedral of St. Nicholas—a massive medieval gem—before sailing for America. Like my uncles, many of the locals are as swarthy as Spaniards. Think Che Guevara, the South American revolutionary, whose grandmother, Anna, was a Lynch from Galway. Her "black Irish" son, Ernesto Lynch Guevara, said on the death of his own son, Che: "The first thing to note is that in my son's veins flowed the blood of Irish rebels."

On Shop Street, a snaggletoothed "traveler" or Gypsy woman begs, her child beside her pounding amateurishly on an accordion. I give the mother a ten-euro note, twice the rate for a palm reading, and ask her to "make it a good one."

"Your troubles are over," she tells me. "But you've got to get home."

At the Ardilaun Hotel, I check in the night before the workshop for the thrill of sleeping with 300-thread-count sheets, the luxury of a shower that's not coin-operated, and the comfort of dining out in the hotel's restaurant. It's good to be sleeping in a real bed for the first time in Ireland. September has been both very wet and the warmest on record, and now I get to crash in an air-conditioned room, drifting off to the blare of the Sky Sports network. Showering in the morning until my skin turns red, I shave for the occasion and even clip my nose hairs like an old bachelor farmer. I don't feel great, but at least I don't look like the grubby van guy when I drop downstairs to the lobby.

There's no reason to add paranoia to an event that features it, but I'm worried about the folks from Schizophrenia Ireland being here. The workshop was advertised in their newsletter, and when we met in Dublin they were about as welcoming as a cup of cold sick. The lobby has upholstered armchairs and neutral art on the walls, the restaurant perky American-style breakfast service. My guess, as I spear my eggs, is that as many as half of the perfectly normal-looking people ambling toward the conference room are being paged by their voices. The event itself is for people experiencing paranoia, voices, and similar symptoms of psychosis, and friends, family members, and professionals are all welcome.

As a few dozen take seats on folding auditorium chairs, a British-born man in his late thirties, with brown hair and a medium build, introduces himself as Peter Bullimore and tells us he's a mental health consultant with the network. For the next two hours, Peter's controlled descent into behind-the-scenes head territory is gripping. As he talks, occasionally walking forward to make a point about the voices he hears, tracing them to trauma caused by abuse as a child at the hands of a babysitter, it dawns that I am in the presence of a rare man indeed. In most cases I've encountered, the only person able to describe the experience of hearing voices is still delusional, making it hard to piece together the sequence of events leading up to the psychotic break. Peter is not. He has the air of a man who knows he is making his points and making them well. He seems to have no trouble straddling both worlds, speaking of the voices as if they were separate things that no longer shake his confidence on a good day.

As he claims, one part of his mind functions in our world quite well, even while the other part is in near-constant communication with these voices. Peter can only suspect—like the rest of us—that somewhere in his mind, although not necessarily in a place science can yet recognize, the voices intrude and cannot be dismissed lightly. If they are not controlled, he says, then they can be bad-mannered, even bullying. He says his first voice came to him as a boy. While he was playing soccer, it urged him to attack another boy. "I heard this voice saying, 'Hit him, hit him,' and so I did."

When the abuse from the babysitter ceased, he says, "so did the voices, and then the paranoia went soon afterwards." The voices were "reactivated" in adulthood, along with extreme paranoia, soon after he became a father; he suspects it was because he was reliving his childhood vicariously. He remembers clearly the day when they returned. He was in the town center, he recalls, when "a booming voice told me I had millions of pounds in gold."

It was a big letdown, because there was no gold, and things got much worse from there. The voices were wild, raucous, and distraught at first. They shrieked at him, disturbed his peace, made him truly unwelcome in his own head.

Naturally, this depressed him. "People would say, 'Can't you smile, you miserable git?' By now I was the archetypal schizophrenic," he says. "I didn't wash. I didn't shave. I became scruffy."

So beaten was Peter by the voices that he would make a suicide attempt. Peter explains that like so many schizophrenics, he was having bizarre religious fantasies. "I thought I was Jesus Christ, so I went to the cathedral. On the way, I stopped at McDonald's for my last supper. I had decided I was born to kill myself. At the cathedral I ran into a priest who exclaimed, 'Christ Almighty.' When I heard him, I thought, Well, at least he recognizes me."

Peter didn't sleep for days and endured increasingly frequent out-of-body experiences. He became convinced that Freddy Krueger, the burnt-faced, metal-clawed movie villain, was on his tail. "I wanted to get it all over with," he recalls, "so I slashed my wrists, but was found by my father."

In a mental hospital he still had night terrors and had to sleep with the lights on. When he looked in the mirror, he saw a long-haired, bearded demon returning his gaze. Wherever he went, whatever combination of medications he swallowed, the disfigured *Nightmare on Elm Street* character stalked him. His voices were all the more persuasive because they possessed an uncanny ability to predict the future. "At one point they told me my mother would die from cancer in six months' time," he remembers. "When she did, they had me convinced. And now they began to say that I was to blame for her death."

After a series of hospitalizations, Peter lied his way out of the last one, he says, "by pretending to be well." When he turned up one day at a Hearing Voices Network meeting, he was floored to find others whose experiences mirrored his own. What a relief to know he was not alone.

At the network, Peter came across a book called *Accepting Voices,* and in its pages he found a way of living with his otherworldly acquaintances. The book challenges psychiatric orthodoxy, which, its authors claim, inhibits rather than stimulates recovery. Peter was thrilled to learn that he could silently control his voices, dismissing them like tiny idols for brief periods at least. He locked himself away for two weeks to listen to them all, giving them free rein for a while, as suggested. "The more I listened to the voices, the more I saw that there was a dominant voice. There's always a dominant voice," he says. "Mine was my abuser. Once I put that in place, I didn't fear it."

It isn't always easy to challenge the dominant voice. "Some people find it very hard because they may have five dominant voices," he says. "And we worry that they'll all go to war with each other. Not true—if you take the dominant voice away, the others will go quietly."

Others share their own experiences about their own voices. Chris Stirk, also from the Hearing Voices Network, dropped the medication too. He says the visual hallucinations are easier to filter out, but audio ones are less avoidable, inducing fear and paranoia as they crowd out other thoughts. His voices slander him, going after perceived personal weaknesses. At times the audio mix isn't simply voices; it's conversations distorted by a cacophonous, discordant score of shouting whispers and whispering shouts.

Through the network, Stirk has learned to live with his voices a day at a time. The clear message here is that you can't knock the hornets' nest out of the tree, but you can coexist with the voices. They may sting occasionally, but they won't kill you, so the best therapy is one that accommodates them. Since Peter stopped taking prescription drugs seven years ago, the voices have settled, but not vanished. His pushing-off point came after a doctor told his father, "Your son is taking enough medication to knock out a horse, but we still can't stop his voices."

It's difficult to quantify, but hearing voices turns out to be a fairly common human experience. Apart from schizophrenics, research shows that many people begin to hear them by dint of stress or trauma. Apparently, the label "voice-hearer" fits far more people than those who would like to claim it. According to the Hearing Voices Network, as many as 10 percent of the population has at some time perceived sensory input when no stimulus was present. In other words, they have experienced auditory hallucinations. Most people hear voices very infrequently—once every few months for four or five years is a typical experience, and those voices tend to be less disturbing.

For the poor schizophrenic, the mind can be a vast vault of many voices. Merging with the world isn't easy when they all begin to talk at once; it's like listening to somebody speaking nine different languages. The voices can be friendly folks or javelins of fear. Simulating the world of a paranoid schizophrenic, Peter inserts a videotape into the player. With conversation barely audible over the blare of Alanis Morissette's old hit single "Ironic," and distorted faces and background noises drowning out a handful of voices, it's like walking into a bad 1990s party. Some voices rise up unexpectedly, others stay loud. The whole video demonstration seems designed to provoke in the viewer the frustrations of psychosis. It is very effective.

Stirk then asks the audience how the experience felt. We supply a host of adjectives: *anxious, frustrated, exposed, rattled, disoriented, disconnected, isolated.* "If this went on for a long space of time, then how would you feel?"

One by one we respond.

"Panicked."

"Confused."

"Defensive."

"Angry."

"Overanalytical."

"Would you turn to alcohol, drugs, or suicide to cope with the symptoms?"

The group goes silent. At length, a middle-aged woman raises her hand to speak. She says she pleaded with her medical team to stop patronizing her. "I keep telling the nursing staff not to reassure me that it will all be fine," she says. "I think it dismisses my experience. There's a flippancy to saying, 'Oh, you'll be grand. Go on then.'"

Another voice-hearer, a bright-eyed woman in her thirties, says she often just wants company. "There's nothing like that feeling of someone being present and just being there with me."

Teeth seem to be a fairly ordinary obsession. "Our sister lost all of her teeth," one woman shares, without elaborating. "We keep getting her new dentures, and she keeps throwing them out. It's getting expensive."

"You've got to give people hope," Peter tells her. "We can never say the voices will go away, but there are ways of living with them and controlling them."

Peter has various coping techniques. One he calls selective listening. "I tell the voices to come back at eight and I'll give them an hour." Another good tip, he says, is to focus on the nice voices. In doing so, he says, "the positive voices become the dominant voices."

A woman named Dora is appalled that her thoughts were being broadcast on TV. Her solution was to watch less of it. Peter agrees. "You may not be able to silence the voices, but you can contain the fear."

A guy named Steve says that satellite signals were bouncing off his head. His ameliorative action was to wear a cap with a protective inside layer of silver foil. Because he believed it would reflect the satellite signals, in his reality it did.

Another suggestion was for schizophrenics to use cell phones to argue with their voices freely and unself-consciously. "Until you go through a tunnel," a woman adds, speaking from her own experience. "A smartly dressed businessman said to me one day, 'Good God, madam, what network are you on?'

"I paused and said to him, 'The Hearing Voices Network.'"

I am not sure what to make of all this. I have no trouble believing that the voices are real or that they get processed in the auditory cortex of the brain, just like ordinary sound, or that they are small "gods" of a sort. The mystery lies in where they originate and what they want. Is there a world of invisible beings who are heard by only some? Epilepsy, which produces extra charges of electrical activity in the temporal lobe areas of the brain, has been known to produce religious visions and voices, just as those produced during prayer and meditation show up in the temporal lobes, on either side of the head, in the same circuits that run language, conceptual thinking, and associations. Dostoyevsky, an epileptic, may be the most famous case. He writes in *The Idiot*, perhaps autobiographically, of the mystical epileptic temple moment when "his brain seemed to catch fire."

The room is uneasy to varying degrees with the label

"schizophrenic." You could argue that there's little difference between a schizophrenic voice-hearer and another type of person who hears voices, but why bother? Peter cites a study conducted in Birmingham, England, of people who heard voices and didn't swoop into a depression until they received the schizophrenia diagnosis. It was the label itself that was isolating and disabling.

It's a shame in a way that Peter distances himself from the label, because he's an excellent ambassador from the schizophrenic side. Here is a person who was hounded and haunted by voices, and yet he's managing them ably. He speaks with clarity and humor, illuminating a world where hallucination can lead to degradation. Voices would make anyone paranoid. What could be more manipulative than an ongoing conference call heard only by you? Peter and others are bridging the gap in fairly good style. One participant says his dominant voice is a real shrew. "I put her on a cliff each day and push her off," he says. "It takes her about six hours to climb back."

Peter takes an informal, show-of-hands poll. "Okay, how many of you believe in ghosts?"

Half the hands go up.

"Fairies?"

A few more hands.

"Life after death?"

Only two people have not raised their hands by now.

"Is there anyone here who can say they've never been paranoid at some time in their life? But when does it become a problem?"

Peter cites a Gallup Poll showing that 45 percent of respondents said they believed in telepathy, 39 percent in life after death, 39 percent in faith healing, and 31 percent in ghosts.

"So it's hard," he concludes, "to distinguish between the two groups of people—the deluded and the undeluded."

It's helpful if paranoid voice-hearers can find someone they trust and with whom they can share their beliefs. Romme felt that suppressing the voices only makes them stronger. Psychotropic drugs, he concluded, could never fix the problem entirely. "Nobody has ever been 'cured' by medication," Peter agrees. "Most people can get by without it. Forcing people to take drugs is a form of abuse."

Instead, Peter devotes time each day to sitting relaxed and listening to his voices. Otherwise, the voices play tricks, knocking down perceptual expectations, plunging him into the dimension-swirling zone of what we commonly call madness. Or, in the case of my sister Austine, challenging her to sink the knife in someone's back for no apparent reason.

The remedy, says Peter, is to listen to the voices in his head and allow himself the choice to respond or not to their instructions, and finally to call his own tune. I take note. It's an idea I might smuggle back home—that reality is in the eyes (and ears) of the beholder.

Research by Dr. David Copolov, an Australian mental health researcher, shows that when the voices are speaking, the brain's temporal lobes become more active. If what you see or hear is not there, says Peter, then you are told you are insane. But what if it is there? That's a possibility he does not explore, but his practical insights fall like gospel on the ears of the faithfully gathered. Despite the hour, he's holding steady, and the crowd clearly likes the notion of managing their voices one day at a time. It puts the keys to sanity in their own hands.

A lovely pearl of thought, that.

CHAPTER SEVENTEEN

⟡

BACK TO ROSCOMMON

I t's a short drive down the Galway Road to Roscommon. When I get to Hodson Bay, the old tortoise Paddy is gone, having closed up his campground back on Labor Day. I try my luck at another site along the lake at Gailey Bay. A dark collie rushes out to greet me. Rock sits with his paws on my lap and wags his tail for food. He'll be my buddy for the remainder of my days here—finally a dog to run over green fields with.

I've missed Roscommon; coming back here feels like coming home (or the closest I'll ever get to an Irish home). I wish I'd gone down to Ennis with Paddy Joe to see the Little Rossies play the Kingdom of Kerry for the All-Ireland football title, but I watched from a pub stool as they won their first minor-league crown since 1951. It says a lot about the pluck of the Little Rossies that more people tuned in to see their victory that Saturday than to watch the Ryder Cup, hosted this year in golf-mad Ireland. Lord knows how many bonfires burned in the roads of Roscommon that night.

That evening, some twenty thousand fans who've had little

to cheer about all these decades come roaring back into the town center. Every pub is wedged with fans wearing the colors of the county, blue and yellow. As the team arrives near midnight in the town square, lightning cracks the skies, as if the gods themselves were noting the win. Emerging from the pubs, a sea of blue and yellow chants, "We are Ros! We are Ros!" as captain David Flynn hoists the Tom Markham Cup, waving the trophy to the throng in the square.

Summer is well over now. Heavy showers have left a third of the fields in Ireland unplantable. By the sounds of the cows, it's mating season again; in fact, all of nature seems to be breeding now, and I'm still chasing Egans. It has taken all this time to locate the other Egan surviving from the parish when my Egans were here, mainly because her name has changed through marriage. At last I catch Molly Egan Mullen down a side road off the N61 in a pink bungalow next to her son's house. She greets me outside in a white sweater with roses stitched in, a red pleated skirt, and brown loafers, and confirms that her people are from the parish, from Cam-Kiltoom, going back to the time when my Mary Egan was there.

Molly is diminutive, her cheeks as red as fall apples. Inside, she has the teakettle on. As she pours water, I look around her tidy home, reluctant to get into exactly why I'm here. I keep mum about knowing already that hers were the Egans rumored to have psychiatric problems.

She tells me she's lived a satisfying life, though she was widowed just as she retired from her nursing career. Her real name is Mary Brigid Egan Mullen, she says, and I may call her Molly. I skirt around the topic, withholding, at least temporarily, my personal details until I press a piece of literature into her hand. It is a notice from Schizophrenia Ireland regarding its fifteenth biennial conference, coming up in Athlone.

I let the slow seconds linger as Molly examines it. She has no idea I've been snooping around. I feel crappy about doing the genealogical equivalent of picking her pocket, rifling through her personal information, and then slipping her wallet back into her purse quietly. But it's my only way in. Cultural etiquette calls for me to find a roundabout approach, never to rake over personal history too directly or exhaustively. I've learned by now you can get only so close in Ireland before flunking the distance test, no doubt a universal cultural rule. It's permissible to discuss personal information first among family members, next among friends and close acquaintances, and finally, if ever, with strangers like me. I'd soon be crossing the line. As she reads the flier, her eyes deepen in her head. "It's a desperate illness," she says looking up at me. "I know 'tis. We have it too."

"I'm sorry to hear that. Who was it, may I ask?"

"My brother, Peter, and an uncle on my mother's side."

Molly composes her face into a perplexed guess about it all. It's best for me not to say a lot. I wait for her to speak. She says she was the oldest of ten. Her brother Peter, "the nicest of them all," was only about twenty when his head started spinning. Not wanting to reveal too much, Molly keeps to generalities. I can see in her eyes she's paid dearly for this madness. Peter was the brother schizophrenia robbed her of. He was the jewel of the family; it's always the jewel, she says. One moment he was as fit as a butcher's dog; the next, like Chelle and Austine, he was so far gone, he rarely left the farm. Peter worked with his father, the chimney cleaner, and was looked after by the other brothers, including Paddy the postman, and was buried just a few weeks ago, in his seventies.

Molly is like a painting, all my attention focused on her sweet Irish face. I can see the pain there, coming back now, arising in her eyes. Schizophrenia is heartbreak and not much more. My insides slosh and roil. I want to tell her I understand. There's no need. She picks up on it. She asks the same disturbing questions. Why does it come on so fast? Schizophrenia is like an invisible force that sidles up—and they are gone before you know it. It sneaks up silently over several months so that we hardly see it coming. With Peter, too, the toppling was total and severe.

Molly lucked out. She married and had one sane son, Tommy, now thirty-eight, well past the average age of onset. "I'm very happy I had Tommy," she says proudly. "He turned out very well, with two lovely children of his own."

From the sound of things, Molly was a devoted mother. "It's something you have to give yourself over to, having children," she says. "You have to embrace it. Being a parent means everything else that you do is on the side."

Molly has no notion of the causes of schizophrenia. She, like me, was a genetic near miss, while Peter was chewed up within the fickle, cruel jaws. "Whether one gets it and another does not may be already worked out at birth," she guesses. "How you're brought up matters, but they come out the way they do."

Molly's father was an Egan, but I'm a little surprised to hear her mother was an Egan too. The Irish know all about kissing cousins, and I suspect Molly senses what I'm thinking, with intermarriage the elephant in the corner of the room. In the wider Roscommon area, there are clusters of Egans everywhere. In the local directory for Athlone, only Kellys outnumber Egans. To some, that insularity has a certain out-of-date quaintness. To me, it's merely worrisome.

Molly offers some advice on my own marriage prospects. "Forget about the schizophrenia," she tells me. "Marry out of it. A man needs lookin' after. Of course, you never know...," she says, her voice trailing off.

Mom married out of it, of course, only to feed schizophrenia's savage lust for more. What Molly has to say isn't surprising. For reasons I can't fully fathom, her words are soothing. Still, what's the percentage in that?

The room goes quiet again, and this time around I think of what my mother used to say whenever there was unexpected silence: "An angel has passed," she'd whisper. The Irish have two words for silence. One is *tost,* which means an absence of conversation; the other is *ciunas,* which means an absence of sound that brings a sense of calm. The latter is what we have now.

Mary Brigid Egan Mullen and I are strangers, yet this force of nature is the biggest mystery for both of us. Without saying so, we are close because we have this in common. The silence is broken with small talk about everyday things. I feel a shift.

Molly opens up only so far. She doesn't take me down through the back stairs and cupboards of her family's mental life, and I understand why. There is a sister who is whispered of in the pubs. For a brief moment I feel Molly will mention her, but she's lifted the veil far enough. It's best to say nothing. Who wants to be put under a microscope, like a bug on a pin?

As I look at her, I wonder if we are related. It would be my privilege. We are members of the same Egan clan, but that does not necessarily mean that we are related by blood ties. I want to check my mitochondrial DNA sequence—the molecule that mothers hand down that allows geneticists to track the maternal line of descent. Short of a hair sample, there is no way to confirm how closely or distantly related we may be. It's extreme nosiness, but it's nosiness emboldened by purpose.

She laughs at the suggestion that I take a hair sample. It's a snip too far. I try to get the DNA word out again, but can't quite say it. A cat has my tongue.

Maybe next time, on a return visit, but for now I'm left wondering if we share the same mitochondrial and whether her family's madness is trestled in mine. There's a good chance of it, with her being a double Egan from my ancestral Egan's parish. It seems more than coincidence that the bread crumbs of my investigation have led back to her. Of the few surviving Egans from this same, small south Roscommon parish, it pans out that one was hit as hard as we were.

At the end of the day what may matter most is that she gets it, knows how it feels, has been there herself, and understands. Meeting her hasn't transformed me, but it has added an important string to the bow. When I leave, I want to plant a kiss on her cheek. We shake hands instead, and I am away. I feel I've gone as far as I can go here, at least for the time being. With her brother laid to rest, the Egan schizophrenia now lingers only as a memory in the parish mist.

Before heading back to London, I drop by the annual Ballinasloe Horse Fair, if only because John and Mary Egan may have toasted their future here, the event being the customary place to arrange marriages. At the fair, in addition to horses, there are ducks, rams, goats, and puppies being auctioned off. Fireworks and magic shows, tug-of-war contests and bungee jumping give parts of the grounds a funhouse atmosphere. Elsewhere, the sight of men in big hats and leather, carrying whips and bridles and walking sticks, gives the place a slightly sadomasochistic vibe.

The fairgrounds is also crowded with nomadic natives

known as travelers and tinkers because they were handy with pots and pans in need of repair. It's a whole class of people who lost their farms in the famine but stayed behind. Only half of their school-age children attend school, and many of the adults are illiterate. Many still live in squalor on the roadside with no water, electricity, or garbage collection, while drawing scorn from the settled community for public drinking, brawling, begging, and letting horses stray. About 3,000 of them still live this way.

Today they've all descended like a horde. It's an ugly crowd, some glaring, others intensely following the action on dice. Loads of hard-looking men race ponies down a narrow lane. I twist an ankle tripping on a curb just as a snarling pit bull on a leash dares me to step closer. A red-haired boy of five or six playing a pennywhistle from the curb hands me my cap and smiles.

By night the moon glows and the fairgrounds have become a place of fear and suspicion. There's a frenzied energy I can't quite fathom until I get closer. Then it hits me like a head butt. Half of the place is jacked up on speed. In this corner of the fairgrounds at least, it's not just drink. Only the kid with the pennywhistle seems clean.

Looking around, I sense it's time to take my leave. It's not any one thing that tells me I'm finished here in Ireland—just a feeling of being done now. The clocks will be going back soon, and it's so cold in the van you could hang meat in there. I will hit the Schizophrenia Ireland conference in Athlone, and then I sense that I am running out of road and weather, and just to be outdoors camping when the trees turn gold is an accomplishment. Time now to go the way of the ancestors, to Boston.

Without a blade of grass to their name, they would have

set off on a journey of 140,000 paces to Dublin, the passenger tickets they held in their luggage their only hope of survival. Off they went with all the others plodding heavily. With their heads bent, they shuffled off in batches east to Dublin. On their way out, they may have squatted with others in "bog-trotter cabins," makeshift homes fashioned into the earth belowground to escape notice. As the wagons crossed back over the Shannon again, this time to escape not the swords of Cromwell but the hunger of the famine, the Egans were but beads in the string skulking across the bogside, the dead and dying all around them.

It took great courage to leave Roscommon for an unknown future in Boston. The peasants of Roscommon had one another at least, and they had the comfort of life's familiar tempo—the celebrations of marriages, the arrivals of newborns, even the threats of eviction would have drawn folks closer. Life had a reassuring procession, a sameness, until the potato fungus hit. Overnight, a third of the crop rotted in the ground. The effect of seeing thousands torn from their huts must have touched them all with a contagious dread. They knew it was just a matter of time before a warrant to evict would be issued by the sheriff, before they'd be turned out to trek the vast vacant spaces in a desperate search for food. If the women and children or the sick and half-witted could not bear it, that was just too bad. They still had to go. It was a drama both personal and epic.

The Egans would have hung on, craving food, through 1846, even as their neighbors lay dying, their faces swollen "grane and yaller," men smashed out of their minds on bad, cloudy *poitin,* drunk in the wet ditches. In the winter of 1846–47, the choice was stark: leave Ireland or die. Inevitably, they went. They had no choice. Ireland was in a state of rot.

To Dublin's Eden Quay they trod, a place whose name, in Hebrew, means "place of delight," though it was anything but. The English landlords must have felt the awful hatred in the Irish just beneath their starving submission. What appeared to be mass resignation was, in fact, bitterness incarnate, the prevailing emotion anger checked by fear.

Fever was more widespread than cholera, but when cholera kicked in epidemically, death became more widespread than fever. With each step they knew they were walking toward death. For so many, the grave seemed but a few paces away. Children would have felt the cold of the roads on their feet, since shoes were rarely worn by them. Since coffins were too costly, special reusable ones were fashioned with a sliding bottom that dumped the corpses into mass graves. To this day, those who cross these old "famine graveyards" are said to be stricken by a spooky hunger. Did Mary Egan, just twenty-four, see the corpses slide off and call to God to take them too? If the hunger and deprivation did not push her past the breaking point, then the loss of others might have. How long before she cracked? How many regrets, how many insults, how many trip wires? Whoever she was, this shrouded figure on her solemn march, she was part of an insanity that swept over Ireland like an almighty blast. The schizophrenia was probably pretty easy to miss amidst the all-consuming famine. But here it was, fed by hunger and crawling eastward to the ferries to Liverpool and the "coffin ships" to Boston.

From Eden Quay, the Egans would have boarded either a sailboat or a steam-powered ferry across the Irish Sea. There is no record of them on this leg, but more than a million who went this way were uncounted. Ship manifests showed a heavy supply of wheat, beef, and pork on the crossings to England. Deck passengers were kept in the dark about the food on board, of course, and within half a day they had their first glimpses of the crowded docks of Liverpool. About a thousand passengers a week were disembarking there, at the most hectic port on the Atlantic, carrying the great bulk of the Irish sea traffic.

Early on the morning of April 1, the *Anglo-Saxon* clipper ship weighed anchor in Liverpool, with John Egan, twenty-seven, listed in the passenger manifest as a laborer, and Mrs. Egan, twenty-four, as a servant, with 359 passengers bracing for a month-long ocean crossing, a carved English monarch gracing her bow under square-rigged masts and topsails. In rough seas, the waves washed over the decks, drenching the ragged refugees, who would have clambered down to steerage. It must've been hell out on the high seas, with nearly a million dying on the journey. Death was the sad lot of so many that sharks could be seen following the coffin ships to feed on overthrown corpses. From the elderly to the newly born, from the half-starved to the stark raving mad, they braved the waves together.

Family lore has it that Mary Egan was fully schizophrenic by the time she hit Boston. She was only a distant ancestor, but it was she who carried our madness to Boston, a strain that runs so strong that, five generations later, it still will not stand down. By the time they disembarked, most everybody in Boston had grown used to the sight of the half-mad, half-full-of-drink Irish immigrant. How much of their physical disability had caused the mental breakdown is anyone's guess. My hunch is it played some part.

PART III

THE HAZE
OF THE
HOMEFRONT

CHAPTER EIGHTEEN

SCHIZOPHRENIA IN WONDERLAND

Ireland was always the warm-up for Boston—for me, the main event. I've been back to visit over the years; after twenty-five years I'm finally moving back, a return I see as waving a white hanky, abandoning the field to a malady that runs over the dead, haunted by thoughts that only as my sisters breathe their last will any real answers be emerging.

Boston's winter feels deeper than Ireland's, the city's trees as bare as old bones as the Atlantic coast passes outside the subway window. It's three Blue Line stops from Logan International Airport to Suffolk Downs—the famous racetrack that was Dad's home away from home—and another three to the Wonderland station, the end of the line.

The North Shore town of Revere was named for the patriotic Revolutionary War messenger immortalized for his famous midnight ride. A few decades after my Egan ancestors settled into the Boston Irish slums, Revere boasted the nation's first public beach. Later, in May Sweeney's day, the world-famous Thunderbolt roller coaster occupied this seaside

239

boulevard at Wonderland Park, the inspiration, decades later, for Disney World.

Seanna moved to Wonderland just weeks earlier, and the moment I see her outside her new seaside apartment, I know I'm home where I belong. Seanna looks better than ever, and Elaine, as always, has a bright light inside her too. All these years, Elaine has served in Boston as the steady valet to Chelle and Austine. She is the oldest, the family matriarch, and I feel obligated to report back to her.

"How was Ireland?" she wants to know.

"A bouquet of barbed wire, to be honest."

"So, what the hell were you doing there?"

"Dabbling in madness, doing the due diligence."

"And?"

I wish I could tell them I've had some great realization, some profound insight about transforming tragedy and insanity into catharsis and understanding. The truth is it isn't easy asking questions into a void, only to wait in vain for an answer. I followed my gut as much as my head, looking for answers, for signposts, and, I suppose, for someone to blame or even to forgive. Tossing a Hail Mary pass to the universe means accepting a long interval between now and the time when schizophrenics receive the benefits of what Dr. Walsh began in Roscommon.

I tell them about lunatic valleys and phantasmagoric caves and my own theory that a desperate history may have twisted the psyche of the Irish. They like the idea of an Irish valley of the mad at the edge of the then-known world. Beyond that, there isn't much to report. Insanity, as it turns out, is no one's national trait. It's universal. One day genetic genealogy may offer clues; for now, the fog that rolled out of the bog around schizophrenia is lifting very slowly.

While there's nothing tangible that can help us deal with the muddle and the fury, I can see my family's frailties in a more realistic light. There's slivers of hope on the horizon, and the Hearing Voices Network's open-minded engagement with the voices seems the clear way forward, if only because the answers lie within voice-hearers themselves, rather than in some half-baked treatment imposed by outsiders. I detail for my sisters the curious coincidence of Roscommon's being, in effect, the epidemiologic catchment area for the discovery of the first gene link. They listen. They laugh. They yawn. They've both seen enough of schizophrenia to take it all in stride.

I tell them about finding Molly, whose Egan clan, like ours, hails from Cam-Kiltoom parish. Elaine wants to fly right over to meet her. Maybe one day we'll nail down a reasonable ancestry, or not, with a hair sample from her, to check the mitochondrial. Seanna tells us about a new class of drugs here in America that might one day offer hope.

We settle in over dinner, and before long we're trading tales of torment the way most families swap holiday stories. None of us has all the family history precisely, but we all have pieces of it, and we exchange humorous notes on things that were not funny at the time. We're all getting punchy now, as we do. We howl at things that most families would rather keep off the dinner table. We laugh because we know that what the bard said was true: laugh and the world laughs with you; cry and you cry alone. By and by we reckon the fairies were framed.

We were transfixed by fairy tales read to us as kids. Now we are the family that feels like a fable: *Once upon a time, many years ago, my sisters wore pigtails and plaid skirts. We were happy. Then one day they lost their minds in a way that was devastating. Because it happened to them, the rest of us never felt right about feeling bad for ourselves. But we did, and we stumbled and recovered and now somehow the threads have woven together into a cord of hope and humor, expressed in our stories—our experience, which is all we have, along with each other.*

In her mid-twenties, Chelle was admitted to Massachusetts Mental Hospital, where she would live for the next ten years until moving into a Vinfen home. Austine lives in a group home for schizophrenics too. Like me, Elaine and Seanna have spent much time wondering why they got so buried in the storm instead of us. We have a survivor's hard humor that masks our guilt.

I still wonder about the dentist getting whacked for taking out May Sweeney's teeth. There's no evidence to speak of, eighty-four years later, until Elaine produces a cryptic handwritten letter to my mother, on Teamsters Union stationery, from another man, begging for his life in a separate matter. It's the final line of the letter that's revealing: "Please understand your father wouldn't believe the truth on that girl," he writes, "and he would have me killed."

Elaine is married and happy without children. Things have not worked out in spectacular fashion for Seanna, though. Along with the rest of us, she has had to deal with the aftermath, and last year it all crashed. In the past two years, she's been hospitalized a dozen times for physical problems—bleeding ulcers, asthma, pneumonia, and malnutrition, to say nothing of the alcoholism and heroin addiction that have put her close to death. Like me, Seanna went from ordinary adolescence to drug addiction on a path parallel to the one that took Chelle and Austine to madness. In that sense, we were the lucky ones.

Seanna now has a year clean and sober, a feat that she believes is a miracle. "A ton of detoxes and quite a few psych wards," she says, and shrugs, dragging on a Marlboro Red. Seanna is not schizophrenic, but she's dodged more bullets than Elaine and I. If one fraternal twin is schizophrenic, the other has a one-in-four chance of also being schizophrenic. By contrast, other siblings face a one-in-ten chance.

Seanna shows no signs of psychosis, but she collects a monthly Social Security check for the depression and anxiety that have mentally disabled her. When I talk to her, I know I come from tough West Irish stock. With her black hair and green eyes, she looks like she's right off the farm from Roscommon. Over coffee in her new apartment, she tells us about her old camp down on the Charles River and how she had slept, literally, on the other side of Boston's commuter rail tracks, drinking rotgut vodka made locally in Somerville. When she kicked heroin this last time, she says, even her face had the shakes.

Seanna has had Last Rites given to her so many times that she's lost count; the most recent visit from a priest was a year ago at Massachusetts General Hospital, when her esophagus burst. She had one pint of blood left in her, and nine toes in the grave. "But I never lost self-awareness," she says. "I'll tell you, I remember lying in that bed. There was no big white light, but the sense of peace was overwhelming. Ultimate, ultimate peace. And I remember thinking what a good place I was in, and this is the way it's supposed to be, and this is how I can be every day, clean and sober."

Seanna could write a book. Her steady mantra is "Yup, it's a miracle." "As a family, we've had some hard times, but we're so lucky to have each other," she says. "And me personally, from a background of someone who knows better, with all the private schools and everything, to go to living on the Charles River with a spike in my arm and a pint of vodka in my back pocket, and to survive all that and come back, now this truly is a miracle."

Elaine nods. All these years she has been here in Boston, keeping the faith. The three of us hang out as easily as can be; there's no subtlety or difficulty in it. We are not a family that quibbles over the small things. We've learned the lesson all families learn to one degree or another—that what tragedy would obliterate, the simple act of hanging out together restores. For this we need no great breakthroughs.

When we catch up to Chelle the next day at her day center, I feel a sweep of emotion as soon as I see her. The place is clean and tidy, but my sister is among the dismal schizophrenics, who all seem out of their skulls. Some rock with their heads in their hands. To say that these voice-hearers are the least of our brethren is a massive understating of how disregarded they are within the culture.

Chelle does not see us enter. Silver hair combed back, on her third Coke of the morning, she has her place in a chair, her mind wandering with its own interior monologue. As she finally rises to greet us, thrilled we're there, I think there is no one in this world so sweet and undeserving of what has claimed her. Chelle has this enduring, childlike innocence that transcends her disorder and is always on view.

She has gained a little weight—a side effect of her medication. Her hair has gone silver, yet, at fifty-seven, she doesn't have a wrinkle. As her kid brother, I idolized her as the bright, artsy sister who made life happy and fun. And I still see her that way. Chelle always puts a positive spin on things. If we can't come to see her on Thursday, she'll say that's great because she'll get to spend that entire day looking forward to seeing us on Friday. Chelle has never hurt a soul, be it human, animal, or even insect.

She talks of returning to the New York stage, and we tell her one day she might, just not today. The meds have calmed her down, and while she still hears voices virtually around the clock, she has managed to shed the intense religious fervor. No longer the shouting bride of Christ, today she is the mildly amusing daughter of Buddha. "He thinks he's God but he's not," Chelle says of Buddha. "In spite of his weight problem," she says, "he's every bit as sexy as Marlon Brando. He just can't go back to India—he's too westernized."

Only part of Chelle is somewhere else, and her voices seem to want what's good for us. "In my own little way, I'm trying to create my own building for all of us, for the whole family to live in," Chelle says, after consulting a voice called Bobby. "Bobby says it's gonna be a banner weekend."

"Oh yeah? What's Bobby like? Is he all right?"

"Bobby is soft-spoken and articulate, but I do most of the talking. He listens. Pretty soon he'll go away. I saw him on the Oscars, so apparently people are aware of him."

Chelle likens schizophrenia to cruising "parallel universes" where everybody is somebody else, some incorporeal personification from a borderland where time is out of sync, space is out of place, and nothing in the physical world has rock-solid meaning. In Chelle's world, we're all famous. Seanna is Joan Baez, Elaine is Julie Christie, Austine is Margot Kidder, and I am now John-John Kennedy. We ask her who she is in schizophrenia's hall of fame. "Marilyn Monroe," she says, who is also the daughter of Buddha. She breaks into her "Happy Birthday, Mr. President" number in the backseat of Elaine's car.

Chelle is one of a kind. She really does break the mold. She lives in fairyland, but she has never lost her joie de vivre. Like anyone, she has her ups and downs. Her ever-elusive search for her mythical white knight goes on. "Last week I died of a broken heart," she says sadly. "I was waiting for Brian Williams to take me back to New York. If he doesn't show up soon," she says, "then that's it for him."

Apart from the national newscaster, Chelle confers on a regular basis with Princess Diana and, in fact, believes that Diana is God. She is also a virgin whose princes, William and Harry, were immaculately conceived. "Charles had nothing to do with it."

In Starbucks, Chelle has trouble sitting still. She repeatedly heads for the ladies' room, to convene with her voices. She misses their company if she disassociates for too long. Back at our table, I give her the well water from Ireland. I don't actually believe the water will work. I wish I could tell Chelle there was a point in the journey where the gates of heaven opened and God spoke to me and I listened, but it didn't happen that way, exactly. All I have is this water in a bottle and some folklore to go with it. "Here it is, Chelle, from the source." I don't want to make a big deal out of it. She doesn't even remember the myth of the well, so I just joke that I have been to the valley of the mad and that I've heard the wings of the angels of sanity fluttering over the healing water below.

Back at the day center, there is plenty of activity, including an open mike. A white-haired woman sings "Molly Malone," accompanied by an amiable staff member strumming his acoustic guitar. Chelle follows with "Over the Rainbow," a performance that touches us all. The next day, at Revere Beach, Seanna sees a rainbow—another of the little synchronicities that have always bound the twins.

A few months later, we get the news that Seanna has first-stage lung cancer. She says she'll beat it: "God doesn't save you from drowning just to kick you to death on the beach."

CHAPTER NINETEEN

§

WE
ARE
FAMILY

In Elaine's car the four of us spin through Boston to Milton, to see our old house on Brook Road between Cape Cod Lane and Frothingham Street, the playground of our early youth. On the way out we pass the Baker chocolate factory, right around the corner from Mom's old law offices, and the Oriental Theatre, where my sisters went by trolley on weekends to catch the rising stars. Off Armory Street, at Stony Brook, we find Austine outside her own Bay Cove day center for the mentally ill; it's part of an old warehouse, now occupied by the Samuel Adams brewery, cheek by jowl with the headquarters of Bikes Not Bombs. It's a nice place, landscaped with tulips and daffodils. Austine, decked out in a Michigan State jacket and a Newport Folk Festival pullover, sits chain-smoking in a hexagonal wooden gazebo. "Hi, Seanna," she says. "Hi, Elaine. Hi, Chelle. Hi, Patrick."

She seems pleased to see us, yet then goes quiet without saying another word, sequestered behind a wall of schizophrenia so solid that no one, not even her fellow schizophrenics, can get past it. Austine has lost all concept of communication. She is older now, her beauty crushed like a fragile flower, and she is losing the last of her yellow teeth. What is it about tooth retention? Teeth are primal, the hardest substance in the human body. Losing them means the hunt is over, the game is up. But who would force the poor kid into a dental chair? She has never consented. Her life is bad enough. Screw the teeth.

In her twilight sleep, smoking cigarette after cigarette, Austine has been on zombie pause for three decades. It's hard to take. As kids, no one befriended me so entirely. Back then there wasn't much that was apt to escape her attention. Now she pays no mind to what anyone says; nothing catches her eye. Her wandering down to Disney World in 1975 turned out to be a permanent disappearance from life.

I feel a distance from her that takes a different shape now that I'm back at home. All the time I was in Ireland or London or Washington or wherever I've lived, I've measured the distance in time, as I did when she first left for those old orange groves. It was one year, two years, and once even five years since I'd seen Austine. Now that time has collapsed, I measure the distance in space. Without a hair snip of time between us, the three-foot gap feels as vast as decades.

I am always unsure of what to do and say and think. Do I remain a little watchful of her next move because I still feel safer that way? Yes, I suppose, and as I move a little closer, I'm hit with a shameful realization: it's not regret of the past but joining together with Austine in the present that is my biggest fear, because I don't know whom I'm joining with. This has nothing to do with her. It's all on me. The past holds the present hostage when the weight of events forces you to look back.

Some of Austine's fellow "clients" at the day center look

just as dazed, staring into empty space, while others chatter away at their phantom voices. Most are on medications that have serious side effects such as weight gain and tremors. Everyone is shocked by how much Austine and I look alike. Austine says nothing, but with the simplest expressions she reveals the terror inside. There is no relief, no break, no interlude from the horror that crowds her mind's dark crevices. She still can't field the simplest question, and we are still left sitting on the edge of our seats, where we have been perched for three decades, more or less. In the end it's easier just to love Austine as she is than to try to figure her out and get sidetracked into despair.

If I could, I would take her schizophrenia and stick it in my own head instead, I want to believe. But would I really? I tell her a little story to bring some relief. "Did you know, Austine, that this life is just a big dream? Did you know that we've all just fallen asleep in heaven, that we're all just taking a little nap? Pretty soon we'll wake up in heaven again, and it'll all be great again. It'll all be grand. You'll see, Austine. It'll all be better than ever."

"Really?" she says plaintively. She seems to get it. She understands the dream concept. She understands ever so briefly, but probably because she recognizes the involuntary nature of both dreaming and hallucinating. Then she goes back to her smoking in her waking-dream state. Her dream keeps going, endlessly, and driven by fairies well beyond me. There's not a lot more to talk about, so I tend to go over the old times, as if by reminding her of them, her old self will snap back. "Do you remember Herb?" I ask about one of our childhood friends.

"Yes," she says, going mute again, but a slight smile means she remembers him fondly. Even when a little laugh or a smile briefly squints through, the death grip of schizophrenia is never shaken. I could remind her of the beaches and the parties. I could go over the time she spent in Florida. I could go on and on, but there's a vast gulf between trying and succeeding. Still, trying has to count for something. As long as there's that slight smile, the light that has not gone out might be relit. Here I have a chance to make things better, so here I sit with a hole in the pit of my stomach.

Before moving to her own group home, Austine lived for ten years with our father in a small apartment in the old Irish enclave of South Boston. Dad died ten years ago, and now Austine's weekday routine is to come to the day center, driven here in a dark van by a young man named Suleiman. A cheerful guy, Suleiman takes Austine and the others for weekly outings in downtown Boston and for swims at the YMCA on Tuesdays and Fridays.

You can't help but like him. The young man exudes good energy with his positive outlook, and it's a relief to see that Austine is in such capable hands. Suleiman understands schizophrenia because he has a family member "in the same situation." Working with Austine and the other schizophrenics who live at the group home helps him to identify. "You learn about their lives and the support they need."

Suleiman says his parents taught him to always expand his horizons, to always learn more. When he asks Austine how many sisters she has, she cannot do the math. "About two," she says, falling one short. With their help, she is looking smart, wearing lipstick and a bit of rouge and new earrings they've got for her.

Austine refers to her time at the day care center as "going

to my job," but she is able to do little here. Inside, a man and woman are playing chess. There's a large room for stretching and exercise, plus a dining area and a series of administrative offices. As lunch gets under way, Austine helps out in the kitchen. "Chopping vegetables helps with her concentration and her hand-eye coordination," says Karen Moore, the center's caring and patient director. "She's good with a knife," Moore says, not knowing the half of it.

An energetic forty-year-old in black stretch pants and a brown top, Moore takes written attendance, circulates the weekly schedules. "It's not a hospital program but a community program, so the emphasis is on getting them back into the community," she explains. "We do Google searches on Thursdays to help people find free stuff to do on the weekend. We talk about everything from shopping and going to the movies to going to play chess in Harvard Square. We might decide to go to the Boston Public Library. They like it there because they have a café. You can tell we're big into cafés."

After lunch, Moore leads an orientation session for new clients. William, a large man with a goatee and a black Adidas cap, says he enjoys doing metalwork. Across the room another large man in a white T-shirt, jeans, trainers, and a black Sean John cap drums his fingers on the table. Trey, bearded, wearing tortoiseshell glasses, sits closer to Moore, saying nothing at all. There's a man named Victor who wears a Boston Red Sox cap and a 50 Cent silver chain around his neck, and he is comparing the 1998 New York Yankees—perhaps baseball's finest team ever—with the 2007 Boston Red Sox. "Nobody can touch us," he says proudly. "You walk Ramirez or Ortiz and another guy will tag you."

Victor seems like the world's most amiable schizophrenic, and maybe it's because of his ability to spot things the rest of us miss entirely. "I saw the heart jump out of George Bush on TV because he knows he'll lose the war," Victor says. He claims he nearly saw action himself in the sands of Iraq. "I was supposed to go to war a long time ago, way before it even happened."

Austine is silent. Yet Moore says she is improving "to the point where she'll actually tell you when she doesn't want to do something. Austine went to an assertiveness group for a while," she says. "She's learning to be more assertive."

Moore tells Austine that her brother had lived away for a long time too. "And when he came back, we weren't too sure of him either."

After lunch, a dozen clients gather in the parking lot to smoke. They all light up at once and Austine takes eighteen drags off her cigarette before anyone else takes a second one. She is silent, unable to respond with anything but a lazy yes or no.

La, Austine's Vietnamese boyfriend, is there. He sits relaxed, puffing away and making coy faces while Austine hovers near him, her fingers wrapped claw-like around her cigarette. "She my girlfriend," he says. "I her boyfriend."

La wears blue jeans, an Operation Desert Storm T-shirt, and a U.S. Army starter cap, his ponytail pulled through the back loop and his Fu Manchu mustache covering much of his face. La talks at us incomprehensibly in Vietnamese, not knowing—or perhaps not caring—that we can't understand him. As if to cross the divide, out of nowhere he starts to sing "Jingle Bells," still in Vietnamese. He gives himself a big hand when he finishes.

In English now, La says he used to live in London, where, he claims, he had fifty-four girlfriends. I gently remind him that he has one very special one now. Austine comes alive briefly at this, smiling knowingly, and her eyes brighten again as Seanna and Elaine give her a bracelet. This is progress. It's been years since we've heard a real laugh out of her—or maybe I've missed it in my absence. I give her my gift from Ireland, the healing water, spilling it in her tea for her. It's a low-key little ceremony. Mighty changes are not quickly brought about by one sip of well water. But it gives me something to give her. Losing her was terrifying, but trying to be there for her is a chance for me to inhabit the worthiest aspects of myself. Through Austine it finds expression, and the walls that divide us become not quite so large.

Our visits seem to make Austine and Chelle happy, so we go as often as we can through the winter. In the spring and summer there's more to do. In mid-July, there's the New England Sand Castle Festival, a hot and hazy Sunday graced by perfect weather. On the hot sand Brazilians are playing beach soccer-volleyball. American flag bunting adorns the Twist and Shake, a pink-and-white cottage turned ice cream shop that's just past Sammy's—a bar where every Saturday night is "sober night." Our favorite sculpture wins the grand prize—it's a man and woman facing each other, casting shadows on each other. Next to it is a sculpture of a cubist self-crucifixion, and not far off are entwined, humanoid-looking fishes carved in the sand.

Throughout the festival, Chelle speaks quietly to her voices. Austine gazes at the haze. We spent so much time on the beaches as kids that it's impossible not to reminisce. Chelle walked there for hours, building castles by day, by night pausing under starlit skies to point out the Big Dipper. Spending time with her then meant much to me. It still does today, right here on the Massachusetts Bay.

Elaine is wearing May Sweeney's wedding band. Seanna is happy as a clam to be living right on the beach for now. Together she and Chelle look as soft and gentle as a pair of woolly teddy bears. A deejay from Boston's Mix 98.5 is here spinning discs, and Chelle suddenly gets her groove on, punching the air and singing, "We are family . . . I got all my sisters with me . . . We are family . . . Get up everybody and sing."

I remember how as kids we all went body surfing while watching the *jets d'eau* in the distance and the rising and plunging of the big, beautiful whales. As the waves lap the shore today, we're all here, together again as family, but just when things begin to feel normal—or at least something orbiting normal—Chelle reveals that Seanna's dog, dead for twenty years, has been reincarnated as a human being with his own acting career in New York. "Tramp's a heartthrob on *The Guiding Light*," she says of the springer spaniel.

I have my own place on the seaside two floors above Seanna's. In the morning the seawall is scattered with clamshells dropped by gulls to crack open. There's great pizza and soft ice cream on the strip, and Kelly's has nothing but the best Ipswich clams, delivered daily. I run on the beach, have a swim, and then go sit on the seawall each morning until the head settles. I close my eyes and try to imagine my sisters bathed in a white light that dissolves all their discomforts, but on many a day, as the Irish like to say, my best prayer is a groan.

Each day I know I am never more than one chance encounter away from the next schizophrenic. In Wonderland, up in our Oak Island neighborhood, it's a man who turns on his own mad axis outside Toddy's convenience store, just around the corner. He is rail-thin, shaggy, and bearded, and hoods his head in an old windbreaker. Sitting on the curb outside, rocking back and forth, he begs for cigarettes. The girl who works the cash register says his name is Roger and he makes his home in the switchgrass that grows in the marshlands off Route 1A. "He's schizophrenic," she continues, ringing up a young boy wearing a backward Red Sox cap. "My mother went to high school with him. She said he was the smartest one in the class, then one day he just snapped. I don't know how it happens."

I am sure it runs in Roger's family. Ireland taught me a few things about schizophrenia, but never enough about why some families who come by the illness manage to cycle out of it after a generation or two, and why other families don't. I may never know what drives us off the road or how to overcome it. Maybe schizophrenia is, in the classic folklore sense found in many cultures, the ultimate trickster that retools reality itself.

In the end, at least, it was the investigation that got me back here with my sisters, and that's what counts. All that time in Ireland I was waiting for the pearl, and here it is at home as I thread myself back into the family skein. The whole purpose was to decide whether to settle in Boston or head back to London. My way is decided. There is no choice to make. I stay here in Boston because today I see the connection between being a good brother and having my own sort of happiness. In my case, they may be identical.

As for the next generation, only Seanna let the cat out of the bag, giving birth to a son, Christopher Donlon, in the summer of 1980 following an unplanned pregnancy. Chris and I are as close as an uncle and nephew can be, because we threw in for a decade or more together when his parents went off the rails. He's the closest I've come to having my own son, and for today, at least, I'm leaving it that way. What's worrisome is the late age of onset—in early adulthood. It's devastating, like the impact of a comet that isn't seen until it hits.

It's been three years since I've seen him last in London, and here in Boston he's sporting the full Irish with a new shamrock tattoo on the right side of his neck, looking like a real Paddy. On one forearm is a "Sinner" tattoo, on the other is "Saint." On his head is a gray cap that his friend literally swiped from the writer Frank McCourt at a December reading he was giving in Harvard Square. "It's what's in your head, not on it, kiddo" is all I have to say on the matter, recalling McCourt's assessment of Ireland as one big open-air lunatic asylum. "Careful what you carry," I tell Chris.

Chris is the next in line, so we're watching him closely to see if he one day gets the tap on the shoulder. At twenty-seven, the omens are pretty good. If Chris hits thirty, he's pretty much in the safe zone. At thirty-four, he's fully cleared the onset years. With each passing year, it's safe to say, schizophrenia is further off his heels. Maybe he'll go on and have his own children, and maybe they'll dodge the carnage too.

Cutting-edge techniques such as pre-implantation genetic diagnosis can't flag schizophrenia yet—that may be decades away. Absent a blood test, intimations of onset are hard to spot. Then again, the whole notion of helping Mother Nature along to detect and treat schizophrenia is fraught with fears that we might end up judging people like horses at the fair— that we might breed out of the population some special people who connect us to another world.

As for me, I sit here tapping at the keyboard, writing this missive with an eye to future generations, because schizophrenia may never be a dead letter. History repeats, yet we evolve by handing down what shabby bits of knowledge we've gathered for the next generation. So here it is, Chris, for you to pass on—some small bits of wisdom for offspring—put into pages with a wing and prayer that things might break your children's way too.

NOTES

3 ***A muddy abyss*** See introduction to the *Tain Bo Cuailnge* (*Theft of the Cattle of Cuailnge*) the central tale in the Ulster Cycle, in two main manuscripts. The first consists of a partial text in the *Lebor na hUidre* (*The Yellow Book of the Dun Cow*), a late-eleventh/early-twelfth-century manuscript; another partial text of the same version is in the fourteenth-century manuscript *Leabhar Buidhe Lecain* (*The Yellow Book of Lecan*), currently housed at Trinity College, Dublin.

4 ***According to 1,100-year-old manuscripts*** See *Metrical Dindshenchas* (*MD*), ed. E. Gwynn (Dublin, 1903–35), III: 51.

4 ***Back when all madness*** See Gabriel Beranger quoted in Sir William Robert Wilde, *Journal of the Royal Society of Antiquities in Ireland*, 1871, 247–49.

See also Joseph Robins, *Fools and Mad: A History of the Insane in Ireland* (Dublin: Institute of Public Administration, 1987), 19.

8 ***She and her fellow patients*** Bleuler first advanced the term *schizophrenia* in 1908 in a paper and then expanded on his work in *Dementia Praecox oder Gruppe der Schizophrenien* (Dementia Praecox, or the Group of Schizophrenias), 1911.

13 ***The toll was so high*** See E. Fuller Torrey and Judy Miller, *The Invisible Plague: The Rise of Mental Illness from 1750 to the Present* (New Brunswick: Rutgers University Press, 2002), 152.

14 ***"We are not so successful*** Mark Finnane, *Insanity and the Insane in Post-Famine Ireland* (Totowa, N.J.: Barnes & Noble, 1981), 71.

14 ***Still, there was*** See *Journal of Mental Science* 13 (1868): 470. See also *Insanity and the Insane in Post-Famine Ireland,* 71.

17 ***Or so the ancient curse*** *Cor Anmann* (author unknown, also known in English as *The Fitness of Names*), 367. (Dublin: Institute of Public Administration, 1987), 3, 19.

65 ***Dysbindin is a gene involved*** The Irish Schizophrenia Research Project is a collaboration between the Health Research Board, the Medical College of Virginia, Virginia Commonwealth University, and Queen's University Belfast, and is funded by the U.S. National Institutes of Health.

NOTES

65 *The research* See Nicholas Wade, "Gene May Play a Role in Schizophrenia," *New York Times,* December 13, 2002. See also Kenneth Kendler and Dermot Walsh, "Genetic Variation in the 6p22.3 Gene *DTNBP1,* the Human Ortholog of the Mouse Dysbindin Gene, Is Associated with Schizophrenia," *American Journal of Human Genetics,* May 10, 2002, 337–48. Essentially, there is a chromosomal abnormality for the gene in a statistically significant number of schizophrenics.

70 *In Mary Egan's time* See William Gacquin, *Roscommon Before the Famine: The Parishes of Kiltoom and Cam, 1749–1845* (Maynooth, Ireland: Maynooth Studies in Local History, 1996), 10.

70 *Today the farms are bigger* 2006 census figures show that the population of County Roscommon now stands at 58,768. In 1841, the county population stood at more than 250,000. Source: Central Statistic Office Ireland, http://www .cso.ie/Census.

72 *Ireland abounds* See *Metrical Dindschenchas,* ed. E. Gwynn (Dublin, 1903–35).

72 *The* dlui fulla *Fools and Mad,* 5.

75 *Archaeologists finding* See Livy, *Historae* (Third century B.C.), written in A.D. 17, which mentions early Celts as removing the skull of their victims, "which thereafter served them as a holy vessel to pour libations from and as a drinking cup for the priest and the temple attendants."

79 *To Jung* See Carl Jung, *The Psychology of Dementia Praecox* (New York: Nervous and Mental Disease Publishing Co., 1936), contained in *The Psychogenesis of Mental Disease, Collected Works,* vol. 3). This is the disease now known as schizophrenia.

79 *If fairy faith remains* See W. B. Yeats, *The Celtic Twilight: Myth, Fantasy and Folklore* (Sturminster Newton, United Kingdom: Prism Press, 1990).

91 *In a nutshell* "Roscommon Suffering from Lack of Support for Mental Health Services," *Roscommon Herald,* April 25, 2006. See also "Appeal to Public to Help Fight Suicide Through ASIST Training," *Roscommon Champion,* Oct. 17, 2006, 21. See also statistics at http://www.ias.ie/stats.htm, the Irish Association of Suicidology Web site.

92 *To keep the roads safe* See Louisa Nesbitt, Bloomberg News, "Irish Drinkers May Hitch Government Ride to Keep Pubs Alive," January 30, 2007.

93 *As recently as the 1980s* The Invisible Plague, 159.

95 *They lived here on the Shannon* See Bryan Sykes, *Blood of the Isles: Exploring the Tribal Roots of Our Genetic History* (New York: Norton, 2006), which includes two chapters on the genetic makeup of Ireland.

96 *In the* Breviarium See *Book of Armagh: The Patrician Texts in the Book of Armagh,* ed. and trans. Ludwig Bieler, *Scriptores Latini Hiberniae,* vol. 10 (Dublin, 1979). Also see text online at http://www.newadvent.org/cathen/11554a.htm.

100 *One small study* Psychologist Ivan Kelly of the University of Saskatchewan conducted a meta-analysis of thirty-seven studies that showed no

Notes

correlation. See I. W. Kelly, James Rotton, and Roger Culver, "The Moon Was Full and Nothing Happened: A Review of Studies on the Moon and Human Behavior and Human Belief," in J. Nickell, B. Karr, and T. Genoni, eds., *The Outer Edge* (Amherst, N.Y.: CSICOP, 1996).

100 **They produced** See "Prehistoric Moon Map Unearthed," *BBC News,* April 22, 1999, at http://news.bbc.co.uk/2/hi/science/nature/325290.stm.

100 **In 1691** See also *Fools and Mad,* 9; Patricia Casey, "Why the Moon Myths Are Pie in the Sky," *Irish Independent,* October 23, 2006, 9.

101 **Moon worshippers** See Sean Cahill, Gearoid O'Brien, and Jimmy Casey, "Lough Ree and Its Islands" (Athlone: Three Counties Press, 2006), 16.

101 **In the translation** See *Sweeney Astray: A Version from the Irish* (New York: Farrar, Straus & Giroux), 46.

104 **At the stub end** *Journal of Mental Science* 44 (1898): 134.

105 **Ruling from Dublin Castle** *Fools and Mad,* 17.

105 **By 1849** Irish Inspectors of Lunatics Report on District, Local and Private Lunatic Asylums in Ireland, 1849 [1054], xxii 53, presented to both Houses of Parliament, 6.

105 **Inspector of lunatics** Parliamentary Papers, 1854–55 (240) xvii, 533, at 34.

105 **By 1861** Anonymous, "Increase in Insanity," *American Journal of Insanity* 18 (1961): 95.

107 **Left to cross the barren landscape** Cecil Woodham-Smith, *The Great Hunger; Ireland 1845–1849.*

108 **Nowhere was "the Irish genocide" worse** National Famine Museum, Strokestown, Roscommon. See also Brian Cunniffe, "Famine Memorial Unveiled at Derryglad Folk Museum," *Roscommon Herald,* April 25, 2006, 21.

108 **Some of the devastation** Schizophrenia has a strong genetic base, but researchers of famine conditions in China and Holland have found that some events in early life, such as maternal malnutrition, could exacerbate a genetic predisposition. The Chinese findings are consistent with those of a much smaller Dutch study, which found a nearly two-fold increase in schizophrenia for those born during Holland's so-called Hunger Winter, a war-imposed famine in 1944 and 1945. See "Rates of Adult Schizophrenia Following Prenatal Exposure to the Chinese Famine of 1959–1961," *Journal of the American Medical Association,* 294, 557–62; No. 5, August 3, 2005.

112 **"Destitution itself was no** An Irish Inspectors of Lunatics Report on District, Local and Private Lunatic Asylums in Ireland, 1849 [1054], xxii 53, presented to both Houses of Parliament, 6.

123 **Roscommon high school teacher** *Cor Anmann* (author unknown, also known in English as *The Fitness of Names,)* 367.

124 **The medieval Brehon laws** See *Fools and Mad,* 3.

124 **The laws had two categories** See *Fools and Mad,* 8.

131 **Checking out** Ken Bruen, *The Guards* (London: St. Martin's Minotaur, January 19, 2004), 117.

Notes

132 *One contemporary scribe wrote* The Parliamentary Gazetteer of Ireland—Ballinasloe in 1846, transcribed and submitted by Damian Mac Con Uladh, http://www.ballinasloe.org/articles/article.php?ID=47.

132 *In* **The Irish Sketch Book** William Makepeace Thackeray, *The Irish Sketch Book* (Gill and Macmillan, Ltd., 1990 [1843]), 234.

133 *This would become* Insanity and the Insane in Post-Famine Ireland, 37.

133 *Nearly half the population* Arnold Schrier, *Ireland and the American Emigration, 1850–1900* (New York: Russell and Russell, 1958), 83.

133 *So many poor were on* John Ramsay McCulloch, *A Descriptive and Statistical Account of the British Empire* (London: Longman, Brown, 1854), 685.

135 *Modern writers such as Michel Foucault* See Michel Foucault, *Madness and Civilization* (New York: Random House, 1965), 61.

135 *The picture that emerges* Fools and Mad, 110.

135 *Bemoaning "the sad evil* Report of the Inspectors-General on the District, Local and Private Lunatic Asylums in Ireland, 1843, Report Commissions, 16, 1844, vol. 30.

136 *One asylum manager* Parliamentary Papers, "Further Report of the Commissioners in Lunacy," 1847, 504.

136 *Her petition to His Excellency* See Convict Reference Book, 1836–39, in National Archives, Prison Correspondence section.

136 *One had to be significantly depressed* See Convict Reference Book, 1836–39, in National Archives, Prison Correspondence section.

137 *While a person* Parliamentary Papers, Accounts and Papers, Reports of the Inspector General, 1849 [1054], xxiii, 53, in letter to Chancellor from the Lunacy Commissioners, 7.

137 *If, after observation* Parliamentary Papers, Accounts and Papers, Reports of the Inspector General, 1849 [1054], xxiii, 53, in letter to the Chancellor from the Lunacy Commissioners, 7.

138 *As did drink* First Annual Report of the County and City of Cork Asylum for Lunatic Paupers, submitted to the governors by Thomas Carey Osburne, M.D., March 1, 1827.

138 *From ancient times* Fools and Mad, 13.

139 *"It would be folly* First Annual Report of the County and City of Cork Asylum for Lunatic Paupers, submitted to the governors by Thomas Carey Osburne, M.D., March 1, 1827.

139 *Ireland's new network* Parliamentary Papers, Accounts and Papers, Reports of the Inspector General, 1849, [1054], xxiii. 53, in letter to the Chancellor from the Lunacy Commissioners, 7.

141 *"In some cases of monomaniacs* Parliamentary Papers, Accounts and Papers, Reports of the Inspector General, 1849 [1054], xxiii, 53.

142 *The staff were warned* Parliamentary Papers, Correspondence on the Subject of Public Lunatic Asylums in Ireland 1828 (234) xxii, 223.

262

Notes

142 *"They shall not bring* Parliamentary Papers, Correspondence on the Subject of Public Lunatic Asylums in Ireland 1828 (234) xxii, 223.

142 *And if a second escape was made* Parliamentary Papers, Correspondence on the Subject of Public Lunatic Asylums in Ireland 1828 (234) xxii, 223.

142 *By 1845, as the famine spread* Reports of the Inspectors-General on the District, Local and Private Lunatic Asylums in Ireland. [645], xxvi (1845), 269.

143 *Many of the patients* Reports of the Inspectors-General on the District, Local and Private Lunatic Asylums in Ireland. [645], xxvi (1845), 269.

143 *The men, who* Reports of the Inspectors-General on the District, Local and Private Lunatic Asylums in Ireland. [645], xxvi (1845), 269.

143 *Not everyone was disturbed* Reports of the Inspectors-General on the District, Local and Private Lunatic Asylums in Ireland. [645], xxvi (1845), 270.

144 *The first ward* Reports of the Inspectors-General on the District, Local and Private Lunatic Asylums in Ireland. [645], xxvi (1845), 271.

144 *With fifty-two more* Reports of the Inspectors-General on the District, Local and Private Lunatic Asylums in Ireland. [645], xxvi (1845), 271.

144 *In a report back to Britain* Irish Inspectors of Lunatics Report on District, Local and Private Lunatic Asylums in Ireland, 1843 [1054], xxii, 53, presented to both Houses of Parliament, 6.

151 *The pledge* John F. Quinn, *Father Mathew's Crusade: Temperance in Nineteenth-century Ireland and Irish America* (Amherst: University of Massachusetts Press, 2002).

159 **Access Hollywood** Anne-Marie Walsh, "Wacko Jacko Discovers His New Creative Home—the Midlands," *Irish Independent,* November 2, 2006, 21.

161 *I had wanted to come here* James Joyce, *Finnegans Wake,* 499–534.

167 *Reading* **Ulysses** James Joyce, *Ulysses,* 157–58.

168 *There's a James Egan* See convict reference book, 1836–39, in National Archives, Prison Correspondence section.

174 *In Ireland's population* Source: Schizophrenia Ireland, 2006.

182 *He believed that "something unusual The Invisible Plague,* 159.

183 *Tim Crow* T. J. Crow, "Temporal Lobe Asymmetries as the Key to the Etiology of Schizophrenia," *Schizophrenia Bulletin* 16 (1990): 433–43.

185 *While his work confirms* Interview following October 12, 2005, lecture of Dr. Daniel Weinberger, chief of the Clinical Brain Disorders Branch of the Intramural Research Program, National Institute of Mental Health, National Institutes of Health in Bethesda, Maryland. Weinberger reviewed literature showing that these four factors increase the risk for the development of schizophrenia.

189 *Predictions of which schizophrenics* "New Tools Aid Violence Risk Assessment," *Journal of the American Medical Association,* August 1, 2007, 499.

190 *In the last year alone* L. Hayes, "Nurse Turnover: A Literature Review," *International Journal of Nursing Studies* 43, 2, 237–63.

NOTES

192 ***In their book*** Michael Corry and Áine Tubridy, *Going Mad: Understanding Mental Illness* (Dublin: Newleaf, 2002).

198 ***"We leave that to*** Joseph Robins, "A Shared Concern: The First Twenty-five Years of Schizophrenia Ireland."

200 ***This echoed what lunacy inspectors*** Irish Inspectors of Lunatics Report on District, Local and Private Lunatic Asylums in Ireland (1849 [1054], xxii, 53), presented to both Houses of Parliament, 6.

201 ***In fact, there is no rise*** Based on discussion with Dr. Aidan Corvin, senior lecturer in psychiatry, Trinity College, Dublin.

206 ***Another schizophrenic sailor*** First Annual Report of the County and City of Cork Asylum for Lunatic Paupers, submitted to the governors by Thomas Carey Osburne, M.D., March 1, 1827.

223 ***Epilepsy, which produces extra charges*** Russell Shorto, *Saints and Madmen* (New York: Henry Holt, 1999), 188–89.

224 ***Peter cites a Gallup Poll*** http://www.gallup.com.

225 ***Research by Dr. David Copolov*** Erica Goode, "Experts See Mind's Voices in New Light," *New York Times,* May 6, 2003, http://query.nytimes.com/gst/full page.html?res=9C05EEDC103CF935A35756C0A9659C8B63&sec=&spon=&page wanted=all.

INDEX

INDEX

Boston Globe, 23, 27
Boston Red Sox, 13
Bo Tain trail, 95
Boyne, Battle of the, 151
Brehon laws, 123–24
Breviarium, 96
Brigid, 126
Bromides, 196
Brothers of St. John of God, 197
Brown, James, 85
Bruen, Ken, 131
Buddhism, 194
Buile Suibhne, 101
Bullimore, Peter, 217–25
Burial mounds, 71
Bush, George W., 153

C

Camus, Albert, 40
Carlow, 204
Carrowell, 104
Catatonic schizophrenia, 50–52, 54–56
Catholicism, 14, 22–26, 72, 74, 77, 78, 80, 95, 96, 102, 107, 121–23, 125
Cave of the Cat (Oweynagat), 3–6, 15–16, 69, 71–76, 80, 97
Celtic Revival, 170
Celts, 72, 74–76, 90, 96, 99, 100, 161
Cerebral syphilis, 196
Channeling, 195
Cholera, 107, 235
Clinton, Bill, 126
Clonakilty, 207
Clonmacnoise, 102
Cluain Mhuire outpatient center, Dublin, 197
Cognitive therapy, 197
Columbus, Christopher, 216

Commission of Inquiry on Mental Illness, 179
Como, Perry, 28
Connaught Lunatic Asylum, 131
Connemara, 216
Consanguinity, 200–201, 230
Copolov, David, 225
Cork County, 99, 198, 205–6
Corry, Michael, 191–95
Cromwell, Oliver, 95, 112, 124, 205, 234
Crow, Tim, 183
Cruchain, 72
Cuchulainn, 74, 102
Culchie Festival, 128
Cystic fibrosis, 185

D

Dementia praecox, 8
Depression, 7, 12, 120, 192, 213, 224
Depression Dialogues, 191
Dervin, Mrs., 109–13
Diagnostic and Statistical Manual of Mental Disorders, 181
Dingle, 162, 171, 207, 215
Dingle Peninsula, 207
Diptheria, 196
Donlon, Chris, 255–56
Donlon, Seanna (Tracey), 20–24, 27–32, 39, 45, 46, 60, 62, 63, 240–44, 246, 247, 253–55
Donnelly, Brian, 168
Doonore North and South, 170, 171
Dostoyevsky, Fyodor, 223
Druids, 4, 5, 17, 71, 72, 74–75, 99, 160–62
Dublin, 99, 162, 164–69, 171, 174, 233, 234
Dubliners, the, 9
Duncarvan, 205

INDEX

S

St. Brigid's asylum, Ballinasloe,
131–36, 139–45
St. Brigid's church, Roscommon,
120–21
St. Patrick's Hospital, 134, 182
Samhain, 5, 76, 80
Schizophrenia.
age of onset, 39, 45, 230, 256
catatonic, 50–52, 54–56
coinage of term, 8
environmental factors and,
185–86, 199–201
evolutionary theory of, 183
genetics and, 21, 22, 45, 51,
65–66, 69, 78, 176–78, 181,
182, 184–86, 192, 241
hallucinations and, 10, 41, 54–57,
62, 182, 183, 191, 220, 221
incidence of, 93, 174, 198
Jung on, 79
management of, 39
maternal malnutrition and, 108
medication for, 39, 45–46, 192,
194, 197, 215, 220–21, 225,
245, 249
paternal age and, 66, 185, 199–200
positive and negative symptoms,
61, 190
psychospiritual viewpoint on, 195
religious delusions and, 42, 53,
141, 186, 195, 219
statistics on, 4
substance abuse and, 185, 199
violence and, 56–57, 189–90, 225
viral hypothesis and, 182
voices and, 7, 10, 37, 39, 41, 44,
45, 48, 51, 55, 57, 58, 78, 85,
86, 151, 174–75, 189–90, 193,
195, 215–25, 241, 245, 246,
253

Schizophrenia Ireland, 93, 196–202,
217, 228
Scotland, 178
"Scream, The" (Munch), 48
Sean's pub, 149–56
Selective listening, 222
Senchus Mor, 72
September 11 terrorist attacks, 153
Serotonin, 45, 87
Shakespeare, William, 21, 74
Shannon River, 71, 93–95, 102,
132, 234
Shock treatments, 137
Skibbereen, 207
Slighe Mhor road, 163
Sligo, 132, 198
Smallpox, 196
Solitary fairies, 79
South Kildare-Carlow, 180
Spiritual possession, 42
Stirk, Chris, 220–22
Stonehenge, 159
Storytelling, 74, 113
Strokestown, 108
Substance abuse, 185, 199
Suck River, 71, 94, 101, 132
Suck Valley, 132
Suicide, 91, 92, 219
Survivor's guilt, 127, 149, 242
Sweeney, Charles, 19
Sweeney, Mad King, 101–2, 211–12
Sweeney, Margaret O'Grady, 19
Sweeney, May (see White, May
Sweeney)
Sweeney family, 168
Swift, Jonathan, 181–82

T

Tain Bo Cuailnge, 74, 75, 102
Tara, 96
Tara Hill, 91

INDEX

Index

ABOUT THE AUTHOR

Patrick Tracey is a writer now living on the North Shore of Boston.